=

L.

Tl.

ACCF

Schools and social work

Library of Social Work

General Editor:
Noel Timms
Professor of Social Work Studies
University of Newcastle upon Tyne

Schools and social work

Margaret Robinson
Department of Social and Psychological Studies
Chelsea College
University of London

Routledge & Kegan Paul
London, Henley and Boston

First published in 1978
by Routledge & Kegan Paul Ltd
39 Store Street,
London WC1E 7DD,
Broadway House,
Newtown Road,
Henley-on-Thames,
Oxon RG9 1EN and
9 Park Street,
Boston, Mass. 02108, USA
Set in 10/11pt English
and printed in Great Britain by
The Lavenham Press Ltd
Lavenham, Suffolk
British Library Cataloguing in Publication Data

Robinson, Margaret

Schools and social work. —(Library of social
work; 0305-4381).
1. School social work—England
I. Title II. Series
371.4'6'0942   LB3013.4   78-40760

ISBN 0 7100 0004 9
ISBN 0 7100 0005 7 Pbk

A race of real children; not too wise,
Too learned, or too good; but wanton, fresh,
And bandied up and down by love and hate;
Not unresentful where self-justified;
Fierçe, moody, patient, venturous, modest, shy;
Mad at their sports like withered leaves in winds;
Though doing wrong and suffering, and full oft
Bending beneath our life's mysterious weight
Of pain and doubt, and fear, yet yielding not
In happiness to the happiest upon earth.
Simplicity in habit, truth in speech,
Be these the daily strengtheners of their minds;
May books and Nature be their early joy!
And knowledge, rightly honoured with that name—
Knowledge not purchased by the loss of power!

Wordsworth, *The Prelude,* V. ii. 411-25

Contents

Contents

Illustrations

Acknowledgments

When all is written and the moment has arrived finally to conclude one's labours, it is a real pleasure to be able to recognise and publicly appreciate the help which the author has been so freely given along the way.

Although the idea for such a book only finally sprouted at the surface some three or four years ago, I can now see that I had actually been germinating thoughts about the boundaries between education and social work for many years. This was doubtless due to my own 'upbringing' and education, both as a child and later as a social worker and a parent myself. It was Dr Kevin Leddy who first encouraged me to reflect upon the importance of boundary issues generally; and I shall always be grateful to him for the help which he gave me over several years.

As the parent of three schoolchildren, I reluctantly had to admit that some of my thoughts about schools were less than rational; and, as many of my discussions about the education of our children proved to be fertile ground on which I began to draw, I should like to thank those professional friends and relations such as David and Rose Spencer and my sister, Joy Clarke, who frequently reminded me that teachers are human too! I should perhaps also extend especial thanks to our daughter Sue, who during the writing of this book grew from an impassioned and at times unwilling consumer of education into an informed and more objective critic of both the educational and social work scenes!

But the event which was responsible for the actual commitment to the definitive idea for such a book was the invitation from the Inner London Education Authority to become involved in a review of their Education Welfare Service in 1973. I spent some three months undertaking the review and all the staff with whom I came into contact not only generously gave me their time and their thoughts on the subject, but also introduced me to a world where everyone was deeply committed to enabling the children of inner London to make the best use of their educational opportunities. I learnt a great deal from all these colleagues, but especially from Miss Joyce Ridding, Miss Ivy Harrison, Mrs Elinor Goldschmied and from my colleague in the review. Though I have made comments on the Education Welfare Service in the text of my book, and in particular in Chapter 4, the opinions I have expressed are my own rather than those of the Authority.

Most of the book was written during my time as director of the Applied Social Studies Course at Goldsmiths' College, conveniently situated for me in the centre of an educational priority area (indeed, I was working in the same house as the Deptford Educational Priority Area team). I should like to take this opportunity of thanking my former colleagues and my students (particularly those who were social workers in the education field) and also my head of department, Peter Baynes, who always gave me both encouragement and support when needed.

Many colleagues have read and advised on sections of the book and, while space does not permit mentioning all their names, I should like to take this opportunity of thanking them for their generosity, even though I may not have incorporated all their suggestions. David Armstrong, particularly, patiently allowed me to correct some of my misguided thinking about counselling and teacher training in discussions with him. I am deeply grateful to my friends Margaret Adcock and Professors Phyllida Parsloe and Bob Pinker, who read drafts of the book and not only made useful criticisms and suggestions, but also encouraged me when I flagged.

Zirphie Parsloe typed numerous early drafts, patiently deciphering my dreadful handwriting, Claire Harbour typed some of the later ones and Shirley White, with great speed and accuracy, typed the final copies. I am indebted to them all. My most heartfelt thanks, however, must go to my husband, Denis, who not only did far more than his fair share of domestic and gardening chores, so that I could actually write the book, but at times even bullied me to sit down and get on with it! Needless to say, the responsibility for the ideas expressed in the book is fully my own.

The author and publishers are grateful to the following for permission to quote from or adapt copyright material: Cambridge University Press for Ian Lister, *Deschooling*; Columbia University Press for E. Litwak and H. J. Meyer, *School, Family and Neighbourhood*; Constable & Co. and Brunner/Mazel Inc. for Robin Skynner, *One Flesh, Separate Persons*; the Controller of Her Majesty's Stationery Office for Karen Lyons, *Social Work and the School*; Little, Brown & Co. for John A. Clausen, *Socialization and Society*, copyright © 1968 by Little, Brown & Co. Inc.; the National

Association of Social Workers Inc. for Harriett M. Bartlett, *The Common Base of Social Work Practice*; the National Foundation for Educational Research for Leeds University Institute of Education, *Teacher Education*; the National Youth Bureau for John Paley and David Thorpe, *Children, Handle with Care*; Penguin Books Ltd for David Head, *Freeway to Learning*; Routledge & Kegan Paul Ltd for David Hargreaves, Hester Stephen and Frank Mellor, *Deviance in Classrooms*, and David Jones and Caroline Mayo, *Community Work One*; Routledge & Kegan Paul Ltd and Humanities Press Inc. for Christopher Beedell, *Residential Life with Children*; John Wiley & Sons Ltd for Gordon Rose and Tony F. Marshall, *Counselling and School Social Work*, copyright © 1974 by John Wiley & Sons Inc.

Introduction: some boundary issues

Social institutions

Social institutions are associated with defining and effecting the system of checks and balances by means of which society regulates itself so that it can actually function. Among these institutions are the social services, and these are generally defined as national insurance, pensions, housing, health, education and the personal social services. It is with the last two that this book is concerned. The educational system, of course, spreads far beyond the school system, which is only one segment of it. It includes further and higher education, adult education and is now extending into pre-school education. This book is directly concerned only with the schools sector of education, and with education provided within the public sector. Whitehead[1] defines education as 'the acquisition of the art of the utilisation of knowledge'. He goes on to stress that 'the central problem of all education' is that of 'keeping knowledge alive, of preventing it from becoming inert'. Whitehead himself had some critical things to say about the performance of schools as 'the true educational unit in any national system for the safeguarding of efficiency' and these criticisms have been developed and expanded since then.

There is no definition of social work in the *Oxford English Dictionary* and no agreement as to what constitutes the task of social work. The *Encyclopaedia of Social Sciences* says the 'objectives of social work are to help individuals, families, communities and groups of persons who are socially disadvantaged and to contribute to the creation of conditions that will enhance social functioning and prevent breakdown'. Boehm,[2] an American social work writer, says: 'The social worker focuses at one and the same time upon the capacity of individuals and groups for effective interaction and upon social resources from the point of view of their contribution to

1

effective social functioning.' In the light of this dual focus, the social worker (alone or with related professional or non-professional community groups) initiates steps (1) to increase the effectiveness of individuals' interaction with each other, singly and in groups; and (2) to mobilise appropriate resources by co-ordination, change or the creation of new ones.

Parker[3] defines the personal social services as 'those lying outside the field of health and education which are adjusted in some special way to the particular social needs of individuals, families and groups, which require personal contact between the provider and the recipient'. 'The skill involved', he adds, 'is often labelled social work.' *Chambers's Dictionary* (1881 edn) quotes J. F. Clarke, writing on self-culture: 'Education in its true sense is not the mere instruction of Latin, English and French. It is the unfolding of the whole of human nature. It is growing up in all things to our highest possibility.' It could be argued that this defines *both* education and social work.

Education and social work are carried out through social systems which are organised for the purpose and which function at national and local levels of organisation. The Department of Education and Science (DES) is nationally responsible for the education system, through the Minister, to Parliament and the electorate. Similarly, the Department of Health and Social Services (DHSS) is responsible for most (though not all) social work. The recent reorganisation of the DHSS reflects the interdependence of the health and social service systems. The boundary issues between them have long been recognised and are openly debated, as indeed is their interdependence. It is the task of this book to attempt to distinguish the social work aspects which have relevance for the schools sector of the education system. Virtually to ignore the health system is in some ways to suggest a false clarity of boundaries, as the health, education and social work systems are interlocking, if not inextricably intertwined with one another. However, it is a worthwhile exercise to try to extract and focus on the boundaries between the education and social work systems. Until recently there has been little recognition that such boundaries have important implications, and sometimes each system functions as if the other does not exist. While the health care system also plays an important part in enabling people to develop to their highest potential, and is itself closely allied to both schools and social work, it may appear as if there is little recognition of the fact in this book.

Redefinition and reassessment

Both education and the personal social services have been subjected to some careful scrutiny during post-war years. There have been numbers of official enquiries, the most notable being those of Plowden,[4] Newsom[5] and Seebohm.[6] Other committees too have not been without their effect on the education and social services. The public enquiry set up by the Minister of Health and Social Security in 1973 to investigate the circumstances of the killing of Maria Colwell by her stepfather[7] has led to searching discussions and renewed public interest, some of it recriminatory. This era of scrutiny and legislative change seems to be culminating in a searching reappraisal of education and social work from both without and within. These two social institutions are not alone in being subjected to such redefinition, but it could be said that the current reassessments are among the most comprehensive and radical. Not only are the social work and education systems redefining their boundaries, but they are also extending them. The education system is beginning to move away from being exclusively child-based, for instance into direct educational intervention with families, hitherto a province of social workers (and, of course, of personnel from the health service, notably health visitors). The social work system, on the other hand, is shifting its orientation into what might be described as educationally oriented activities, for instance day care; and also perhaps into the more politicised aspects of (adult) education, raising the level of political consciousness among socially deprived community groups. The reasons for these reappraisals are manifold and complex, but some of them are connected with the apparent failure of the systems: so many young people leaving school 'uneducated' (i.e., unable to read), and so many people, groups and communities apparently still unable to function socially even if social work help has been available.

Clegg and Megson[8] wrote starkly (if simplistically) of children in need of help: 'Children who are criminal or vicious or ill-adjusted to the society in which they move, or even children who are merely badly behaved, have often served a long apprenticeship of distress.' They point out that 10-20 per cent of all children need preventive or curative help—about 2 per cent of them receive such help.

The current concern over the care of children and in particular their needs and rights as individuals has led those who are concerned with schoolchildren and their families to look to the defects and failures within their own system, as well as pointing out those 'over the garden wall'. The increasing demand by society for public accountability has begun to highlight not only the conflicts and dilemmas of both the schools and the social work systems, but has also thrown some boundary questions into relief.

At present, each of the two systems is apparently separately and individually concerned with redefining its boundaries, often ex-

3

tending them while so doing. Both systems frequently behave as if their sister-organisation did not exist, or alternatively almost generalise each other out of existence! Education literature typically refers to the Welfare Services, presumably meaning health services such as health visitors, the probation service and all other kinds of social workers. Similarly, until quite recently, social work literature consistently failed to recognise the importance of the impact which the schools have upon the family life of their pupils, referring to them in equally blanket terms as Education or The School.

The boundaries between education and social work in fact overlap, often at the most crucial and vulnerable points. It is an indictment on both systems that too often the boundary of one is extended as if in ignorance of the work of the other; or perhaps in rivalry, as if to indicate that anything it can do they can do better. Too little attention is given to these areas of overlap, to the reasons why such an overlap has occurred, to the effectiveness of either or both systems, to the ways in which they might work together or separate more distinctly, and to the question of the public's right to make informed choices.

Goldstein,[9] while commenting that 'everything has a label, a descriptive term which enables us to "know" its purpose or substance', agrees that 'the term social work emerges as ambiguous and non-descriptive, revealing only that it has something to do with human relations.' He himself attempts to capture some of the subtleties involved in the social work task by the following definition:

> Social work is a form of social intervention which enhances, conserves and augments the means by which persons individually and/or collectively, can resolve disruptions in their social existence. The nature of the profession is governed by the combined recognition of the individual as a unique and active organism, the social environment as a dynamic force, and the effects of their interaction.

Goodacre[10] considers that the functions of the school are fourfold: instruction, socialisation, the classification of children and promoting social welfare. She also considers that schools have an autonomous function in that they should set themselves apart from the culture pattern which they serve in order that a social climate can develop in which teachers and pupils can work together in harmony.

While teachers, social workers and others are likely to be critical of both these definitions, they are nevertheless the result of careful considerations by respected researchers of each 'profession', and they serve to demonstrate the possible areas of overlap. It is with some of the issues resulting from the overlap of schooling and social work that this book is concerned.

Part one discusses social functioning and social breakdown. Chapter 1 considers the tasks of education and social work in relation to schoolchildren and their families and discusses the areas of overlap. The family life-cycle is described with particular reference to crucial periods of stress when family functioning might become impaired. Chapter 2 takes up the question of social breakdown, considers some of the difficulties of arriving at a satisfactory definition of social breakdown, and also attempts to describe a model of the process of social breakdown in relation to individuals, families and schools. Part two is concerned with some current issues in connection with the overlap between schools and social work, and considers some specific boundary areas where confusion appears to be highlighted. Part three considers the repertoires of intervention to enhance social functioning and to prevent and remedy social breakdown. Chapter 4 is specifically concerned with the role and function of the education welfare service and Chapter 5 with the people in the system, namely teachers and social workers. Part four, Chapter 6, makes some concluding comments and points out some of the trends already developing which are likely to influence the future development of both schools and social work and their attempts to perform their tasks in relation to schoolchildren and their families.

Part one

Social functioning and social breakdown

Chapter one

The area of overlap between school and social work

As has already been implied, both teachers and social workers are agents of society. The tasks which they undertake are delegated to them through the systems within which they work. Organisationally, these systems are departmentally separate even when co-existent in the same local authority. Though in much of their practice they serve the same demographic area, the geographical location of offices is frequently separate and discrete. Teachers and social workers are concerned about the same children from the same families, often those very children who both fail to attain their educational potential and also break down socially. Yet despite this concern and the good intentions which accompany it, communications break down, misunderstandings occur and there is even neglect of the very tasks which the schools and social work systems are required to carry out. This book is an attempt to shed some light on the reasons for these misunderstandings, failures in communication and neglect.

Recipient sector of society

Broadly speaking, educationists are preoccupied with and oriented towards schoolchildren and their education; and social workers with breakdown in social functioning and with preventing such a breakdown. The school system is primarily concerned with the educational needs of schoolchildren. However, there is currently a spirited and at times acrimonious debate within the education system itself as to what constitutes education and how 'educational needs' should be met. The debate around narrower or broader definition of education, at times flares up into actual conflict, either between schools, or even within the same school, as the recent inquiry into William Tyndale Junior School has revealed.[1] The narrow definition of education could be described as focusing on the cognitive and developmental needs of children, while the broader definition includes, or even emphasises, the socialisation aspects. While such a definition may be a question of the values and philosophy which underlie educational principles, some educationalists consider that the type of school and the demographic area in which it is situated should also influence the balance between cognitive development and socialisation. At a grammar school in a middle-class area, for example, the socialisation of the young people could more or less be taken for granted, whereas at a comprehensive school in a socially deprived inner city area, aspects of the socialisation task would almost inevitably fall upon the school. However, the primary orientation of the school system is towards the needs of groups of children, who may vary both in their capacities and in their emotional development and also according to the stage of development which they have reached.

The social work system, on the other hand, is more oriented towards the individualised needs and social functioning of families, groups and communities. Similarly, too, there are debates not only on the relative value (in terms of long-term effectiveness) of intervention at group or community level, but also on the definition of social work intervention—and most hotly on the question of intervention at the community work level. Many community workers, notably those who are politically motivated social activists, do not consider that what they are engaged in is social work at all. Other politically conscious community workers consider that such intervention subscribes to social work values, and is a social work activity. A key factor in this debate, also at times reaching conflict proportions, seems to centre on the importance which the worker gives to the self-determination of the client. Preoccupation with the social functioning of people and their individualised needs does lead social workers into some invidious situations, particularly in families where the needs of individual members may not only be different, but also in conflict. Educationists are concerned with *all* children from five to sixteen years old, for whom they have a statutory responsibility to provide education (under the 1944 Act), whereas social workers have statutory responsibility for *some* children who have been defined by varying criteria (some of which are legal) as being at risk or in need of care. The education department is not absolved from responsibility when social work is involved, though in some cases its power may be superseded by that of the social service department. For instance, if a care order is made it is the social service department which has the power to decide where a child resides, though the education department still has a statutory obligation to provide schooling for the child (even if the child's family home is in another authority).

Both the teachers in the education system and the social workers in the social work system may also be indirectly concerned with the same family: the teacher with the children or some of them, the social worker with the parents (or even grandparents) and with other pre-school or post-school children. Whereas the statutory responsibilities of social workers in regard to children usually lie with the social service department of the local authority, the statutory responsibilities in relation to the other family members may also or instead lie with the probation service. There are, of course, also voluntary social work agencies (such as the Family Welfare Association or Family Service Units) which, while not having statutory responsibilities, may exercise both concern for and influence with and on behalf of families. This concurrent involvement with schoolchildren and their families can lead to shared mutual concern which is on the whole beneficial to the families, though the orientations are different; but it can also prove disadvantageous to the family.

The family may be 'caught' between the different orientations of the two systems, one concerned primarily with the children's educational needs and the other with the social functioning of the whole family. Alternatively, the family may stand 'isolated' between two systems which are both involved but, because of lack of communication, fail to provide effective help where and when needed, as was the case with Maria Colwell.[2] Some families stand 'pig in the middle', waiting and in need, while the vested interests of both departments are being argued out around them. Whichever of these situations prevails, the confusions, inconsistencies, activities and inactivities which arise from failures of communication can be deleterious rather than helpful to the families concerned.

Families, then, can be of simultaneous or concurrent concern and interest to the two systems, but they can also be involved with the two systems at different times, objects of what might be described as consecutive concern. These families are perhaps more vulnerable to the effects of different orientations, for they tend to be seen as the failures of the other system and perhaps even may be subtly used as pawns in internecine 'wars' between departments of the same authority. Schools may well regard the children of a multiple problem family which is 'ticking over' quite well in social work terms as being let down by their feckless parents. Or the children of an ex-prisoner, who seems to be committing further but legally undiscovered offences, may be viewed by teachers as victims of a soft probation officer. Social workers, on the other hand, may consider that the teacher's preoccupation with the child's cognitive development is unrealistic, particularly perhaps in situations where the social worker considers that the child's emotional needs are not being met at home.

There is abundant evidence that schools and social workers concurrently involved with schoolchildren and their families have allowed their stereotyped pictures of each other to influence the definition and the process of their task. Unfortunately the school and social work systems as currently organised subtly encourage such stereotyping. In the Maria Colwell case, for example, the education welfare officer went to the school but met only the headmistress, and not the class teacher who had repeatedly expressed her concern for Maria. Nor did the social worker responsible for the supervision of Maria ever meet the education welfare officer. While it is difficult to obtain direct evidence of situations where teachers or social workers have reinforced parental prejudices regarding the other system, there can be little doubt that this does happen, and also that it can lead to schoolchildren failing to get the help they need at the time when it would be most effective.

While some schools (perhaps many) do indeed fail to meet the needs of the children who attend them, most schools struggle to do so. The average social worker is not usually sufficiently well informed to make this kind of judgment in relation to an individual child and his or her school. Yet many do so, without ever visiting the school or checking carefully with colleagues, thus basing their judgments on discussions with their clients and their own stereotypes and experience. This can and does lead to social workers colluding with schoolchildren and their families over non-attendance at school. Of course, teachers, too, make judgments about families without being in possession of sufficient facts and frequently without anyone from the school system ever visiting the home and fully informing the school of the home circumstances; and they often fail to take into account how child-centred they are. So both systems often lack knowledge of the family members in the other situation (whether school or home) in addition to not knowing how the other system functions. This reciprocal ignorance provides a fair breeding ground for the development of prejudice and stereotyping on the part of the people within the system, as will be discussed in a later chapter.

Who are these children who are the cause of concern to both the education and the social work system? Wedge and Prosser[3] write of the socially disadvantaged and quote the facts gained from the sample of eleven-year-old children who were the subject of the National Children's Bureau Cohort study. They outline the following:

1 *Family size:* 1 in 4 of the children studied come from large or one-parent families;
2 *Low income:* 1 in 7 of the children come from families who are in receipt of free school meals or supplementary benefit.

3 *Poor housing:* 1 in 4 have spent a significant proportion of their childhood in overcrowded conditions and lacking hot water.

They define socially disadvantaged children as children experiencing all these conditions and find that 1 child in 16 is socially disadvantaged, an average of 2 to every classroom! We can *already* distinguish many socially disadvantaged children and monitor their progress; but there are many others whom we fail to detect or who are at risk in other ways. Whatever our views on heredity or the transmission of deprivation, these children are tomorrow's parents.

Role and function of education and social work—the concept of socialisation

It has already emerged that school education and social work are frequently concerned directly or indirectly with the same population, and their functions may be carried out consecutively or concurrently. While the functions of the two systems may be relatively constant, their aims and objectives vary according to shifts and changes in societal standards. These are usually reflected in legislation and directives which have to be interpreted. The guidelines which evolve in order to aid interpretation are by no means always clear and often fail to take account of the different orientations of the different systems.[4] An example is the difficulty of collaborative action even in relation to suspected non-accidental injury to children, as recent enquiries reveal.

While the family is considered to be the primary socialising agency, the school is considered to be the major secondary agent of socialisation. Social workers, too, could be considered as agents of socialisation, even as tertiary agents, where the families and schools have failed. Goldstein[5] points out that certain systems, such as mental hospitals or prisons, have a resocialising function, for their formal purpose is to make up some deficiency in early socialisation. He considers that social workers have a particular additional task, that of socialising the socialising agencies.

This concept of socialisation is of equal use to teachers and social workers and may provide one of the bridges towards the development of mutual understanding. Socialisation is the development of the person as a social being and participant in society. It is a process in which different social institutions have their part to play; and these institutions may vary as to the importance of their role at different times during the process. The patterns of social learning, the acquisition of language and of selfhood, the learning of social roles and moral norms are largely learnt in the family and perhaps in the neighbourhood. However, the process of enculturation and social learning in the wider world takes place in the school and beyond; and, from the societal perspective, socialisation is the medium by which social and cultural continuity are attained. Socialisation, therefore, implies learning, but in the broadest sense; and in particular learning that bears on future role performance.

Socialisation and social control

Socialisation includes the transmission and maintenance of existing moral norms. Such norms are, of course, constantly being redefined and reshaped, and another aspect of the socialisation process is to enable the evaluation and innovation of social norms. It is in this aspect of the redefinition and innovation of social norms that socialisation agents, such as teachers and social workers, may become responsible for tasks of social control. As Clausen writes:

> Socialisation and social control go hand in hand; they are complementary bases for social order and continuity, but they are by no means identical. In addition to the norms that constitute moral imperatives, all societies have a variety of arrangements which tend to insure the support of the moral order . . . the means of support or enforcement include not only such highly institutionalised social forms as the religious and legal orders, but also the informal controls and sanctions that operate within kinship, occupation, and local community relations. The effectiveness of social control rests, in the last analysis, on the transmission of moral norms through the socialisation process, on the recruitment and socialisation of (witting or unwitting) control agents and on widespread acceptance of the legitimacy of the norms and sanctions.[6]

Socialisation agents, when acting also as agents of social control, have responsibilities in relation to maintaining the prevailing moral norms as decreed at macro level.

Consensual agreement about such moral norms does not necessarily exist at micro levels and, of course, these are the levels at which most teachers and social workers operate. Clausen's use of the phrase witting and unwitting agents of social control is interesting. Whereas the police could be described as witting agents of social control, doctors, social workers and teachers could sometimes be described as unwitting agents of social control. In some circumstances such agents have legally backed powers which they are expected to use in order to ensure the maintenance of the prevailing mores of society. Moreover, they are publicly accountable for the use of such powers. For example, compulsory admission to mental hospital, compulsory school attendance and the reception into care of children, are all situations in which teachers and social workers are acting as agents of social control. However, there are many other ways, often much less explicit, where socialising agents also act as agents of social control, often without realising it themselves. There are not only dissonances about prevailing moral norms in a pluralistic society such as ours, there are also differences as to how norms should be encouraged or ensured; and furthermore there are disagreements in our expectations of ourselves and one another at the personal level of functioning.

The aims of socialisation—some problems of definition

The aims of socialisation are inevitably imprecise. Not only are there particular differences of opinion over the question of social control, but there is also lack of general agreement about the aims of the process in relation to children. The definition of a good citizen is more likely to be couched in terms of such prohibitions as, does not break the law or act cruelly towards his or her children, than in affirmations. It could be said that the process of socialisation is to enable individuals to achieve an approximation of those social norms which seem to be implicitly expected by society at any one time. This implies that people are expected to develop sufficient abilities to function as a physical, economic and emotional unit as well as contributing to society, perhaps changing it for the better. Such a loose definition, of course, begs many questions, like the criteria for an adequate contribution to society, or change for the better. Further questions are raised, such as what constitutes a unit and whose definitions should prevail? Nevertheless, it is on the basis of some such goals that our society is endeavouring to function; and it is on some kind of tacit acceptance of these goals that our social structures are based.

While the values which determine the goals of the socialisation processes are so implicit they often remain unclarified and un-challenged by the people within the system. It is therefore difficult to identify their influence on the functioning of the social structures, and differences and conflicts of values about the basic assumptions which underlie such socialising agencies as schools and families often lie dormant yet cause dysfunction in the system.

In some aspects of their task, schools and social work agencies may have very similar goals—for instance the promotion of social competence—and yet failure to recognise and make explicit the values on which such a goal is based can lead to failures of communication, confusion or even conflict. Even where both the values and goals are explicit and tacitly agreed upon, the means by which such goals may be reached may be vastly different and remain misunderstood or unquestioned. Sometimes too, values operating at different levels within the same system may lead to ends which are contradictory to its avowed goals.

A current example is the placing of young people in bed and breakfast hotels. While everyone concerned with the young person (teachers, magistrates and social workers alike) might agree that removal from home is the best decision, most would agree that to place a young person who is in need of care and control in a bed and breakfast hotel is unlikely to be the best solution to their difficulties. How do such situations then arise? This may well be because there are no vacancies in appropriate homes or hostels for such young people. Or, if there are, there may not be sufficient residential social workers to work in them. At the level of both social service and education committees, choices have to be made in terms of costs. Often such choices are made on political grounds rather than grounds of need. Provision for disturbed adolescents, which is very expensive, may be considered inexpedient from the point of view of vote-catching. While at grassroots level teachers in schools and social workers in the field may agree that the needs of adolescents are of paramount importance, within the finance committee of their shared local authority different projects may vie with one another for funding, the eventual decision being made as the result of political bargaining.

Socialisation, social interaction, social functioning

Despite the difficulties in defining the goals of the socialisation processes and the conflicting values on which these goals are formulated, Clausen points out that society depends on some consensus about present and emergent goals and the means for achieving them. Socialisation is currently taken to mean the process of training a human being for social participation in his group. McBroom[7] writes: 'Broadly therefore it is the acquisition of knowledge of self and others in social interaction, the process by which the human being attains his most fully human potential and level of functioning.'

While some writers, like McBroom, consider that social workers may be involved in compensatory socialisation (role learning because of missed opportunities) or resocialisation (efforts to alter deviant behaviour), others, like Goldstein, are less specific about the social worker as a socialising agent. In education there may be debates about the amount of emphasis and time given to socialisation or, for instance, the cognitive development of pupils, but most teachers would agree that schools have some responsibility for the development of their pupils' capacities for social interaction.

An alternative description of competent social interaction might be social functioning. Boehm[8] considers that the primary focus of social work is on social interaction, the interaction of the individual with his or her environment. He writes:

The nature of any problem in the area of social interaction is determined both by the individual's potential capacity for relationships in the performance of his social roles and by the social resources he uses to satisfy his needs for self fulfilment.

The concept of tasks

The idea that there are tasks which must be delineated and performed by social systems may help to define the role and functions of the various socialisation agents concerned with schoolchildren. While the concept of task may be criticised on the grounds that it implies doing things to or with people rather than providing opportunities for them, thus devaluing the facilitative role of both schools and social work, it does nevertheless afford an opportunity for focusing on key issues. Rice,[9] in writing of business enterprises and educational institutions, postulates the idea of the primary task—that which an organisation must perform in order to survive. The definition of such a primary task has to be inferred from the behaviour of the organisation, but failure of leaders to define the primary task appropriately, or lack of agreement on its definition, will jeopardise the survival of the organisation or enterprise. Society requires families, schools, social work agencies (and others) to perform tasks in relation to the socialisation of schoolchildren. Even if these three social institutions perform their tasks appropriately, they differ in the emphasis placed on various sub-tasks and on the processes and methods whereby such tasks are performed. Underlying the performance of these processes are the value systems of the social institutions, the ideological basis which informs and underpins their actions. A way of looking at the schools system would be to consider the five-year-old pupils as the through-put (which is how Rice describes the 'material' on which an organisation carries out its primary task), with teachers interacting with them in such a way as to produce socially functioning (socialised) young people at sixteen. Some schoolchildren also require social work intervention, as do some of their families; but all children of school age go to school, and most schoolchildren have families or substitute families with whom they also interact. See Figure 1.

Clausen[10] has formulated the tasks which families and schools must undertake as part of the socialisation process. Adapting their material to make it more relevant to the situation in Britain, and

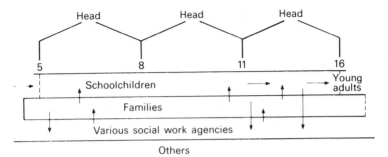

Figure 1 School throughput

formulating social work tasks in a similar way, Table 1 demonstrates both the overlap of tasks between the systems and the process of socialisation.

The initial tasks of the family system are to provide nurturant and physical care for the developing child and training in his or her physiological needs (tasks 1 and 2). In the ordinary course of events, the school system is not involved at this early stage, except indirectly through older siblings. The social work system is, however, likely to be involved if the family is socially deprived, and particularly if it is likely to become homeless (task 8). The school system is not usually involved until the child is about five years old, although the White Paper *A Framework for Expansion*[11] stressed the need for resources for the pre-school child. Unfortunately, the recent swingeing cuts in the educational services have made such an expansion highly unlikely for the present generation of pre-school children. Roughly speaking, the provision of nursery classes favours the institution- and profession-centred approach (as described by Van der Eyken),[12] and these may be provided by the school system, thus extending the tasks of the school to include the training in physical tasks and some nurturant and physical care (tasks 1 and 2). On the other hand, where families are failing to discharge these tasks, social work agencies (usually the social services department) may become involved in providing play groups, day care (the home and community approach described by Van der Eyken), or even residential or foster care for under-fives, in order to protect them and provide for their development. Such intervention could be considered as enabling individuals, families or groups to subscribe to the dominant or cultural values of society or to overcome as far as possible any gross deficiencies in development which may hinder their social functioning (tasks 4 and 8). The question of schools' or social work agencies' involvement in these early tasks will be considered further in the section on Educational Priority Areas.

TABLE 1 *Overlap of tasks between the system and the process of socialisation*

Family tasks	Educational tasks	Social work tasks
1 The provision of nurturant and physical care		
2 Training in physiological needs, e.g., learning toilet training, etc.		
3 Teaching and skill training in language and perceptual skills and self care	To teach specific cognitive skills such as reading, writing and to impart information	
4 Orienting the child to his/her immediate world of self, family, neighbourhood, community and society	Orienting the child to his/her intellectual heritage and seeking to commit him/her to its ends	To enable individuals, families and groups to subscribe to the dominant cultural values and goals of society
5 Transmitting culture and subculture goals and values and motivating the child to accept them as his/her own	To teach child cultural goals and values and to make clear their relevance	To provide information relevant to the resources needed in order to subscribe to those values and goals
6 Promoting interpersonal skills, motives and modes of feeling and behaviour in relation to others and acting as role models	To provide guidance and models for problem solving and for role taking	To provide guidance and models for problem solving and for role taking
7 Guiding, correcting and helping child (and later adolescent) to formulate his/her own goals and plan his/her activities	To provide an atmosphere which is conducive to learning	To provide a relationship which is conducive to enabling the other tasks to be carried out
8	To overcome any gross deficiencies in development which may hinder child's performance in role taking	To overcome as far as possible any gross deficiencies in development which may hinder social functioning
9		To act as an agent within society so as to promote a fairer distribution of the resources needed in order to allow individuals, families and groups to subscribe to the dominant cultures and values of society

19

The teaching of skills in relation to language, perceptual and physical skills and self care (task 3), while certainly initiated within the family, is reinforced within with schools system, particularly in infants' schools. The teaching of specific skills (task 2) is considered by many primary school teachers as their major task. Social work agencies have not traditionally been involved in any formal teaching of skills to schoolchildren, although for children who have suffered gross deficiencies in development which may hinder their social functioning (task 8), they have often found ways of reinforcing such teaching. Social workers are becoming increasingly involved in community projects and can therefore find themselves both indirectly concerned with such tasks and sometimes directly involved, particularly with young children and adolescents: in organising activity groups for them after school hours or during the holidays, for instance.

The task of orienting a child to his or her immediate world of self, family and neighbourhood is a primary task (task 4) and could be said to include the all-important task of helping the child to make relationships. Ruddock[13] describes the essence of relationship as reciprocity, and a capacity for making relationships is of primary importance to the developing child. The task of orienting the child to his or her immediate world of self and family is reinforced and extended by the school system, and includes community and cultural goals as well as orienting the child to his or her intellectual heritage (tasks 4 and 5). It is in attempting to teach the child culturally acceptable goals and attitudes that schools may be introducing values which are dissonant with those of the child's family (task 5) and thus initiating a conflict for the child. There is increased debate among teachers at the present time about their power to decide cultural goals and values of their pupils; and it is in this aspect of the curriculum that the school system becomes involved in political issues. It is particularly the task of the school to demonstrate the relevance of these cultural values to the developing child, and when both family and school have failed to do so the social work system becomes involved. It is when a child translates what is in effect a value conflict into socially unacceptable behaviour that the social work system intervenes to enable individuals, families and groups to subscribe to the dominant cultural values (task 4).

The social work system is in a similar political dilemma over whose value system should prevail. Obviously, if there is already a clash of values between the school and the family, it is even more important that the child should be enabled to subscribe to the cultural values and goals of society. Yet who decides what these are? The social work agency, whose policies may be dominated by political issues (the social service departments), employs social workers—who are expected to subscribe to its policies. The final decision as to whose values should prevail often rests with the courts, which frequently become involved at this stage. It is in this area of deciding what are the dominant cultural values that there is so much current difficulty, as is demonstrated by the interpretation of the 1969 Children and Young Persons Act.

The task of providing guidance and role models for problem solving and role taking is, of course, initiated by and within the family (task 6) but may be reinforced or extended within the school system. Indeed one of the current criticisms of schools is that if sexist stereotyped roles are not introduced within the family, they are in the schools, particularly in relation to girls. Most families have particular 'styles' of problem solving and schools have the opportunity to extend the range of problem-solving activities. Here again, if there is dissonance between the school and family styles of role taking or problem solving, the social work system may eventually become involved, either during the pupil's school life or later.

The final family task, that of guiding, correcting and helping the child to formulate his or her own goals and to plan his or her activities (task 7), is sometimes initiated by the school (as part of orienting the child to his or her intellectual heritage) (task 4). The schools are also criticised for their attempts to seek to commit the pupil to its (society's) ends. The prevailing debate about the schools selecting the slots into which the child as an adult may fit, falls into this aspect of the school's tasks. (See also E. Goodacre, *Home and School,* National Foundation for Educational Research, 1970.) Nevertheless, it is often during the phase of adolescent rejection of and rebellion against family values that schools can and do play a vital part in performing this task. Here, too, the social work system may become involved.

It is in the school and social work tasks in relation to overcoming any gross deficiencies which may hinder the child's learning or the client's social functioning that much ambiguity lies (task 8). If it is the child's cognitive development which is hindered, then the task falls to the school. There is, however, increasing criticism that the schools are failing to teach some children enough to enable them to take their appropriate place in modern society. This has been substantiated by the Bullock Committee.[14] It is in relation to this task that less structured agencies are developing, some of them wholly or partly financed by social services departments or education departments. Such agencies could hardly be described as social work agencies or schools. They will be considered later in the section on the boundary issues.

The school task of providing an atmosphere which is conducive to learning (task 7) would presumably entail the teachers developing and using their relationship with their pupils. It is in the execution of this task that the problems related to discipline, class control and the choice of teaching methods fall. There is also currently much debate about the indoctrination of clients by social workers' use of their power within the social work relationship. The social work task of creating a relationship which is conducive to carrying out the other tasks (task 7) need not be so different from the relationships of teacher and pupils, particularly when the social worker is working with groups of clients. This aspect will be considered further in the chapter on the people in the system.

The school, then, usually acts as an extension of the family, reinforcing, elaborating and building on the tasks of socialisation already begun within the family. The school, too, may initiate where the family has failed to begin or perform its tasks. The school may also provide compensatory socialisation in the form of remedial help; or even resocialisation in order to undo developmental deficiencies caused by the familial socialisation processes. For the majority of children the task performance of the school as a secondary agent of socialisation is enough, perhaps particularly as regards their cognitive development. If, however, the failure of the family task performance has been gross, then the social work system, by acting as an extension and back-up service to both the family and the school, may provide the socialisation (amelioration and support) or the resocialisation (change of family socialisation patterns). Frequently the failures in socialisation processes which lead to social work intervention are those which involve the area of emotional development and the social functioning of the child, though such failure can lead to inhibition of cognitive development.

Where the social work system seems to have a unique contribution to make is in providing information to families and schools about the resources needed and/or available in order to assist (them) in the task of enabling families or groups to subscribe to the cultural goals of society (task 5). It is here that Goldstein's[15] view of the social work task being to socialise the socialising agencies may be considered. While it is the task of social workers to be informed about benefits (such as free school meals, clothing, family income supplements and rent rebates, etc.), they must also know about family rights and protection, for instance as regards custody and security of tenure (or at least where to get information about such rights). In addition to such knowledge, the social workers in the social work agencies are also expected to use this knowledge in accordance with such social work principles as respect for persons and the individual's right to self-determination. It is in applying these principles that the social worker may undertake the task of socialising the socialising agencies.

The task of acting as a change agent within society in order to promote a fairer distribution of resources (task 9), while not unique to social work, is not a family task, nor is it on Clausen's list of school tasks. While social workers would probably agree that changing society in order to promote a fairer distribution of resources is a social work task, it is also a political one and some would consider it best undertaken within the political system. However, there is a growing indication that schools might take a more assertive role in executing such tasks, instead of passively accepting their role in handing on dominant cultural attitudes in relation to the allocation of resources. As will be shown in the section on community schools, the opportunity exists for schools to become involved as change agents within society, even though this may cause conflicts within the schools over the execution of other tasks, for instance the transmission of cultural values. The problem of determining what the prevailing cultural values are is increasing, for both teachers and social workers. In pluralistic societies such as ours, just whose views should prevail? This dilemma will be discussed further in the chapter on the people in the system; but it should not be overlooked that it is just those children who are of most concern to teachers and social workers who need clear and coherent discussion and demonstration of these values.

Therefore, the analysis of tasks carried out by the family, the school and the social work system shows considerable overlap. The schools and social work systems share similar dilemmas in their attempt to introduce or reinforce the task of enabling the child to subscribe to the dominant cultural values and goals of society. Even the law does not always provide such useful guidelines, not only because the law is inevitably open to differing interpretations, but also because there are conflicting philosophies underlying laws in relation to children (for instance those of the 1944 Education Act and of the 1969 Children and Young Persons Act).

Where the school system and the social work systems do differ is in the emphasis which they may place on different tasks. There are debates within education about the importance of weighting the curriculum towards the cognitive or emotional development of children. Generally speaking, the primary educationists would give more weight to the latter and the secondary educationists to the former. Within the social work system there is also considerable debate about whether social workers should spend more of their time acting as change agents within society and less time on enabling individuals, families and groups to subscribe to the dominant values of society. The criticism here is that many of the prevailing values merely serve to shore up the standards of a capitalist society and therefore maintain the unequal distribution of resources.

Another difference centres on the methods which the school

system and the social work system use to carry out their tasks. This is particularly apparent in the relationships which the teachers and social workers develop and use to carry out their tasks. It is also apparent in the structure of the organisations which are created in order to carry out the functions expected of the systems. These issues too, will be discussed later, in the section on the people in the system.

It is, therefore, when the school system, too, is failing (or has failed) to fulfil the tasks expected of it that the social work system usually becomes involved. This may have something to do with the complaint frequently made that schools do not refer children early enough. (No one likes to admit failure and perhaps more especially when it means that someone else will be trying to pick up the pieces.) The fact that public expectations of the school system are often unrealistic only serves to compound this conflictual situation. Indeed, it may actually exacerbate the tensions between the school and social work systems.

The primary task of the school is to reinforce and extend the socialisation processes begun within the family system. The primary task of the social work system is to engage in compensatory or resocialisation processes not only of individuals and families, but also of other socialising institutions. Goldstein writes: 'the profession's commitment to the social well being of persons demands continuous examination of existing policies, programmes and services of institutions and their impacts on special populations in functional, ethical and value terms.' It could be argued, therefore, that while schools are concerned with developing capacities for social functioning, the social work system is concerned with the breakdown (possible or total) of social functioning. Therefore the considerable overlap between the tasks of the schools and the social work system in relation to some children could lead to reinforcement of their task performance or, at the other extreme, to conflict and confusion.

Kellmer Pringle writes:

Children have four basic needs: 1) the need for love and security in which parents, teachers and other care givers play their part; 2) the need for new experiences, in which both play and language are important; 3) the need for praise and recognition, particularly for effort rather than success; 4) the need for responsibility appropriately recognised and given strengthening co-operation rather than competition.[16]

Some children, she points out, appear to be at risk and 'it is often for just these children that schools and social work agencies find themselves most inextricably involved in tasks of compensatory or remedial socialisation'. Kellmer Pringle sees the issues in this way:

If later malfunctioning or handicap can be predicted with a satisfactory degree of probability then three consequences would follow: Firstly, it would be necessary to refine methods for identifying 'vulnerable' or 'at risk' groups at the earliest possible time. Secondly, it would be important to devise procedures to prevent harmful effects altogether, or at least to mitigate their severity. Lastly, it is crucial to evaluate both the short and long term effectiveness of any interventionist procedures.

One way of predicting possible malfunctioning is by identifying periods of stress, both in individuals and families. All individuals go through periods of stress as part of the process of living. Most of us weather these storms, others falter and recover, still others founder. While Kellmer Pringle has pointed out the life situations in which children may be at risk, she also points out that early identification is crucial. A framework which is of assistance in guiding us towards a more precise identification of children at risk of breakdown in social functioning, is the concept of the life-cycle. Individuals and families could all be described as going through a pattern of life-cycles—they are part of everyone's psychic and social development.

Individual and family life-cycles

In every life-cycle there are particular transitional periods and it is often at just these transitional periods that individuals or families seem to make changes which result in spurts of growth of a bio-psychosocial nature; but it is also sometimes possible to trace breakdowns of a similar nature to these periods.

Erikson,[17] an anthropologist and psychoanalyst, writes of the development of individual identity as passing through a series of crises which he calls 'Life Crises' or Crises of Identity. He describes eight stages through which individuals pass during their life-cycle. At each stage there are certain components of identity which come to ascendancy and present the individual with the challenge of reconciling two opposing polarities. The needs of each stage lie dormant, coming to ascendancy only at times of heightened preoccupation. At each phase a crisis develops, until a lasting solution is found by the individual. Only when a solution is found which achieves a dynamic balance between the two opposing polarities, is the individual able to move freely towards the next stage. At each stage the environment, too, particularly in the form of important others (parents, teachers, etc.) impinges on the individual, conveying to him or her both expectations and feedback on performance. Each life crisis affords fresh opportunities for reconsidering 'old' solutions, so that crises which have been maladaptively resolved at stages of development may be resolved afresh during subsequent identity crises. Erikson sees these life crises as period of hope and challenge as well as times of confusion and distress. There are problems to be confronted, tasks to be carried out and new possibilities discovered, each of which can add to the development and enrichment of the identity: 'Each stage becomes a crisis because incipient growth and awareness in a new part function together with a shift in instinctual energy and yet cause a specific vulnerability in that part.' According to Erikson, the crisis is a turning point which results in a radical change of perspective.

His eight stages roughly correlate with certain ages of physical development and also with the role changes through which most of us pass. In describing each stage, Erikson has selected two key descriptive modes which envisage the struggle between the extremes and which ultimately lead to a satisfactory balance between the polarities.

Table 2 outlines Erikson's stages, together with the social roles appropriate to them. Also included are the components of identity in the struggle relevant to each stage as well as their contextual place within the social system. In this way the table not only demonstrates the crises through which the individual passes (and which must be resolved for satisfactory development of identity), but also that the social systems impinge on the resolution of these crises.

TABLE 2 *Individual life-cycle*

Stage	Tasks	Social system
1 Babyhood	Trust—mistrust	Family
2 Toddler	Autonomy—shame and doubt	Family
3 Playground/nursery	Initiative—guilt	Family/playgroup
4 School child	Industry—inferiority	Family/school
5 Adolescent	Identity—identity confusion	School/work/family
6 Young adult	Intimacy—isolation	Work/marriage
7 Family life	Generativity—stagnation	Work/family
8 Old Age	Integrity—despair	Family

Erikson considers life crises in individual and developmental terms; his theory shows a way in which individual indentity develops towards ultimate maturity. While he recognises the influence and impingement of the family and of the wider society, his theory holds them constant while considering the dynamic bio-psychosocial development of the individual.

On the other hand, Turner,[18] a social anthropologist, writes in terms of the nuclear family life-cycle, which he sees as linked with the other social systems of which it is a part. In considering the developmental cycle of the household as a domestic group, with special reference to nuclear families as household units, he distinguishes between normative patterns and forms of deviation. Turner focuses particularly on patterns of kinship and outlines four phases through which families usually pass: (1) the courtship phase; (2) the initial phase of marriage; (3) the child-bearing and child-rearing phase; and (4) the phase of disintegration. Other writers, too, distinguish phases of family life, but the Rapoports,[19] a psychoanalyst and a sociologist, particularly link these phases with personal and interpersonal tasks which must be performed within each phase, as part of the role transitions integral with the phase. The idea of linking roles, the social patterning of behaviour and the tasks which the role holder is expected to carry out, can be useful in the study of the family life-cycle. Perlman,[20] a social worker, writes of vital roles as having four dimensions: (1) to carry a role means to act or do something, actions and behaviour being part of role performance; (2) to carry a role means to do something in relation to one or more others—interactions and transactions between and among people; (3) transactions between people are shaped and governed by their ideas and expectation and judgments or the attitudes and behaviour of the self and others; (4) ideas, expectations and judgments are charged with drives and emotions, feelings and their accompanying pushes and pulls being integrally involved. The Rapoports' study of role transition is related particularly to the tasks of engagement and marriage, but it seems that it would be quite possible to extend this concept of role transition with accompanying tasks in which the role holders' expectation of themselves and each other affect the performance.

Figure 2 shows the pattern of events in their customary sequence within the life-cycle of a family. Ten phases are outlined, the pattern of development and the role changes which occur being viewed primarily from the point of view of the original couple.

Though we distinguish ten phases within the average family life-cycle, the role changes with their accompanying tasks tend to occur in clusters which affect the whole family. Focusing on the nuclear family in Figure 2, there is a cluster of role changes occurring either simultaneously or in quick succession around the time of the child-bearing and child-rearing phase and when the children first go to school. There is a second cluster during the years in which there is another period when several members of the family may experience role changes. Adolescent children move out, their parents readjust, become parents-in-law and later grandparents; and about the same time or not too long after they may retire and also lose their own parents. All these role changes involve the completion of certain tasks—personal tasks, interpersonal tasks and tasks involving the whole family.

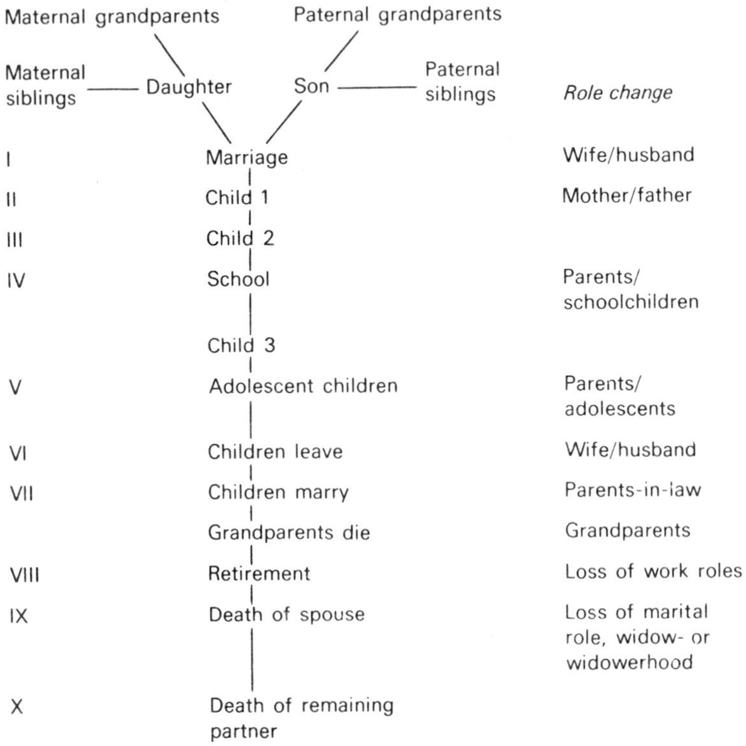

		Role change
Maternal grandparents	Paternal grandparents	
Maternal siblings —— Daughter Son —— Paternal siblings		*Role change*
I	Marriage	Wife/husband
II	Child 1	Mother/father
III	Child 2	
IV	School	Parents/ schoolchildren
	Child 3	
V	Adolescent children	Parents/ adolescents
VI	Children leave	Wife/husband
VII	Children marry	Parents-in-law
	Grandparents die	Grandparents
VIII	Retirement	Loss of work roles
IX	Death of spouse	Loss of marital role, widow- or widowerhood
X	Death of remaining partner	

Figure 2 Family life-cycle

Crisis situations

In addition to the individual and familial crises which occur naturally as part of the developmental cycles of living, there are other hazards and stresses which most of us are subjected to from time to time. Caplan,[21] a specialist in community mental health, defines these crises as loss situations or those in which there is a threat of loss. In loss situations a person may lose resources essential to his or her needs, such as the loss of a parent or of a job. In other situations there is the threat or fear of loss of essential resources, such as a child's fear that his or her mother may not return home from hospital. Caplan sees such crises as relatively unexpected and causing a period of confusion and stress while the individual attempts to cope. Like Erikson, he considers crisis situations to be those which temporarily present people with problems and tasks for which they have no current repertoire of coping mechanisms. He, too, sees them as opportunities not only for developing new skills and attitudes which will stand the individual in good stead in future situations of stress, but also as a means of acquiring additional strengths and flexibility of personality and thus the qualitative range of living. Some of these crisis situations are unprovoked and occur naturally, for instance the loss situations described above, which are dealt with by grieving and mourning, the situations involving threat of loss being dealt with by what Caplan calls 'worry work'. There are, however, other crisis situations which are provoked either by individuals or by families. These may be provoked by individuals for reasons of their own, either deliberately or because of the psychic structure of their personality. For instance, a child may stay away from school either because he or she is phobic about school, or because either he or she and/or the family do not agree with compulsory school attendance. Similarly, families provoke crisis situations either unwittingly or because of a clash of values, which may or may not be the result of deliberate choice. This may result in a crisis situation in which the wider social system—whether family, school or society—will duly respond to the provocation. However, even such provoked crisis situations can result in the acquisition of new skills, attitudes and wider horizons for the individual or family involved.

Marris, a community sociologist, in writing of conservatism, change and innovation at the societal level, considers that changes when the familiar pattern of life is disrupted can also be understood in terms of loss and bereavement followed by grieving:

> Grief can be evoked not only by death, but by any profoundly disruptive loss of meaning . . . . In response to an event, we identify it as belonging to a class of events and then discriminate the best action in the circumstances. This behaviour will break down, first, if there is no best action, whatever the event, because the actor is robbed of essential purpose, as in severe personal bereavement. Second it also breaks down if the event cannot be identified and every attempt to classify it is proved by what follows to have been mistaken . . . . Third, besides the

loss of attachments and disintegration of a predictable environment, the meaning of life may be threatened prospectively . . . . there is a fourth kind of loss, which destroys only the meaning of a relationship, not the relationship itself. Behaviour may break down, for instance, when the same event falls into more than one category. There may then no longer be one best action, but two or more which mutually exclude each other, according to how the event is interpreted.[22]

In summary, there are transitional periods both in individual and family life-cycles when changes of a bio-psychosocial nature impinge on the individual or family in such a way as to cause a crisis situation which, while temporarily resulting in confusion, stress or even breakdown, can eventually result in innovation which qualitatively improves the life style. Natural or provoked crisis situations can also have similar effects and results, both for individuals and for families. Marris's theory postulates that innovations at societal level, too, are the response to loss or threatened loss or disintegration of meaning both in personal careers and societal terms. It is at these times of crisis, whether individual, familial or even societal, that appropriate and planned intervention can both prevent further breakdown and produce innovative change.

While some of the at-risk situations are situations of privation in economic as well as bio-psychosocial terms, there are others which are the result of events of crisis proportions which change the life-cycle pattern. The loss of a parent by departure or death, which turns the family into a one-parent family, is a crisis which may result in chronic deprivations in economic and psychosocial terms. The knowledge that a child is mentally or physically handicapped is again a crisis which affects the bio-psychosocial development of that child, but also has psychosocial reverberations throughout the whole family. Both these situations result in losses which must be faced and met with appropriate grief and mourning in order both to come to terms with the loss and to re-establish changed patterns of life-style which take the losses into account. The circumstances of some parents and children are such that separation even for relatively short periods can precipitate a dangerous situation that has to be worked at by all concerned if the life-cycle which has been even temporarily interrupted is to be resumed and the original life-style reinstated.

In order to show the crises which all individuals and families ordinarily go through as part of their identity and family life-cycles, Table 2 and Figure 2 have been put together as Table 3. This shows the stress points at which *all* families are vulnerable because of psychosocial stresses (often bio-psychosocial stresses) which occur at

TABLE 3 *Family life-cycle in social context*

Maternal grandparents / Maternal siblings — *Paternal grandparents / Paternal siblings*

Personal social services	Stress points (Individual, family)		Wife—husband	School	Other social services
					Particularly Health, Housing, Supplementary Benefits, etc.
(peak stress)	1, 6	I	Marriage		
	1, 6	I	Parenthood child 1		
	1, 2, 3, 7	III	child 2		
	1, 2, 4, 7	IV	School child 3	Infants	
(peak stress)	4, 5, 7	V	Adolescent children	Junior Secondary	
	6, 7	VI	Middle age (health hazards)		
			Death of grandparents		
	6, 7, 8	VII	Children leave home	Higher and further education	
	8	VIII	Retirement		
	8	IX	Death of one spouse		
		X	Death of remaining partner		

31

that time. It also reveals the two periods of peak stress, when the family members as individuals are not only undergoing stresses relating to physical and psychological tasks which need resolution as well as role transitions in relation to one another, but at the *same time* the whole family is undergoing a major developmental transition phase. It is these phases of agglomeration of bio-psychosocial stresses which require rapid and major changes within the family members as individuals and as a group, which are the periods of peak stress. The first period of peak stress usually follows the birth of the second child and lasts up to and including the admission to school of all children. For some young families the period of peak stress may begin with parenthood or even marriage, particularly for those couples who have incompletely managed the separation from their own families of origin. During this *'young family peak stress period'* all the family members are rapidly experiencing identity crises, role transitions and pressures from society in the form of expectations and feedback. The intensity of this stress depends on many factors, but children very close together in age is one important factor and another is the age at which the children make their first foray from the family into the outside world, for instance to a play group or nursery class. The second period of peak stress is around the time when the adolescent children leave home, and the parents are coping with their own mid-life crises and may also be experiencing the loss of their own parents. This is often followed in quick succession by becoming grandparents and the retirement of one or both partners. The order of these crises may be varied, but there is also an agglomeration of bio-psychosocial stresses at this *'mid-life family peak stress period'*, a period which may be prolonged or relatively short and exceedingly intense and is often dependent on the ages of the family members involved and also on their physical fitness.

If at the same time as any of the normal crisis periods, but particularly at those of peak stress, the family is also experiencing privation or deprivation, then the hazards for them are greater. Large families with low incomes, for instance, may find the young family period of peak stress particularly difficult; and if these families also experience additional unexpected crises, they are very likely to fail. Crises which result in loss or threat of loss situations are also much more likely to result in the breakdown of social functioning of individual family members at these periods of stress. The young family peak stress period is, therefore, one of maximum vulnerability; the mid-life family peak stress period is preoccupied with losses anyway, but if the loss is by desertion or death of a partner or the parent of an adolescent, it would be crucial.

Table 3 not only puts the individual and family life-cycles

together, but also places them in their social context, showing the availability of the social services at times of stress.

While showing the availability of support services at stress periods, the table demonstrates that the school as a support system is not available at that time when the family most needs the school's reinforcement in terms of secondary socialisation tasks. Indeed, for the young family period of peak stress, it could be argued that compulsory admission to school (with its possible consequent hazards in terms of value conflict between school and home) can constitute precipitate role changes with which the family may be unable to cope. For instance, for parents who cannot share their children or have low self-esteem (or both), entry to school can constitute an additional hazard rather than a reinforcement. While the development of voluntary pre-school programmes is beginning to provide much-needed support, too little attention is paid to ways in which schools could provide psychosocial support for young families at this period, although the community school movement is showing interest in such developments. At the mid-life family period of peak stress, too, the potential support of the school is being withdrawn just as the adolescent children are most in need of external supports and most estranged from their parents. This is also the time when parents are most preoccupied with psychosocial tasks of their own and have least to spare in terms of the needs of their adolescent children. Insufficient attention is given to ways in which difficulties of this kind may be alleviated. The young people have, after all, been within the school system for eleven years during which there must have been at least some recognition of the pattern of their life-style. Yet it often seems little more than fortunate chance that youth workers become involved at this period of stress. The school system therefore becomes linked with the family developmental life-cycle during the first period of peak stress and often severs these links, thus terminating its responsibilities towards the family during the second period of peak stress. For some families both entry to and exit from the school system add to the strains of these peak periods of family stress. The school system, therefore, becomes involved with families during the first period of peak stress and terminates its responsibilities during the second period; in other words, both entry to and exit from the school system are integral parts of the family developmental life-cycle.

Social functioning and the prevention of social breakdown

If the aims of families, schools, and the social work systems as agencies of socialisation are promoting the social functioning of individuals (however defined), then it is essential to try to distinguish not only how they achieve such ends, but also to evaluate both success and failure. While the life-cycle theory gives some indication of periods of stress at which individuals and families may be vulnerable to breakdown, there is insufficient knowledge as to why some families seem to manage to transcend these periods of stress and others do not. While Kellmer Pringle[23] has indicated groups of children who are at risk of failing to have their needs satisfied, there is little indication of how remedial or resocialisation processes might prevent or ameliorate the possibility of their social breakdown.

Table 3 reveals the availability of support services, giving particular weight to the schools and social work system in relation to the family, but there is no indication of whether these systems do in fact provide the secondary socialisation processes needed and in ways that allow the families and children who are at risk of social breakdown to use them.

Bartlett,[24] an American social work writer, considers that social work is concerned with social functioning; but, as has been shown, this is not the unique province of social work, for schools too are concerned with social functioning. He describes social functioning as concern with people coping with life situations. The concept of coping is a loose one, which might best be defined as managing to function well enough within one's own expectations and those of society (Figure 3) (this will be discussed further in the next chapter). Bartlett particularly stresses the balance between the demands of the social environment and people's efforts to cope. It is the understanding of this balance which Bartlett considers to be the province of social work. She also uses 'orientation' in a rather specific way so as to mean 'the social worker's position and perspective in relation to the people and social phenomena in his or her practice'. It is in the balance between those demands that the first difference between the school system and the social work system becomes apparent. On the whole, the school would give more weight to the demands of the social environment: this is the task which society expects of the school as its agent of secondary socialisation. On the other hand, the social work system might give more weight to people's coping efforts: society requires the social worker to mediate between the individual who is not coping and societal institutions of all kinds.

While the ultimate aims of the socialisation processes of both the schools and the social work systems may be similar, the orientation which they adopt is different. Teachers are primarily oriented towards all schoolchildren aged from five to sixteen. Furthermore, these children are seen as functioning until evidence arises to the contrary. Social workers on the other hand are oriented towards people of any age, but only those who are perceived to be in some difficulty with social functioning. Thus teachers could be said to be oriented towards all children, often to the point of minimising the importance of their family relationships, while social workers could be said to be oriented only towards children who are at risk or malfunctioning, often to the point of accentuating the needs of such children at the expense of other 'ordinary' children. While teachers and social workers may draw on similar areas of knowledge (for instance, psychology and sociology), the values on which they base their use of that knowledge will be different and, in particular, will

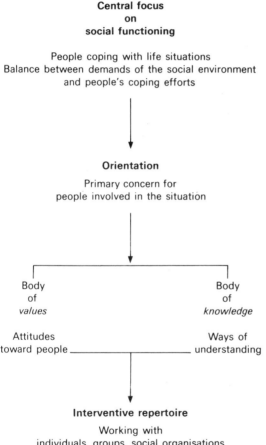

**Central focus
on
social functioning**

People coping with life situations
Balance between demands of the social environment
and people's coping efforts

Orientation

Primary concern for
people involved in the situation

Body
of
values

Body
of
knowledge

Attitudes
toward people

Ways of
understanding

Interventive repertoire

Working with
individuals, groups, social organisations
directly and through collaborative action

Figure 3 The common base of social work practice
(Source: reproduced by permission of the National Association of Social Workers from *The Common Base of Social Work Practice* by Harriet M. Bartlett, NASW, 1970, p. 130)

be influenced by their respective orientations. Teachers, for example, are likely to emphasise the needs of average individual children, or groups of children of a particular age group; while social workers are more likely to consider the needs of the family (which may be in conflict) or the needs of natural though deviant groups of children (such as the delinquent gang). The ways of understanding the people with whom they are concerned will, of course, be influenced by the respective attitudes of both teachers and social workers. These in turn will be heavily influenced by the socialisation processes of their own training. In particular, teachers' modes of intervention are primarily concerned with individual children, or children of the same age who are together in artificially constructed stranger groups (i.e., classes or tutorial groups) of median size (approximately 18-30). In contrast, much of social work is concerned with individuals or natural family groups, or with small groups who have specific problems (such as the after-care of psychiatric patients). These differences also inevitably give a different perspective and orientation to their work. Teachers, too, are usually the focal point of the system of which they are a part. For instance, they are usually the only adult with a child or group of children, a factor which greatly influences the dynamic of the situation. Social workers usually attempt to make their 'client(s)' the focal point of the system and may be but one adult among several, as well as the child(ren). Thus the ways in which teachers in schools and social workers in social work agencies carry out their socialisation tasks are usually very different and much influenced by the organisational structure of the system (as will be discussed later in the chapter on the people in the system). Figure 4 adapted from Bartlett's diagram (Figure 3), gives some indication of the overlap between schools and the personal social services, both of which are concerned with the social functioning of people coping with life situations.

In summarising the issues in relation to the area of overlap between schools and social work, they are both concerned, as agents of socialisation, with the social functioning of individuals. Schools are concerned with the social functioning of all schoolchildren, social work agencies with the social work functioning of some children and their families as well as other pre-school children and adults. The area of shared concern is for some schoolchildren and their families. This concern may be concurrent or consecutive and it is operative with children and their families who are experiencing social breakdown as the result of faulty or failed socialisation processes. Although there is considerable overlap in the task performance of both the schools and the social work system, the social work system tends to become involved when the schools are failing to carry out their tasks. While there is similar knowledge available to both teachers and social workers, they may select and pattern the use of that knowledge differently. This is probably because their orientation and ways of understanding are different, teachers tending to be child-centred and oriented to a school-based value system; social workers, on the other hand, tend to be oriented towards individualised concern with people in the community, whether as individuals, families, groups or communities. The methods of intervention which schools and social work agencies use their tasks of socialisation are usually different and are influenced by the orientation, attitudes and value systems of the two spheres of operation. While both schools and social work agencies may be required by society to act as agents of social control, the societal expectations of their task performance seems to require each to contain conflicts which are inherent in a pluralistic society; these conflicts may also be 'held' between the systems.

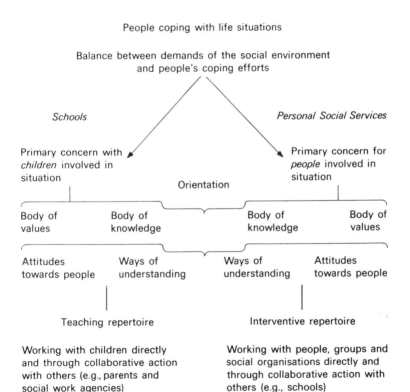

Figure 4 Social functioning
(Source: adapted from Bartlett's diagram, reproduced as Figure 3)

Chapter two

Breakdown in social functioning - social breakdown

Adequate social functioning might be described as an ability to cope with life's tasks and the pressures of environmental demands within the mores of contemporary society. Such a description could be applied to schoolchildren and their families, but it is not yet possible to develop a similar set of ideas in relation to social organisations, such as schools or social service departments. There are, of course, other theories which have been developed for this purpose (see for instance the work of Rowbottom, Billis and Hey[1] in relation to social service departments, or Litwak and Meyer[2] in relation to school community relations; the latter will be discussed later in Chapter 6).

When it comes to the question of a breakdown in social functioning, or what might constitute a definition of social breakdown, there is little satisfactory or comprehensive theory developed. However, since, as will be shown later, there is little doubt that some such phenomenon does exist and that society, or agents on behalf of society, take action in order to deal with it, an attempt must be made to describe such situations. Evans, in a helpful discussion on models and theories in social science writes:

> Models are used by way of an analogy. They are conceptually complex ways of describing social reality. A model . . . may describe elements . . . without necessarily explaining the relation between those elements or the social processes which are necessary to sustain or change them. A theory, on the other hand, attempts to go beyond simple description to (often causal) explanation.[3]

In this chapter an attempt will be made to develop a model of the *process* of social breakdown. The model will describe the gradual process of breakdown in social functioning in relation to individuals, families and schools (although it might also be developed in relation to other social institutions) and pays particular attention to the part which the various agents of social control might be considered to play in such a process. The model discussed here is in the form of a continuum, ranging from 'adequate social functioning' on the one hand to 'total social breakdown' on the other. The model features four intermediate stages: Risk of Social Breakdown, and the Primary, Secondary and Tertiary (final) Stages of Social Breakdown. While the model can be reasonably clearly developed in relation to individuals and families, it is less precise in relation to schools, partly because such a process is rarely clearly documented. However, as will be discussed later, the recent careful and coherent inquiry into events at William Tyndale School clearly reveals some such process unfolding.[4] It is intended that the model should demonstrate that such a process not only does occur, but also that the various agents of society play an important part in it. But before describing the model, it is necessary to digress in order to direct attention to some definitions implicitly used in the model.

Failures in social functioning

In the model, failures of social functioning are taken to be acts or omissions of performance which in themselves constitute a failure to live up to the expectations of society and/or those of the self. Such failures might be deemed delinquent acts, neglect, derelictions of duty, and so on. It can already be seen that moral dilemmas in relation to the definition of the norms as to what actually constitutes social functioning are already compounding the attempt to define such failures. Society's view as to what constitutes such failures is in some situations clearly defined in legal terms (as, for instance, in the definition of criminal acts of child cruelty, or as failures of responsibility under civil law in the case of parents' responsibilities with regard to the education of their children). However, even in such situations the agents of society responsible for executing the law are allowed varying degrees of discretion. In other situations the definition of failure in relation to social functioning becomes a question of what is the moral norm and whose view of this should prevail in the given situation. Nevertheless, by implication society *does* make all kinds of definitions as to what constitutes social breakdown. While these are commonly accepted perceptions, even they may vary considerably from group to group, and other perceptions are often a matter of the more powerful imposing their view on the less powerful. Nevertheless, the role of socialisation agents, and particularly the power they wield when acting as agents of social control, is clearly of great importance in the process of social breakdown.

Role of socialisation agents as agents of social control

As was discussed in Chapter 1, teachers and social workers have tasks to carry out in relation to their role both as socialisation agents and as agents of social control when exercising certain responsibilities with regard to maintaining the prevailing moral norms. Furthermore, they are frequently held accountable for carrying out these responsibilities, despite the difficulties of defining just what form some of these norms should take (also discussed in Chapter 1). These aspects of the teachers' and social workers' roles often place them in moral dilemmas (as will be discussed in Chapter 5), especially in a number of situations where the hitherto accepted moral norms appear to be changing, or where there is radical disagreement about whose perception of what is right should prevail. Nevertheless, such activities are clearly part of their role and it could be argued that, along the continuum of social functioning to social breakdown, these agents of social control are stationed, en route as it were, in order to carry out these tasks. Such agents have varying authority and powers (source, legitimation and constraints pertaining to them will be discussed later in this chapter): they are able to make definitions, according to the rules of society and the roles and functions allotted to them. These definitions may take the form of descriptive 'labels' based on the professional judgments of the agents. Such judgments inevitably involve perceptions which are affected by the value base of the agent making the judgments. Some of these definitions are merely descriptive, others may require prescriptions or interventions which necessarily follow the making of the definition. In either case, if other members of society see an impingement upon their own interests in the situation, the descriptions—and more especially the prescriptions—may be accompanied by attendant publicity. In some circumstances the prescriptions are carried out by the agent making the definition; in others, the prescriptions are carried out by other agents to whom the subject (or subjects) of the definition are referred. In such instances the prescriptions are usually redefined in terms appropriate to the second agent (who is likely to be operating from a different set of value assumptions) before carrying out the prescriptive intervention.

Definitions of social breakdown are therefore being made implicitly all the time. Heraud,[5] in describing similar complex processes, points out that the same behaviour can be treated as an infraction of rules at one time and not at another. Nevertheless, such definitions frequently result in action being taken with the intent of ameliorating the now defined breakdown. These implicit definitions are made at all levels of the social system, not only at the individual or family level, but also at levels which involve other social institutions, such as schools. They appear to be made on the grounds that the person (or the family or institution) who is the subject of the definition is failing to cope 'adequately enough' with the tasks expected of him by the larger and wider society. Further, that such failures are more or less publicly noticeable and that some other person(s) or the community at large is considerably inconvenienced or impinged upon. These failures, thus publicly recognised (whether or not so recognised by the media and thus further highlighted), are in turn adjudged by society's agents of social control, who, according to their role, make explicit definitions of social breakdown of varying degrees of severity. Such degrees of severity are dependent on the role and tasks of the agents of social control, and particularly on the powers which they wield in relation to the prescriptions they proscribe. Thus, while teachers are agents of social control and act in such a capacity in relation to *all* schoolchildren, their definitions of social breakdown are less seriously considered than those made by other agents, such as social workers (or doctors). Social workers, on the other hand, by their role are involved with children and/or their families who have *already been* so defined—by the very act of referral to a social work agency.

Strictly speaking, social workers and teachers could not be said to be agents of social control in relation to schools, although they do have some powers in connection with defining social breakdown (in the case of teachers by adding to the staff turnover, in the case of social workers by passing on evidence of serious cause for criticisms to higher authorities). Nor perhaps is it appropriate to describe the higher reaches of the education system or the political system (in the shape of democratically elected education committees) as agents of social control, although they may perform similar functions in relation to schools. Such definitions of social breakdown are eventually followed by prescriptions in relation to the subject(s).

As has already been stated, the perceptions of the agents making the definition on behalf of society may differ from those of the subject of the definition. While it depends on the extent of the discrepancy between society's agents and those of the subject, inevitably some negotiation is required in order to minimise or contain this discrepancy. It is in situations when socialisation agents are also required by society to function as agents of social control that the powers of such agents are likely to be brought into use. These are also the occasions when the rights of the subject, both for protection or to challenge the definition of the agent, also 'come into play'. The more the power which is accorded to the agents of social control, the more such a definition of social breakdown is likely to affect the subject. Hence referral to a social work agency is a major step in this direction. While society has developed controlling

41

mechanisms which restrict the powers of its agents—legal prescriptions and public accountability among them—nevertheless such agents inevitably exercise elements of discretion in relation to their tasks of definition.

Power to define social breakdown

The model makes frequent references to loss of power(s) on the part of the subject; and by implication, with regard to definition and prescription in relation to social breakdown, to the powers held by the agents of socialisation (especially when also acting as agents of social control). It is therefore important, before proceeding with a detailed discussion of the model and its possible usefulness, to consider the question of power both in relation to the autonomy of the subject and with regard to the powers of definition of social breakdown which are held by the school and social work systems. It is not possible to engage in what would be a lengthy and discursive consideration of the power of the subject, for this would certainly entail philosophical and political argument. It must therefore suffice to give a simple explanation of the changes in the state of relative freedom of the subjects under consideration in the model, the subjects being the child, the family and the school. It can be seen from the model that as the definition of social breakdown progresses, so the power of the subject *decreases*, and the use of power on the part of the socialisation agents *increases*. It can also be seen that the introduction of additional socialisation agents (i.e., referral from school to social work agency, or definitions made within the legal system) drastically reduces the autonomy of the subject.

As has been shown, the powers to define social breakdown are related to those aspects of the roles of social workers and teachers in which they are acting as agents of social control. Toren,[6] in discussing the power of social workers, writes of remunerative, coercive or normative powers. Remunerative power involves the dispensation of money, other goods and services. Coercive power is exerted in the form of protective services which involve increased surveillance. Normative power involves both the manipulation of self-esteem by giving various rewards (flags or a benediction are suggested), and social power which is mediated through interpersonal relations, an important aspect of which is the subject's wish to gain social approval. There seems every reason to think that a similar approach would be equally appropriate in relation to teachers.

For simplicity of discussion, power is here considered as being of two kinds: professional power, which would include what Toren describes as remunerative and normative power; and statutory power, which is the coercive power delegated by society to those professions. (Power and authority will be discussed further in Chapter 5.) Professional power is important in the discussion of the model in that this is usually considered to be knowledge and expertise which society traditionally accords to various authority figures. It is, however, important to comment here that even such long-respected figures of authority as doctors and judges are increasingly subject to attack as regards their professional power. The universal value of education is also under question, and this naturally affects the status and professional power of the teacher. Social work too, is coming to be seen in a much more negative light, instead of as a profession of benign do-gooders as was the tendency in the past. Nevertheless, while such professional power may not necessarily entail automatic acceptance when used to define conditions of social breakdown, it is still considered worthy of consideration.

Statutory power is that delegated by society to specific professions and is usually backed by the possibility of reference to the courts and the application of legal sanctions if necessary, though this is also subject to appeal. Some of the statutory powers are relatively minor while others, seemingly minor, are subtly subject to interpretation which in fact gives a good deal of discretionary power. For instance, the head of a school is legally considered to be *in loco parentis* while a child is in school. This has been so since the case of Williams *v.* Eady in 1893 when the Master of the Rolls delivered judgment with the words 'as to the law on the subject there could be no doubt. It was correctly stated by the learned Judge that the schoolmaster was bound to take such care of his boys as a careful father would take of his boys'. Clearly the definition of a careful father would be open to considerable discretionary interpretation. The education authorities also have powers to prescribe certain kinds of educational provision, for instance, special education of various kinds, although this is of course usually finally the result of medical recommendation. Perhaps the most unpopular power of the education authority is that of compulsory attendance at school between the ages of five and sixteen under the Education Act of 1944 (as amended to include the raising of the school-leaving age in 1972). Parents may be prosecuted for failing to see that their child attends school under this Act (Section 39). Such powers give the education system statutory authority to make reference to the court, so beginning the process of definition of social breakdown. The social work system now has considerable powers in relation to children at risk or in trouble.

Under Section 1 of the Children and Young Persons Act 1969,[7] magistrates are empowered to make care orders or supervision orders when the following conditions exist:

(a) The child's proper development is being unavoidably prevented or neglected or his health is being impaired or neglected or he is being ill treated, or

(b) it is probable that the conditions described in (a) will be satisfied having regard to the fact that the court (or another court) has found that the condition is or was satisfied in the case of a child or young person of the same household;

(c) he is exposed to moral danger;

(d) he is beyond the control of his parents or guardian;

(e) he is of compulsory school age and is not receiving efficient full-time education suitable to his age, ability and aptitude;

(f) he is guilty of an offence excluding homicide

and also that he is in need of care and control he is unlikely to receive unless the court makes an order.

If the court makes a supervision or care order in relation to a child then the parental rights in respect of that child are effectively diminished and the state's agents, in this case social workers of the local authority, have particular powers vested in them by the court and thus share the rights. In the case of supervision orders, the social workers of the social service department, while not having the right to remove that child from home, have a duty to advise, assist and befriend that child and have considerable discretion in the interpretation of such authority. In the case of care orders, the social service departments also have the right to decide where the child should reside, whether for example the child should be fostered, live in a community home or be allowed home on trial. Section 29 of the Children and Young Persons Act 1975 provided some checks on this power by giving other people caring for the child (e.g., foster parents and residential staff) more opportunity to state their views to a court before irrevocable decisions are made.

An example of the social workers' powers in relation to defining social breakdown at a family level is the compulsory removal to mental hospital of someone considered to be mentally ill. While such powers are shared with the medical profession, the social implications for family life are considerable and it is the considerations based upon this area of the patient's life which are the responsibility of the social worker. Under the 1959 Mental Health Act, compulsory admission to mental hospital can be effected on the grounds that a patient is (i) suffering from mental disorder of a nature or degree which warrants his detention in a hospital under observation for at least a limited period, and (ii) that he ought to be so detained in the interests of his own health or safety, or with a view to the protection of other persons. Either a social worker or the nearest relative may make application to admit a person compulsorily for observation (sec. 25 or 26), though if the former the relative must be consulted where possible. Such an applicant must have seen the proposed patient within the previous fourteen days. The proposed patient must also have been seen within the previous seven days by two medical practitioners (one of them approved as having experience with mental disorder) on whose written recommendations the application is based. The admission to mental hospital of one member of a family cannot be without affect on the rest of the family, and as a result they are likely to experience further erosion of their autonomy as a family group.

As is perhaps already evident, such statutory powers are often shared between two or more systems and the professional groups who work therein. This has arisen partly because of the development and evolution of social policy and various care-giving systems in response to the emergence of new problems. It means that the tasks in relation to the amelioration or alleviation of such problems are inevitably fragmented and thus made the responsibility of different organisational systems. There are, of course, advantages in that no one system has unlimited power, and while any agency may make definitions regarding the various stages of social breakdown, only specified agencies can carry out the prescriptions which may be required by such definitions. Thus the prescriptions which follow the definitions may only be carried out by those agencies which are empowered to do so, as in the case of a transfer to another school. In some situations, notably those where the power of the subject is curtailed by the definition, the agencies must negotiate an agreement over the definition (often with a system outside that of which their own agency is a part) in order for the prescription to be carried out. This is the case before a subject can be compulsorily admitted to mental hospital, where both the health system and the social work system must agree that this is appropriate and necessary.

The various care-giving systems, however, are frequently linked at junctions at such high levels in the systems that often the people concerned with all kinds of decision making are remote from those whom the systems are required to serve and service. This can result in confusions and uncertainties about responsibilities, including the power to allocate resources. It does, however, also imply that it is virtually impossible for any one part of the care-giving system (or even any one system) to have either total responsibility or total power for defining a family as experiencing a severe level of social breakdown.

While such fragmentation is inevitable because of the complexity of our society, it can constrain the conflicts between competing care systems which have defined social problems differently. While such conflicts can result either in inappropriate interventions, or neglect to intervene at all because of failure to acknowledge the responsibility for doing so, they do also allow for co-operation between systems and for innovations to develop. Different definitions and prescriptive interventions can lead to comprehensive care if they are the result of genuine exchanges of information.

It is therefore against the background of the use of professional and statutory powers that much of the definition of social breakdown takes place. While citizens may be aware that they have some rights, such as the right of appeal against most legal definitions, many are ignorant about the extent of their actual rights in any given situation, or in relation to their needs. The question of rights will be considered in the next section and the negotiation of social breakdown later in this chapter.

Rights of the subject

Society has enacted legislation designed to protect vulnerable members of the population. For instance, all children are at risk of social breakdown and they are therefore protected by society by means of socialising agents indicated in Chapter 1. They may, however, also need protection from acts of fate, from the vagaries of their parents or, indeed, from the consequences of their own acts, and there is, of course, specific legislation to achieve this protection, notably the various Education and Children and Young Persons Acts. Recent policy has stressed the rights of the child, particularly in situations where natural parents have not been able to meet the child's needs. Various agents of society are given powers in relation to such legislation and their task is to ensure that such vulnerable members of society are indeed protected; if necessary by using their power to refer to the courts, who make the ultimate decisions regarding the use of legal constraints and sanctions.

What is important in considering the process of social breakdown is that many agents may be involved in the final definition. The more advanced the process, the more serious the definition, the more agents will be involved in the process. The police, of course, are the main law-enforcing agents, but many other professional groups, including doctors, social workers and teachers, might be described as having a hand in the process. At each phase of the process, the social status of the subject is redefined in some way.

Social breakdown may be viewed as a process beginning with the failure(s) of the subject; the definition of having failed, which is made by the agents on behalf of society; the acceptance (of varying degrees) of such a definition, voluntarily or involuntarily; the prescriptions carried out by society's agents in order to mitigate or relieve the process, which inevitably curtail the powers and freedom of the subject, until the ultimate definition of serious social breakdown is reached. The more serious the process of social breakdown becomes, the more agents of society are involved in the definitive aspects of the process, and this in turn intensifies the process and its wider implications for the subject concerned. The more people involved, whether as agents or subjects, in the process of definition, the wider the ramifications will be. However, in the case of children defined as subjects there are greater protective devices created by society in order to minimise some of the additional adversity resulting from such definition. An example of these devices is the confidentiality which pertains to all court proceedings concerning children and young persons. Society, through its legal framework and its democratic political institutions, does attempt to both restrain its agents and protect the rights of its members.

Autonomy of the subject(s)

While, generally speaking, an adult individual is considered to be autonomous as regards power, this is not so in the case of children. As has been mentioned, *children* (and other vulnerable members of society) are specifically protected by various legal enactments until such time as they are considered old enough to take responsibility for themselves. This is sixteen in the case of compulsory education and marriage and eighteen for most other matters, such as the right to vote. During the pre-school years, while the primary power in relation to socialisation rests with the family of a child, if the rights of that child as laid down by society are threatened in any way, other socialisation agents will become involved, the social work system being the one most likely to be invoked for the child's protection. However, as soon as *any* child reaches school age, socialisation responsibilities for that child remain with the family, but are shared with the school as a secondary socialisation agency (see Chapter 1). Thus the power of the family in relation to a child of school age is automatically shared with the school that child attends. As was also shown in Chapter 1, it is when the family reaches Stage III of the family life-cycle that the school becomes involved not only as a socialisation agent, but also as a potential agent of social control. Such a situation pertains throughout the whole of a child's school career, only ending when that child leaves school (although the powers of the school in relation to social control diminish sharply after the age of sixteen).

The position as regards *family autonomy* is in fact more complicated in that other socialisation agents (not strictly relevant to this book) exercise considerable powers in relation to it. For instance, work roles, or the lack of them, exercise considerable socialising forces upon the family, but there is insufficient space to discuss them here. As has been shown, all families are autonomous up to a point in relation to the use of what power they have until their children reach school age. However, families too are protected from loss of autonomy, since the use of sanctions is defined by law. At the same time, as has been shown, recent legislation (i.e., the Children Act 1975) reveals a philosophy which seeks to give much greater protection to the individual child, sometimes even at the expense of the parents.

As might be expected, the power and autonomy possessed by a *school* is very complicated indeed. Events at Tyndale Junior School revealed a situation in which this whole question was highly confused. It must therefore suffice to say that the head of a school is believed to have absolute power in relation to the curriculum that is taught there. Indeed heads have been described as the last stronghold of absolute power; and even before recent events seem to have questioned the veracity of this statement, there was considerable criticism of the extent and range of the power of the head.

Theoretical perspectives

To explore the importance of the relationship between the agents of social control and the subjects they define as experiencing social breakdown, some potentially helpful theoretical perspectives will be considered. So far the relationship between the different 'levels' of definition have been implied. In that the model describes definitions and prescriptions of social breakdown as being made at individual, family and school 'levels' in the social system, there is an assumption that these may be linked, and yet there is no evidence that this is the case. While the following section describes two theoretical perspectives which may eventually prove useful in illuminating these relationships and links, they are discussed only in an oversimplified form and no claims are made concerning their actual utility.

(a) Deviancy theory

A theoretical perspective which may help to explore the relationship between the agents of social control and the individual subjects they define as experiencing social breakdown is the interactionist approach to deviancy and in particular that perspective known as 'labelling theory'. Hargreaves *et al.* in a critical introduction to labelling theory describe the key questions such a theory poses as follows:

> What are the circumstances under which a person gets set apart, henceforth to be considered deviant? How is the person

cast in that social role? What actions do others take on the basis of this redefinition of the person? How does a person judged to be deviant react to this designation? How does he adopt that deviant role that is set aside for him? What changes in his group membership result? To what extent does he realign his self conception to accord with the deviant role assigned to him?[9]

As Hargreaves points out, there are two features which are outstanding in this perspective:

First, deviance is seen as a question of social definition. Deviance does not arise when a person commits certain kinds of act. Rather deviance arises when some other person(s) defines that act as deviant. Second, deviance is seen as a relative phenomenon. If a deviant act is an act that breaks some rule, then since rules vary between different cultures, subcultures and groups, acts which are deviant (i.e., which break the rules) in one culture, subculture or group may not be deviant in another.

Hargreaves *et al.*, in writing of deviance and education, add that while Becker

uses the concept 'rules', which is one of the most basic concepts in labelling theory, one could substitute the word 'laws' without in any way impairing the sense of the text. So whilst the analysis can be applied to non-criminal deviance—which is why the more abstract concept of rules is to be preferred—it is this more criminological model of deviance which is heavily implicit in the literature.

Hargreaves stresses that three key writers who take this approach, Becker, Kitsuse and Kai Erikson, emphasise the 'societal reaction' to the act rather than the act itself as the generation of deviance. He continues:

In other words, the social reaction to deviance [the labelling] creates, under certain conditions, problems for the person who committed the deviant act which can be resolved by the commission of yet further deviant acts and by a self designation as a deviant person. The paradox is that the social reaction which was intended to control, punish or eliminate the deviant act has come to shape, stabilize and exacerbate the deviance.

This sensitivity to the possibility that social control can, in certain circumstances, lead to the amplification of deviance has, however, led to an under-emphasizing of the idea that social control can lead to an elimination or attenuation of deviance—perhaps because this is the common-sense assumption about the relationship between social control and deviance which was adopted in an unquestioning manner by earlier sociological theories. Nevertheless, there have been too few studies which demonstrate the attenuative rather than the amplificatory aspect of social control.

This comment will be received as balm by teachers and social workers, still smarting from batterings by theoretical sociologists who are often sharply critical of their activities as agents of social control. (This, despite the fact that children can hardly be described as making choices in the same way that adult deviants, such as alcoholics and drug takers, are described as doing.)

Deviancy theory has not yet been developed in relation to families, although Hargreaves and his colleagues have begun to develop this in relation to classrooms (as will be later discussed). Nevertheless, it is possible to hypothesise that such a labelling perspective may have its usefulness in relation to both those social institutions as well as in relation to the individual, whether adult or child.

(b) Systems theory

In this book so far the word 'system' has been used particularly in connection with education, schools and social work, without any theoretical explanation of the term. What follows is a necessarily simplistic and brief account of the systems approach, which is becoming an increasingly popular perspective in relation to social work, and the work of family therapists with whole families. It is possible that the systems approach may provide a means of bridging the area of overlap between the education and social work systems so that a theory of common usefulness can be developed.

Forder writes of general systems theory as developing in order

to find a way of analysing complex situations of interaction in which the whole is greater than the sum of the parts . . . . A central tenet of general systems theory is that all systems but the very largest are themselves subsystems of other systems and all but the very smallest are the environment for smaller systems. Among the higher systems certain characteristics prevail as distinct from the traditional closed systems of the physical sciences. These systems are open—they maintain themselves by a flow of material in and out; they may be goal directed—such a goal may be the maintenance of a homeostasis (a steady state) by means of rigidly defined limits (as with thermostats). Such goal directed systems may show a tendency towards increasing elaboration of organisation. In the closed system of physical science the tendency is towards an equilibrium of maximum entropy or measure of disorder. Living systems however demonstrate negative entropy—they import into themselves to grow and develop.[10]

Forder points out that 'human beings who are themselves composed of cells, organs and members, are subsystems of families, small groups, organizations, communities and states. Moreover the boundaries of open systems cannot be clearly defined'. Skynner, also writing of systems theory in relation to living things, seems to disagree with the last statement, for he writes:

at the limits of the living thing, dividing it from the surrounding world, is the *boundary*. This boundary permits, or ensures, that certain materials pass across it, entering the organism from the outside or passing from it out into surroundings, while restricting or preventing the exchange of other elements. Failure of the boundary to restrict exchange across it leads to a loss of difference between the living thing and its surroundings, of its separate identity; instead there develops an identity of inside and an outside, one meaning of death. Too impermeable a boundary, preventing any exchange brings another form of death.[11]

Skynner elaborates systems theory in relation to the psychological level as follows:

the formation and preservation of individual identity similarly requires effective boundaries or defences, ensuring sufficient communication to transmit information adequately from one generation to another, while at the same time permitting each individual to select some influences and reject others and retain some information within a private sphere not open to the inspection of his neighbours.

Skynner gives a helpful diagram, which is particularly useful in demonstrating the overlap between individual, family and school systems. This is reproduced as Figure 5.

Forder, Skynner and others (including Goldstein)[12] commend the usefulness of systems theory in devising a model for practice; Forder and Goldstein specifically in relation to social work, and Skynner (a psychiatrist and family therapist) in relation to work with individual children, whole families, groups, and in consultation with schools.

The usefulness of systems theory in relation to the practice of intervention, according to Skynner, lies in recognising the boundary characteristics of the level of system where the intervention is taking place. He sees each level as having its own boundary 'across which

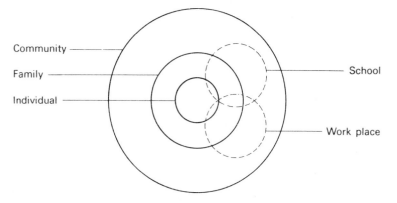

Figure 5 Systems, order, hierarchy
(Source: Robin Skynner, *One Flesh; Separate Persons*, Constable, 1976)

the passage of information is restricted relative to that occurring beyond the boundary region whether inside or outside'. Skynner considers that

> we can recognise a boundary within the individual, separating those aspects of his psyche which are unconscious from the contents of his conscious awareness; another between him as an individual and those around him, guarding and maintaining his separate total identity; yet another around the family as a whole, governing its exchange with the wider world and both expressing and maintaining its difference from other families.

He goes on to say: 'Not all systems show this simple arrangement whereby one is included in the other. Schools . . . do not show a simple Chinese box arrangement but overlap in a more complicated way.'

In social work there are still many unresolved problems in the use of systems theory in relation to social work intervention, notably a lack of criteria to guide the choice of level at which the social worker might intervene—for instance, as a caseworker with an individual or a family, or as a resocialising agent in relation to the school. Nevertheless, the systems approach has its uses and there seems no reason to doubt that it could also be adapted for use in the school situation.

It could therefore be considered that interventions (whether of teaching or social work repertoire) at individual or family level have ramifications throughout the system. Although, as Skynner says, the systems overlap in a more complicated way in schools (and in other social institutions, from which one could assume social work organisations might be included), there are also repercussions in one such system from interventions carried out in another.

The process of social breakdown

It is now possible to discuss in more detail the model of the process of social breakdown, which is outlined in Table 4. Each phase will be taken separately and ways will be indicated in which the theories described might usefully illuminate the issues. While each stage of the model will be considered separately and at each level of definition—that is, individual (child), family and school—an attempt to link the levels will also be made. Although the model describes four stages, these are by no means clear cut and there are no obvious boundaries between them; as will be revealed in the ensuing discussion, each stage begins to take on characteristics of the next one, before it becomes clearly recognisable as a stage of social breakdown of greater severity.

(a) At risk of social breakdown

This is the first stage of the continuum of social breakdown and the one which is most difficult to recognise. It is perhaps more recognisable as a phase, rather than a stage, and is often only clearly discernible through hindsight when a further stage has been reached. After all, there are occasional 'minor' failures amongst all schoolchildren, families and schools; these are part of everyday life and they are usually coped with, contained, managed and recovered from as a matter of course. Indeed some of them could be subsequently described as growth points for the subject. However, sometimes these failures move slightly beyond being described as 'minor', or the minor failures become rather more frequent; even so these may be explained away as lapses, aberrations, misguided incidents, and so on. Of course, the difficulty in defining and describing what does constitute adequate social functioning adds to the complexity of such situations, which, while often recognised, are often the subject of debate, arising from the different perceptions of those concerned. Nevertheless, closer examination (and particularly retrospective examination) often reveals incipient patterns of social breakdown. Study of some of the recent carefully documented inquiries into situations which have resulted in complete breakdown, such as those relating to Maria Colwell[13] and Tyndale Junior School,[14] reveal that the seeds of the subsequent disasters were present long before any 'official' actions were taken.

What are these seeds and how may they be recognised early

TABLE 4 *Model of the process of social breakdown*

Stage	Individual	Family	School
AT RISK	Dawning recognition by subject No definitions made Other primary socialisation agents 'alert' All rights and powers retained	Dawning recognition by some subjects No definitions made Other primary socialisation agents 'alert' All rights and powers retained	Dawning recognition by the social institution No definitions made Socialisation agents 'alert' All rights and powers retained
PRIMARY	Primary socialisation agents active Definitions made within the system Prescriptions made within the system Power of subject constrained	Primary socialisation agents active Definitions made within the system Prescriptions made within the system Some powers constrained	Socialisation agents active Definitions made higher up the system Prescriptions made within the system Some powers constrained
SECONDARY	Primary and secondary socialisation agents active Definitions made within and outside the system Power of subject limited	Primary and secondary socialisation agents active Definitions made within and outside the system Powers limited	Primary and resocialisation agents active Definitions made within and outside the system Powers limited
TERTIARY	All relevant systems active Definitions made within the legal system Prescriptions involve 'custodial' care Power of subject seriously curtailed	All relevant systems active Some definitions made within the legal system Prescriptions involve custodial care for some members Powers seriously curtailed	All relevant systems active Definitions made within the politico-legal system Prescriptions involve major restructuring Powers seriously curtailed

enough? Kellmer Pringle,[15] a trenchant and controversial writer on the needs of children, states that we do not even use our existing knowledge about which children are likely to be at risk. She lists the following as being particularly vulnerable: (i) socially and culturally underprivileged children; (ii) families where personal relationships suffer from some degree of impairment or where there is some emotional neglect; (iii) families where there is serious or irreversible physical or mental illness or disabling handicap; (iv) the child who has one parent only (whether because of illegitimacy, separation, divorce or death); (v) families affected by sudden and disrupting crises. While not all the care-giving professions would agree as to the causes underlying Kellmer Pringle's list of children at risk, most of them would probably agree as to the vulnerability of such children—and yet these same professions could hardly be said to be 'alert' in their concern for such children. Certainly with regard to co-operative effort in working together across the boundaries of their own care-giving systems, it could be argued that they are at times more concerned with preserving their own professional principles than with the needs of children.

Holman,[16] also an impassioned writer, though taking the line that it is the family at risk who should be given priority, on this occasion takes a more sociological view. He describes the twilight zones of the inner city areas as follows:

(i)   geographically located in between the business centre and the outer rings of our cities;

(ii)   having a relatively high number of immigrants;

(iii) home conditions characterised by overcrowding and lack of amenities;

(iv) higher (than average) proportion of unskilled and semi-skilled workers;

(v)   higher (than average) proportion of families receiving state benefits;

(vi) higher (than average) proportion of large families;

(vii) higher (than average) proportion of fatherless families;

(viii) lack of play space and facilities;

(ix) poorer health than is found in the population as a whole;

(x)   high incidence of child deprivation and delinquency;

(xi) some evidence that the areas have the worst social services.

The Plowden Committee had in 1966[17] recommended that Education Priority Areas (EPAs) (many of them situated in the twilight zones described by Holman) should receive positive discrimination in order to combat the vicious downward spiral of poverty and deprivation. More resources, buildings, new and additional equipment, extra more-skilled teachers, and so on, should be given to these areas, over and above the national average. The EPA projects (which will be discussed in Chapter 3) have now been completed and the definition extended to include many inner city priority schools, both primary and secondary; yet many of the problems remain.

In the model the phrase 'dawning recognition by the subject' (subjects or social institution) has been used. This is a somewhat ambiguous phrase which deserves further explanation. Again, hindsight often reveals that children, families or even schools have given indication that they recognise that all is not well. Some kind of 'message' is often sent to socialisation agents from the child or the family which perceptive teachers, particularly those who are in direct contact, are able to pick up; families, too, also make appeals both directly or indirectly to other care-giving agents, for instance those in the primary health-care team who have responsibility for the primary health care of the whole population. The appeal for help may not be direct; quite often it is in the form of a disguised SOS. Some common instances are excessive or unrealistic complaints (both from or about the child, family or the school); 'absenteeism' (at all levels of the systems, whether by truancy, frequent desertions by or hospitalisations of family members, staff turnover or sickness in school); frequent petty delinquencies (again at all levels—a high delinquency rate in a school indicates that all is not well); a high rate of 'failure' (whether for an individual child, a family, or for a school as evidenced by its low popularity to attract pupils or staff). All these are indicators that the subjects at risk recognise for themselves (at some level, anyway) that there is a problem.

While no official definitions of social breakdown are made at this stage, the model indicates that primary socialisation agents are 'alert'. Those relevant agents of society take up what may be described as a 'watching brief', which may take the form of alert concern. The recent work of Hargreaves et al.[18] suggests that teachers do in effect pick out the children who are at risk of social breakdown. His research into deviancy in the classroom shows that teachers, by such imputation, may also affect the future career of pupils labelled as deviant. Hargreaves and his colleagues became somewhat enmeshed in their attempts to define rules and their relation to deviant acts; and they also ran into difficulties in getting the teachers to give a coherent and explicit account of the rules they were invoking. However, they were able to develop an interesting hypothesis concerning the grounds on which teachers made their early judgments about pupils. These were in five areas: (i) appearance, (ii) conformity to discipline role aspects, (iii) conformity to academic role aspects, (iv) likability, (v) peer group relations. They discovered three key factors which led to certain pupils standing out at an early stage. First, 'sibling phenomenon' (that is, the teacher's previous experience of a particular pupil's sibling(s)); second, 'staff discussion' (perhaps in the form of passed-on documents, or prior information, but particularly the comparing of notes in the staff room); and third, the knowledge that 'a child may have a particular problem, about which the school is informed and which becomes widely disseminated amongst the teachers'.

This work of Hargreaves *et al.* does reveal the attendant difficulties in all situations where definitions of deviancy are made. While social breakdown, as described in the model, is not synonymous with deviancy (which often seems to lead to imputations of delinquency), there are similarities in that once a child, a family or a school are defined as experiencing social breakdown, then an inevitable process of setting apart (in sociological terms 'alienation') appears to begin. This Catch-22 situation seems inescapable and may result in understandable reticence on the part of socialisation agents to make any definitions at all. There also seems no doubt that as the process of social failure progresses from primary to secondary and finally to tertiary breakdown, so also do the ramifications of such a process extend and deepen in their severity. The systems approach would provide an explanation of this phenomenon. Furthermore, it would appear that definitions made at higher levels in systems have more far-reaching and longer-lasting repercussions than those made at a lower level. It is one thing to define a child as experiencing social breakdown (if only because a child is protected from adverse publicity); it is another to define a whole family as experiencing social breakdown (if only because of the varying levels of opprobrium which may result from other members of the community); and it is quite another to define a school as experiencing social breakdown.

Mention has been made of schools in priority areas where the education system has already established what could be described as a state of alertness. It could, of course, be argued that once schools are ranked as schools entitled to additional privileges over and above other schools, then they are already defined as experiencing social breakdown. The concept of positive discrimination does, however, go some way to meet the criticism of labelling as described above. Nevertheless, there are some indications that schools which could be considered at risk of social breakdown are not defined sufficiently early in the process as experiencing primary social breakdown.

Power's[19] research conducted in an inner London borough found that there were very large differences in the delinquency rates of the secondary schools and that these could not be explained by taking the neighbourhoods into account. Nor where these differences related to the formal characteristics of the school—age or design of buildings, co-educational or single sex, etc. Rutter *et al.*[20] came to similar findings in relation to primary schools; and also concluded that the teacher/pupil ratio appeared to make little difference. As Rutter says: 'None of these studies was able to prove that the schools actually influenced the children's behaviour and attainments, although this was the inference.'

Phillippson[21] (who worked with Power) came to the conclusion, however, that some schools apparently protect their pupils from delinquency while others put them at risk of it. He suggests that

both the pedagogic and unpedagogic values of the school and the way they are handled may be related to delinquency, but that the pedagogic being more stable and more or less common to all parts of a given stratum of the educational system are more likely to exert a relatively constant influence.

High staff turnover and absenteeism, for example, he suggests contribute to 'low institutional pride which is shared by both teachers and pupils'. Such a view is, of course, controversial.

Nevertheless, a recent Gulbenkian-sponsored conference on Education and the Urban Crisis[22] considered that some evidence exists to suggest that there is a larger proportion of maladjusted children in our inner city schools than elsewhere. Rutter's findings indicate that, whereas the percentage of pupils rated as maladjusted in the Isle of Wight is 10·6 per cent, the same operational definition related to primary schools in an inner city borough over the same period revealed 19·1 per cent.

In the introductory essay to his book on the conference on Education and the Social Crisis, Field points out that though there is a

fundamental question about whether the purpose of the education system is to ensure a pool of ability which will sustain the economic system or whether it is to gain mastery over key areas of life together . . . most schools appear to be a million light years from a situation where they gear their education programmes to the needs of the wider labour market.

It could be that the 'low institutional pride' in a school described by Phillippson is reinforced by other factors within education and other systems. For instance, the refusal of places at the school, or the steady removal of children by their (often middle-class) parents is an indication that the school is either at risk or has even moved into the stage of primary social breakdown.

As will be discussed in subsequent chapters, there may be reason to think that greater involvement of social workers within the school system could play a considerable part in promoting more effective social functioning by schools, particularly in those educational priority areas.

(b) Primary social breakdown

In the model, which starts from the level of schoolchildren and their families, the social work system is not usually involved in the definition of primary social breakdown, for that definition is made within the school system. The social work system may, however, be involved at the family level; for instance, one parent may be on probation or a grandparent may be admitted to an old people's home. Such a situation introduces some complication into the model and seems to indicate that such a family is already experiencing social breakdown. However, there are good grounds for thinking that, while schools are making definitions and prescriptions within the school system in relation to some of their pupils, social workers may simultaneously be making definitions and prescriptions within the social work system in relation to other members of the same family. Therefore, it could be said that, only when the situation is such that the school considers it a family problem of some severity and/or the social worker considers that the school should be alerted to the family situation, that the stage of secondary social breakdown is reached. This will be discussed further in the next section. At primary social breakdown it is clear that something is 'wrong' with the child, or indeed with the family, and so affecting the child. There is open recognition between the school and either the child or the child-in-the-family that a problematic situation exists, whether or not each accepts the perceptions of the other as to what it actually is. If it is the school which is being defined as experiencing primary social breakdown, then this is recognised in other parts of the school system. Either the inspectorate is becoming concerned about the state of a school, or the neighbouring schools who may be involved with some of the children at other stages in their school career are expressing their concern about what is happening within a particular school. Such a situation clearly prevailed at some stage with regard to Tyndale Junior School.[23]

Another characteristic of primary social breakdown is that, in addition to the definition of primary social breakdown, prescriptions are also made to alleviate, mitigate or correct the situation. These prescriptions are made within the same system. In the case of a school child experiencing primary social breakdown, there are many prescriptions which may be made within the actual school. Special remedial teaching may be recommended, or the child may be admitted to a sanctuary (a small, closed unit for teaching pupils with difficulties, usually behaviour problems). Other prescriptions of a more radical nature, but still within the system, may also be prescribed, thus intensifying both the definition and the process. For example, a child may be recommended for admission to another school, a tutorial class or even a special school, or excluded from school altogether. To put into effect any such prescription which requires the child's withdrawal from the school will (in some measure at least) involve other members of the education system in addition to the head; for instance, the local education officer, the educational psychologist, a school medical officer or psychiatrist, or the school governors or managers. It could be said that such eventualities are moving the child steadily towards being defined as experiencing secondary social breakdown.

It will be seen that when definitions of primary social breakdown are made within the system, then the autonomy of the child is being curtailed or constrained. It is here that labelling theory might prove to have some usefulness. Sarri,[24] in describing what she calls 'malperformance' in schools, points out that 'even when malperformance is recognised in schools the response may range from indifference to supplying a full complement of remedial services to loss of status, privilege and perhaps essential exclusion'. She amplifies this by adding that the school 'defines the conditions under which the behaviour becomes deviant as well as defining deviancy as such'. Finally, once the pupil 'has been identified as deviant, this may significantly affect his public identity, his self image and his motivation to achieve'. Earlier work by Hargreaves,[25] an action research project among the fourth year at Lumley Secondary Modern School, found that the pupils could be divided into two sub-cultures, the academic and the delinquescent. The academic sub-culture was located primarily in the upper stream and subscribed to such middle-class values of the school and the staff as ambitiousness, individual responsibility, self-reliance, etc. The lower-stream boys, on the other hand, were deprived in three ways: (i) their lack of conformity to teacher expectations led to their being evaluated negatively and thus to their developing a sense of inferiority; (ii) because they were the objects of discrimination, privileges open to higher-stream boys were not open to them; (iii) the range of occupations open to them became increasingly restricted.

If the implications of systems theory can be accepted, such definitions and prescriptions relating to the child-in-the-family would also have repercussions within the family itself. This is especially so when social opprobrium is attached to the prescription, such as admittance to a school for the educationally sub-normal or maladjusted. There may also be implications for the pupil's future school career or even intergenerational repercussions. Such an example was demonstrated in a recent BBC programme on the Children's Charter.[26] This portrayed Dean Riley, a teenage boy who played truant on 73 out of 100 days, preferring to play pinball machines rather than go to school. He saw his future as getting into the navy. His father went to the same school (though now updated and converted into a comprehensive), also played truant, spent time in an approved school and was in and out of unskilled jobs all his life. The boy's mother's attitude to school was simple and uncompromising: fifteen years is long enough to keep anyone. One of his teachers 'hopes for the best but fears the worst. I'm afraid he's going to be in and out of work. I hate to say it and I hope he isn't, but he may well be in and out of prison and really have the most dreadful kind of life.' The headmaster of the vast complex of new and old buildings thought the school was too big. On the television programme, Dean Riley was understandably inarticulate. 'What are schools for?' he was asked. 'Learning, I suppose.' 'Don't you want to learn?' 'Dunno—not really.' 'What will you do if the navy won't have you?' 'Dunno.' 'He's me to a tee,' said his father. The process predicted by the schoolmaster seems inevitable, given Dean's attitude, that of his parents and the school, yet the social forces impinging on them would seem to require political and economic intervention rather than that of a social worker whose powers of intervention are likely to be equally limited, given such cumulative negative reinforcements in all the systems involved.

The definition of primary social breakdown in relation to a school has already been shown to be much more imprecise than in the case of children or families. The question of who has the power to make prescriptions regarding schools even when they could be described as experiencing primary social breakdown appears to be even more confused. The Tyndale enquiry in 1976 seems to reveal that school inspectors (anyway, local authority inspectors) only have powers to advise, and cannot impose any form of alleviative or corrective action. Nor does there seem to be much experience (documented, at least) of measures which might prove helpful in such situations. Berg,[27] in an unashamedly prejudiced and somewhat simplistic account of the failure of a new comprehensive school, Risinghill, which was opened in 1960 and closed in 1965, describes it as the death of a school. The pupils were drawn from four feeder primary schools and there followed a period of disagreements, deterioration, defensiveness, accusations and witch-hunting, which, Berg claimed, centred on hostility on the part of both the staff and the education authority towards the head's policy of abolishing corporal punishment.

Before proceeding to discuss secondary social breakdown, which involves the introduction of the social work system into the process, it is useful to pause in order to consider some of the aspects of the delay in referring pupils outside the educational system; and in particular outside their own school.

Some of the reasons for this reluctance to refer children elsewhere have already been raised (both in Chapter 1 and in the early part of this chapter), but there are two further key factors. First, there is the tendency of schools to function as relatively closed systems. Goffman's[28] work on total institutions would seem to have considerable relevance for schools. He describes one category of closed institutions as 'purportedly established the better to pursue some work-like task and justifying themselves only on these instrumental grounds'. He lists boarding schools amongst these. However, many of the characteristics which he considers as common to such institutions could also be said to apply to day schools, particularly the large secondary schools which are so characteristic of our educational system. Indeed, most large schools need to pay close attention to their organisational structures if they are to avoid the situation Goffman describes:

> The handling of many human needs by the bureaucratic organisation of whole blocks of people—whether or not this is a necessary or effective means of social organisation in the circumstances—is the key fact of total institutions . . . . When persons are moved in blocks, they can be supervised by personnel whose chief activity is not guidance or periodic inspection, but rather surveillance—a seeing to it that everyone does what has been clearly required of him . . . . In total institutions there is a basic split between a large managed group, conveniently called inmates, and a small supervisory staff.

Although the Child Care Service was established in 1948 and the Social Services Departments in 1971, the extent of ignorance within the education system about the tasks and functions of the social work system is extraordinary. The failure of the social work system to define its task clearly may compound such ignorance; and there is also a fluidity about both teaching and social work which makes it hard for teachers and social workers alike to take hold of any situation and define what is actually happening. Nevertheless, the major reason for such a marked reluctance to refer children outside the school system could be attributed to the tendency of schools to function as closed systems.

Teachers are also reluctant to act as agents of social control. They are not of course alone in this, as will be seen later; social workers, too, are often reluctant to act as such in situations which call for them to take up an authoritative stance in relation to their clients. Nevertheless, referral of a pupil outside the school system often involves the explicit use of the authority which teachers do have. To act in this way not only means some acceptance that such powers of referral rest with them, but often also entails some kind of confrontation either with another teacher, or with the subject who is to be referred, sometimes both. Part of this reluctance on the part of teachers to refer a pupil may be due to concern that he or she (and family) might become stigmatised as the result of such a referral. There can be little doubt that stigmatisation is often the result of referral to the social work system, where the powers as agents of social control, real or imagined, are certainly greater than those of the teacher, and are therefore considered more stigmatising.

If the model of practice based on systems theory described earlier is valid, then it could be said that the information needed to inform the education system has not passed through the boundaries. By and large it is the younger and more recently trained teachers (including those late entrants who are parents themselves) who are not only aware that an educational relationship with a child cannot bypass his parents, but also that the other care-giving systems in the community have an important part to play in enabling the education system to carry out its tasks.

Children who have behaviour problems tend to be seen as 'bad' by the school system because their behaviour makes it difficult for teachers to carry out their tasks, while children who are isolated and withdrawn may hardly be noticed because they make fewer demands on the teacher and are less disruptive in class. On the other hand, children whose behaviour is seen as bizarre, and especially those whose parents are known to suffer from psychiatric disorders, are often seen as 'mad'. While ultimately such children are often referred outside the education system, this step is often taken too late for the most effective remedial intervention to be taken. There seems no reason why children who are giving cause for concern should not be discussed with the social work system, which could then act in a consultative capacity. In effect this is what happens with many children who are referred by schools to child guidance clinics where the psychiatric team (which includes social workers) redefine the problem, and quite often their prescription is to help the school to contain the problem and the child. (Skynner, incidentally, gives an amusing account of such a consultation carried out in school, where a child's persistent screaming in school led him to comment that he'd like to wring its neck. This spontaneous comment enabled the school staff to confess to similiar feelings and led to a very profitable discussion which seemed to lead to beneficial results for the child at school.) Of course, not all problems can be solved by informal consultation with the social work system. As will be discussed later (in Chapter 4), the Education Welfare Service is already beginning to play just this kind of role. In many areas too, the social service area teams have built up co-operative and mutually supportive consultative relationships with the local schools, which can only prove advantageous to both and ultimately beneficial to the children and families about whom they are both most concerned.

(c) Secondary social breakdown

When a subject is defined as experiencing secondary social breakdown, both primary and secondary socialisation agents are actively involved. In this model the secondary socialisation agents are taken to be social workers, both those with statutory powers and responsibilities (such as social workers in social services departments, probation officers and the National Society for the Prevention of Cruelty to Children [NSPCC]) and those without (predominantly those working in independent social work agencies such as the Family Service Units). For the purposes of this model, social workers working in the education system (such as education welfare officers and youth and community workers) are considered as primary socialisation agents, in company with the rest of the education system. Social workers attached to child guidance clinics (whether employed by the education system or by the social work system and seconded to the health care system) are in an interestingly anomalous position (in this model), on the boundary, where they are in a position to act as primary socialisation agents together with the education system and also as secondary socialisation agents together with the social work system. In such a boundary position they can at times make it possible to contain the definition and prescription of schoolchildren and their families at the level of primary social breakdown and at other times act in a consultative capacity to the education system over the question of speeding the process of definition of secondary social breakdown. It is the *psychiatrist* who has the power of definition and prescription (although the social worker takes a part in this) and, of course, the possibility of a psychiatric definition of breakdown influences both the referring agents in the school system and acceptance of the definition by the subject (in such a situation, the child-in-the-family). (If voluntary psychiatric referral is refused and the school system consider some definition is necessary, then they must proceed with referral outside the system—either to the health system or to the social work system, who may prescribe psychiatric care as part of their prescription.)

One of the key factors of secondary social breakdown is that the definition is made *outside* the school system. With regard to schoolchildren, this means that they are referred to the social work system and it is this act of referral which indicates that the stage of secondary social breakdown has been reached. As has already been stated in the case of families who are already known to the social work system, the phase of secondary social breakdown is reached when either the education system or the social work system make the decision that a contact with the other system is necessary, because the situation now requires some kind of definition to be made as regards the family. Such a situation might be the case when a social work agency has been working with a pair of parents, the focus of the work being the couple's marital problems, and the social worker forms the opinion that the schoolchild is likely to be affected adversely by the situation between the parents. Or in the case of the school, where the education system is of the opinion that in a single-parent family, the mother's preoccupation with blind granny is leading to neglect of the schoolchild. It should be noted that in neither of these situations (and there are many others) is any kind of statutory compulsion involved in the referral.

Prescriptions are made both within and outside the systems. It may be that referral outside the school system is made to allow a prescription to be carried out which is either inappropriate or, more probably, unavailable to the school system (for instance, skilled family social work by a social worker). Indeed the recognition that such a prescription may be needed may precipitate the definition. Once a referral is made then the other system (in this case the social work system, but of course many referrals are made for medical definitions and prescriptions) needs to redefine the subject in its own terms and from another orientation. For example, a family may become homeless, which may lead the school to refer its members to the social work system. The social work system then redefines the subject and makes a prescription, which may be quite contrary to what the school staff had in mind when making the referral. For instance, in the case of the homeless family, the school may see the prescription as finding a foster home near the school so that the child can continue attending, while the social work system may see the prescription as keeping the family together because the mother is inclined to become seriously depressed and relies on the teenage daughter's support, and the teenage daughter needs the reinforcement and support from her role in the family because there is a real danger of promiscuity. Of course, this is an oversimplification of the kind of decision making involved, but it serves to illustrate a common situation where differing orientations between the systems lead to different prescriptions, and at times contention or even conflict.

With regard to both children and families, the early stages of secondary social breakdown are not likely to involve the invocation of statutory powers, although of course this possibility is ever-present and will be discussed further in the section on negotiated social breakdown. The power of autonomy of the individual child as well as the child-in-the-family is reduced by the definition of secondary breakdown because now there is the distinct possibility that statutory powers may be invoked as regards the child. Their privacy is also impinged upon in that they are expected to become involved with the social work system, which implies both a degree of dependency on it and any change which may take place in the image of the family either in relation to itself, or as seen by the neighbours.

Before leaving the issue of defining the family as experiencing secondary social breakdown, it is worth considering the *meaning* for the family, which may well differ depending on whether the intervention comes from the education system or from the social work system. Families, too, are aware that the education system has responsibilities which require it to take an active interest in *all* schoolchildren. And they are aware, too, that the social work system (generally seen as an agglomerate—the welfare) is only interested in *some* families, and that when things are not right. It could perhaps be assumed that interventions by the education system are experienced in a less alienating way (i.e., the family perceive themselves as less deviant) when definitions and prescriptions are carried out from within the education system. It may well be true that teachers are seen as rivals for their children and as people who may well give them more effective 'parenting'. As will be discussed later (in Chapter 5), research by Lynch and Pimlott[29] indicated that parents were surprisingly ambivalent to home visits being paid by the *teachers* of their children. It could, however, be inferred that intervention from the education system in the shape of education social workers (i.e., the Education Welfare Service) might be less damaging to the self-esteem of the family than when the same intervention is carried out by the social service system (in this case the social service department). Thus, from the family's point of view, one form of definition and its resultant prescription is possibly more acceptable than another, and this may make a difference. Of course, individual families take distinct and idiosyncratic views of the two systems, but such an argument does indicate that a family would have some choice in many situations of primary and secondary breakdown. This factor of choice would then imply that the family's power and autonomy are less eroded. Naturally, such thinking remains speculative, and in any case is highly dependent on the organisational state of the systems, and of course the competence and skills of the social workers involved.

It is not at all easy to describe the definition of secondary social breakdown with regard to schools, if only because situations which might be described as being at this stage are rarely documented in ways which are easily accessible to the general public. However, such a situation might be seen as the alerting of the political system, as happened in the case of Tyndale Junior School.[30] The structural system which exists between the Inner London Education Authority and the local boroughs tends to complicate the discussion in this particular instance, however, since the local boroughs are not discrete education authorities, although they all have representative members on the council of the ILEA. However, it might be said that the alerting of the local borough Labour Party and other local authority officials could be seen as defining a stage of secondary social breakdown. Other schools and community homes (where education is provided on the premises) could also be described as having been defined as experiencing secondary social breakdown when decisions were taken to notify DES inspectors or (in the case of community homes) the social work services officers of the DHSS. There have recently been one or two school situations where such definitions could be said to have been made, usually in situations where there was a history of assaults or sexual offences against children in the 'school' and it was considered that insufficient action had been taken within the (local) system.

In relation to schoolchildren and their families, secondary social breakdown might be seen as occurring in two almost distinct phases. The first phase, which has already been described, involves only the education and social work systems; although the health system often also plays a part in both definition and prescription, for at the phase of secondary social breakdown it is often remarkably difficult to disentangle what is medical or psychiatric and what is social. Nevertheless, this first phase does not take into account any *direct* connection with the legal system. Before discussing such a link, which distinguishes the second phase of secondary social breakdown, it is necessary to refer to recent social policy in relation to the care of children.

Packman's[31] excellent account of child care policy from the Curtis Committee (1946) to the Houghton Committee (1972) documents this very fully and it must suffice here to comment all too briefly on the frequently impassioned debate as to the precipitating causes and appropriate treatment for children in trouble (this will also be referred to later in the section on intermediate treatment in Chapter 3). Packman, commenting on the Children and Young Persons Act 1969, writes: 'the Act's intentions are clear. The Juvenile Court should be a place of last resort'. And later 'Delinquents and deprived children are all children in trouble and, as far as possible, should be treated alike'. It was originally the intention of the Act that children of ten to fourteen who have committed a criminal offence should not come before the court unless they are also in need of care and control which they are unlikely to receive at home. The intention here seems clear—that children and their families who can be worked with on a voluntary basis need not appear before the court. Second, with regard to offenders of fourteen to seventeen years of age 'Prosecution should be retained but restricted in ways which would cut down its use and spare a number of offenders a court appearance'.

Unfortunately, because of political differences which were reflected in the debate during the passing of the Act and because of an unexpected change of Government, the Act was never fully implemented and an emasculated version is the basis of much current law in relation to children in difficulties. The age for criminal prosecution remained at ten and there were other features, too, which were not introduced. The present position with regard to the appearance in court of juveniles remains complex and at times confused, as for instance in relation to truancy, where a recent review (*Observations on the 11th Report from the Expenditure Committee on the Children and Young Persons Act 1969* [1976]) commenting on the application of the care and control test in relation to truancy admits that there is some uncertainty over the interpretation of the Act. Earlier in this chapter (in the section on the power to define social breakdown) allusion has already been made to the grounds on which supervision and care orders may be made by the juvenile court. However, many children who commit indictable offences are not brought to court, the police being able to exercise considerable discretion in relation to cautioning the youngsters rather than charging them. Packman comments that the use of police cautioning was another unimplemented Section of the Act and during the debates it did not seem that it was intended that police cautions should be used as the means for keeping children out of court; this was envisaged as the province of the social worker. The guide to the Act (Part 1 of the Children and Young Persons Act 1969), in discussing consultation procedures before bringing care proceedings, refers to the need to satisfy the care and control test which

> relates to the whole of the child's relevant circumstances, so it will normally be essential for any person who is considering whether to bring care proceedings to ascertain any relevant information about the child's circumstances which is possessed by other persons. Such persons may include local authorities, the police, schools, probation officers, child guidance clinics, other services and voluntary organisations. It may normally be convenient for the local authority to collect information from other services with knowledge of the child. The care and control test debars the court from making an order unless this is necessary to ensure that the child receives the care or control which he needs, so it will likewise normally be essential for a

person who is considering the initiation of proceedings to ascertain also whether any other person or body is taking, or might be in a position to take, action likely to provide the child with the requisite care or control without the need for a court order.[32]

In practice, the police, the education system and the NSPCC usually consult with the social services department before bringing proceedings.

In returning to the discussion centring on the introduction of the legal system into the process of definition of secondary social breakdown, it is important to stress that here again there is a distinct orientation and value system. In a recent article, Parsloe,[33] in writing of the different approaches of the law and social work, points out that the justice model 'explains crime as freely chosen action against the rule of law', whereas 'the welfare approach views criminal behaviour as a symptom of emotional and/or social disturbance'. She also stresses the demands of society which 'require the criminal justice system to act as a meeting point for these different approaches and to arrive at decisions which do not ignore the rights or the needs of individuals'.

Therefore, the final phase of defining secondary social breakdown is one where the definitions are made in a juvenile court incorporating a legal approach and where the prescriptions are backed by the possibility of greater or lesser legal sanctions. In these situations, of course, the powers of the subject—that is, of the child and of the family in relation to that child—are increasingly limited.

It is perhaps interesting to comment here that despite the intention of the original Children and Young Persons Act 1969, the courts eventually retained their discretion to select probation officers (who are court officers and therefore part of the legal system) as supervisors for children of ten upwards. The use of this discretion, which has been upheld in the recent review (1976) of the working of the Act, seems to vary widely from court to court and is probably as much dependent on the availability of trained social work staff as any other reason. However, in relation to its meaning to the families concerned, it could be conjectured that supervision by a probation officer is indicative of a further phase of definition of social breakdown.

(d) Tertiary social breakdown

Tertiary social breakdown can be said to have occurred when the stage of social breakdown has been reached which the defining agents consider requires radical corrective action in order to restore the possibility of social functioning. By the time such a stage is reached, the definition is likely to include at least three systems (and therefore additional agents rather than the customary socialisation agents), one of which is likely to have the power to make definitions with legally backed sanctions. Usually this is likely to be by reference to the court, but in the case of the definition of families, it may be that the health service takes the major role in the definition (perhaps under the Mental Health Acts). A distinguishing feature of tertiary social breakdown is the considerable and serious curtailment of the power and autonomy of the subject. The effect of this curtailment is likely to involve the whole process, the definition, the prescription and also the role behaviour of the defining agents in relation to the task. While definition of secondary social breakdown is a serious consideration for the defining agents, it is in tertiary social breakdown that the powers in relation to the task are shared between the agents and their powers of discretion subject to more restrictions and scrutiny. While this sharing of power serves to protect the subject from too much high-handed use of power, it can also lead to uncertainties and discrepancies as between the defining agents. Ormrod, speaking on the role of the courts in relation to children comments:

> Our society has reached a stage in which its courts are being called upon more and more to make value judgments. For some purposes the values of the existing courts of law are mistrusted and so special tribunals are set up like the Rent Tribunals or the Industrial Tribunals and many others . . . . But the involvement of the courts in personal relations of many different kinds is steadily increasing. Judges have to be prepared, therefore, to make value judgments in all kinds of situations . . . in the sphere of value judgments, each judge, inevitably, brings to every case his own set of values, built up out of his knowledge and experience of life and influenced to a greater or lesser extent by personal qualities such as insight, the capacity to understand the motivations of other people, social and moral attitudes . . . . One can make allowances for those personal idiosyncrasies of which one is conscious, but every individual carries with him through life a complex of subconscious experiences of which he is largely unaware, but which, particularly in moments of stress, influence his behaviour and attitudes, and, therefore his decisions. An unfettered or unstructured discretion to do what is right and just inevitably involves this twilight area of the personality.[34]

Ormrod is writing as a judge, but such comments might also apply to others. He goes on to say:

the quality of guidelines or the practice now becomes of crucial importance to the validity of the decisions . . . value judgments in inter-personal or social relations cannot be formally validated. One can agree or disagree with such decisions, but it is not possible to demonstrate that they are correct or incorrect because it is never possible to see what would have happened if a different decision had been made.

Another important feature of tertiary social breakdown is that the subject's self-image is usually radically redefined as part of the process. While in primary and secondary social breakdown the subject's self-esteem may suffer to a varying degree, when tertiary social breakdown is defined, there is no escaping from the accompanying sense of failure, whether this is acknowledged or not.

In the case of schoolchildren, the stage of tertiary social breakdown is usually reached when a child is compulsorily required to spend more time away from home in some form of custodial care than he or she spends at home. Indeed, one reason for such compulsory care may be that the home or family of the child may no longer be functioning in such a way as to provide him/her with the care and control he/she is considered to need.

There are some difficulties in defining custodial care in view of the ambivalent attitude which society adopts to juveniles in trouble, as has already been discussed. While children are partially protected from some of the stigmatic effects of court appearance by the fact that juvenile court hearings are held in camera, there can be little doubt that there is some effect. Both the child and the family are left in no doubt as to how seriously the magistrates view a particular situation. The very fact that a child is compulsorily removed from home is also not without its effect on the family and also on the neighbourhood and the child's peers at school. Finally, when the child does arrive in a residential establishment, it is usually quite clear both from his (or her) contemporaries and by the degree to which his freedom is restricted just how serious his position is now considered to be.

In terms of deviancy theory, tertiary social breakdown is the final step on the road to becoming deviant: being labelled as deviant by society and experiencing oneself as deviant. This is more apparent at the family level, although with the present state of theory in relation to the family this is more difficult to describe. In sociological terms the family could be described as alienated, no longer accepting the norms of society or accepted by it. In psychological terms the family is totally failing to function as a natural group or to carry out expected tasks. The definition of a family as experiencing tertiary social breakdown is a very complex procedure. The model states that some definitions are made within the legal system, but it seems very unclear how many family members need to be so defined before the result is complete family failure. We know that a good many of the families described as being at risk by Kellmer Pringle[35] do ultimately end up at the tertiary stage of social breakdown, but it is often difficult to distinguish aspects of the process. For instance, the definition of a child in one family would seem to be sufficient, and yet other families can apparently survive a number of children being so defined and removed. One of the problems in trying to distinguish the process is the number of defining agents involved, who in various and apparently unconnected circumstances may be steadily affecting the family's self-image without being aware of it. It is not uncommon among families at serious risk for a child to be seen in a juvenile court, and a parent in an adult court (or compulsorily admitted to mental hospital) all in a matter of weeks. Another factor is the break-up of families either by divorce or desertion. There are increasing numbers of reconstituted families (such as some with step-parents) which are not functioning effectively as such and may decline into a state of tertiary social breakdown, almost without the defining agents realising what is happening. Because of the number of care-giving agents who might become involved with a family, many of them carry out their interventions from a different theoretical and value base, without reference to one another (even those working within the education or social work systems) and without realising that by such lack of co-ordination and co-operation they are failing to take even the most obvious steps to prevent the family's process of social breakdown. The Colwell/Kepple[36] family at the time Maria was home on trial was clearly a family suffering from tertiary social breakdown, as was the Meurs family[37] when Mrs Meurs was looking after Skinner children in addition to her own. Yet the subsequent enquiries showed that critical information, involving key facts, was not available to the defining agents (in both these cases, the social services department) who had both the power and the responsibility. Family therapists basing their work on systems theory would probably say that the lack of a coherent system within such families is likely to be reflected among the care-giving agents, who will carry out their tasks in isolation from one another, thus mirroring the disintegration among the family members. Those who have worked in such situations state that they spend as much time disentangling and trying to understand the situations such families get *them* into, as in trying to intervene directly with the family.

(The systems approach might well be useful in relation to possible non-accidental injury to children. The small research study of Stevenson and Desborough on 'Case Conferences in relation to Non-Accidental Injury'[38] seems to indicate that the appropriate people are not always invited to attend; that communication failures occur at the conference itself often because medical or legal terms are insufficiently understood; and that there is a need to clarify the status of the conference in relation to certain types of decision-making.)

Definition of tertiary breakdown in relation to schools is perhaps less difficult because, although here, too, at least three systems are likely to be involved, the powers and responsibilities are less fragmented and shared out. Nevertheless, as the Tyndale inquiry seems to have shown,[39] it is very unclear just which authority has the ultimate power to define a school as experiencing tertiary social breakdown. Incidentally, the enquiry gives a graphic account of a school system beginning to fail from within, in its description of the staff walking out of a parent-teacher meeting because they considered their professional competence was being questioned, and of the circulation by one of the teachers of a document highly critical of the school's educational policy. It would seem to be that if definitive measures had been taken following these incidents, such measures, while they would clearly have defined the school as experiencing social breakdown, might also have led to prescriptive remedies that could have saved the school and ILEA and many of the individuals involved from ultimate public humiliation.

Rights and negotiation in relation to social breakdown

It is against the background of such powers of definition and prescription that much of the definition of social breakdown takes place. As has been indicated, many citizens are not only unaware of their rights, they are also inclined to exaggerate the powers which the defining agents actually do have. For instance, it is commonly thought that teachers have unlimited power in relation to transfer to special schools, or even with regard to exclusion from school, whereas actually such power is subject to various constraints, including forms of appeal. Social workers, too, are often seen to have the power to remove children from home, or to 'give' a foster or adoptive child. As has been seen, the power to remove children is subject to many provisos: even the power to remove a child temporarily to a place of safety under the Children and Young Persons Act 1933[40] requires the granting of a warrant by a magistrate; adoptions must be approved by an adoption sub-committee of the local authority social services committee; and fostering arrangements must conform to the boarding-out regulations. Nevertheless, these and similar perceptions on the part of the general public play their part in influencing situations where teachers or social workers are trying to negotiate with families over the education or care of their children. It should be remembered that all teachers and social workers are members of the public and are just as likely to adopt similarly stereotyped ideas, *particularly* in relation to the powers of the other system, of which, as has already been said, they are often woefully ignorant.

The public are particularly unaware of the rights they possess in relation to resources and their own protection. As was shown in Chapter 1, part of the task of the social work system is to inform or guide the public so that they may take advantage of these rights, say in relation to housing, unemployment or supplementary benefits. The whole rights field is now so complex that specialist Welfare Rights Workers are emerging, who not only inform and guide, but also act as advocates for their clients at the many tribunals to which appeals can be made, particularly in relation to the areas mentioned above. With regard to children, the Child Poverty Action Group and the recently formed Family Rights Group is able to give a very comprehensive service in this area if families are referred to them, as do Gingerbread and the Council for One-Parent Families. In many instances parents can be assisted to put their views before the court effectively. The National Association for Mental Health is also taking a leading role in advocacy for psychiatric patients, particularly those detained under the controversial emergency compulsory admission procedures under the Mental Health Act 1959 (sec. 29).

Another important factor in negotiating with families who are experiencing social breakdown is that the complexity of rights and powers which are available to the professionals and 'client(s)' involved in such situations are not always known to all the professionals either. For instance, it is unlikely that the teacher who is negotiating with a parent over a suggested placement in a residential school is aware of all the social resources which may be available to assist the family, for instance funds for visiting the child. It is equally unlikely that a social worker is aware of educational resources that may provide the parents with a greater range of choices in considering the future of their child.

While teachers and social workers are expected to clarify the rights available to 'clients' in situations where definitions of social breakdown are being made, failures in communication frequently arise. Some of these failures are unavoidable and inevitable, but there are other areas where a great deal could be done to improve the situation. For people who are familiar with the processes involved, their complexity becomes simplified and it is easy to forget, for instance, that carefully designed legal phrases are often confusing to clients who are not using them daily. Reference to sections of Acts of Parliament, the use of letters to abbreviate important titles are all easy habits to fall into, and even when clients are courageous enough to ask the meaning of 'ESN', 'Section 1 money', or 'deemed maladjusted', their pain and anxiety may be such that they quickly 'forget' again. In listening to families where definitions of tertiary social breakdown have been made by professionals, it is not unusual to learn that they were unaware of their rights of appeal, or even understood what was happening at an early stage of the procedure. Of course, distortions inevitably occur, people misconstrue, mis-hear or deny what is said to them; but social workers and teachers, along with other professionals, also fail to repeat or spell out the rights and the powers involved in such situations. Unfortunately, this occurs too frequently in just those areas where there is conflict and feelings are running high in the family or the individual. For instance, under the 1944 Education Act,[41] a teacher may (via the head) refer a child for a statutory examination for an educationally sub-normal or maladjusted school. The parents must be informed and the child examined by a psychologist and a school medical officer, who will make the recommendation to the parents and the school medical authorities. The parents usually eventually accept such a recommendation, although of course they have the right of appeal. It would be foolish to deny the weight of power that such expertise carries for most parents, but it is all too easy for these professional judgments (for that is what they are) to be so intimidating that they are not properly understood or accepted. A (psychiatric) social worker in a child guidance clinic spends a fair amount of time discussing, explaining and listening to parents whose children are in the process of being classified as maladjusted. Such cases rarely come before the courts but the definition of experiencing social breakdown is being made all the same and the process could be described as negotiating social breakdown. There has been distress, among West Indian parents in particular, and complaints that they accepted such a definition of their children and allowed them to be admitted to ESN schools without fully realising the implications of such a label and the repercussions it might have later.

Handler,[42] writing of the work of social workers (child-care officers) with families with multiple problems, points to the use of financial assistance under Section 1 of the Children and Young Persons Act 1963, which could be described, he says, as 'a coercion to bribe such families to mend their ways or else . . .'. The implication being that unless the families subscribed to the suggestions made by the social worker they were in danger of having their child(ren) taken into care. Similarly, an offender over seventeen years old may be offered probation instead of a prison sentence, a 'suggestion' which theoretically they have a right to veto, the clear implication being, nevertheless, that they may lay themselves open to some other punishment (fine, prison sentence) if they do not accept. In the case of voluntary admission to mental hospital, too, an implied threat of compulsory admission at some time in the future lies in the background of the negotiations.

These are examples of the definition of social breakdown, where the subject apparently accepts the definition and yet is unaware of the full facts or even their rights in the situation. Subtle pressure is put on the subject who agrees to the recommendation, feeling that they have little power to make a choice which is often implicit and not explicitly discussed. As a result of the complexity of welfare rights and of discretionary dispensation of both allowances and information, 'clients' are not infrequently relatively powerless in such negotiations. Increasingly, other interested persons, particularly community workers and lawyers (notably those from legal action centres), act as informants and advocates to the client. It is, however, important to recognise that teachers, social workers and others are often unaware either of the power relationship which prevails or of the possible consequences of such definitions and prescriptions.

Social workers, particularly, are now becoming much more aware of the slippery slope to social breakdown and the part that they may unwittingly play in speeding this decline. It is only relatively recently that deviancy theory and other relevant sociological approaches have begun to influence social work practice. It is only fair to say that such knowledge has come as an unwelcome shock to a profession which regards itself as altruistic and caring and it is to its credit that the social work system is struggling to incorporate such thinking. But it is not easy; social workers are often in an untenable position, particularly with regard to schoolchildren and their families. On the one hand, informed current thinking indicates that the child's needs are urgent. Clegg and Megson,[43] for instance, when writing of the schools' responsibility for the welfare of the children in their care, point out that when children are in need of social help their need is often clamant and pressing: every day counts. They cannot wait for their parents to be helped; by the time that happens they may be severely damaged either emotionally or even physically. The authors seem to overestimate the skills of both social workers and teachers to provide adequate help even if children at risk are referred to the appropriate source of help; but the message is clear. Evidence of lasting damage to children 'in care' is given by Rowe and Lambert[44] in their study of children in care. They found that once they had been in care for six months, only one in four such children had a chance of returning to their families. The implications here are also clear: social workers concentrate too much and too prolonged effort in attempting to improve or maintain the social functioning of the *family* at the expense of the child. Goldstein, Freud and Solnit (a lawyer, a psychoanalyst and a psychologist)[45] state two value preferences:

> First we take the view that the law must make the child's needs paramount . . . . It is in society's best interests. Each time a cycle of grossly inadequate parent-child relationships is broken society stands to gain a person capable of becoming an adequate parent for children of the future. Second, we have a preference for privacy. To safeguard the right of parents to raise their children as they see fit, free of government intrusion, except in cases of neglect or abandonment, is to safeguard each child's need for continuity.

They go on to stress that in these extreme situations it is important for society to decide which is the least detrimental alternative for the child, as the child's development is at stake. Such a philosophy can be seen to underlie the most recent Children and Young Persons Act, that of 1975. On the other hand, social workers are also aware that there is a good deal of circumstantial evidence that in some cases the definition and resultant prescriptions of social breakdown in relation to a child of the family can have serious repercussions on the rest of the family, which frequently includes other children. Recent inquiries into cases where children have died as the result of non-accidental injury (for example, Maria Colwell,[46] Susan Auckland, Steven Meurs[47]) reveal this only too clearly. Thus social workers in serious cases of social breakdown are almost always on the horns of a dilemma realising, as they now do, that definition of secondary or tertiary social breakdown as regards an individual child may also have the effect of pushing the whole family further along that path also.

Unfortunately, when teachers are involved in such delicate negotiations of social breakdown, it is the head or even the educational administrators who wield the actual power in the negotiations. Frequently they are not personally known to the parents (or even to the child or young person) and thus the negotiations start off with the subject feeling intimidated by the power that is attached to the role of these authorities, and also by the social distance between such powerful strangers and himself.

In other circumstances the power of the agent of social control may be much more obscure and there may be a chain of processes through which negotiations might have to pass before the ultimate sanctions can be reached. For instance, a social worker in a voluntary agency, such as Family Service Units, could be said to be negotiating a contract of breakdown in social functioning with a family with multiple problems who have been referred by the school to the education social worker who, assessing the family, needed intensive social work help and referred the family to the FSU as a preventative measure. Such a situation has less coercion implied in the definition and could be said to subscribe to the criteria of voluntary definition of social breakdown, although the level at which such a definition is made would be relevant to the stigma which resulted.

Parents (or a parent in a one-parent family) have certain expectations in relation to their own well-being and that of their children. For instance, parents who have to go into hospital may ask the social service department to arrange for the care of their child or children. Under Section 1 of the Children and Young Persons Act 1948, if it appears that a child in their area under the age of seventeen

(a) has neither parent nor guardian or has been and remains abandoned by his parents or guardian or is lost; or

(b) that his parents or guardian are, for the time being or permanently; prevented by reason of mental or bodily disease or infirmity or other incapacity or any other circumstances from providing for his proper accommodation, maintenance and upbringing; and

(e) in either case, that the intervention of the local authority under this section is necessary in the interest of the welfare of the child,

It shall be the duty of the local authority to receive the child into their care under this section.[48]

A similar situation may prevail in the case of parent(s) admitted to mental hospital. Homelessness and unsatisfactory home conditions (including chronic ill-health) may also prove to be criteria for the voluntary definition of social breakdown. How 'voluntary' such a definition may be considered to be is currently being hotly debated, but legally the parents and the authorities (in this case usually the social service department) have contractually agreed that a social breakdown has occurred. A third condition which may lead to voluntary definition of social breakdown is when one parent deserts the family or dies or when the family unit has always been incomplete.

There is currently much spirited public debate about the pressures of society which may force a definition of social breakdown on such families who, while apparently being 'helped' by the various social agencies involved, may simultaneously be becoming publicly labelled as experiencing social breakdown, which in turn has further deleterious effects. For instance, it is common knowledge that in prison those who are convicted for offences against children are ostracised and not infrequently are attacked by the other inmates.

Families on housing estates who become 'well known' for their outward evidence of social breakdown (probation, prison, special schools, children's periods in care, admission to mental hospital, etc.) are often treated with hostility and obvious contempt by other apparently or actually more 'respectable' families. Jordan,[49] in writing of poor parents, dismisses the current policies of selective benefits for the poor as a political response to a social and economic crisis and as a return to the spirit of the poor law. He writes:

> a personal social service which had no connection with poor relief would not be in danger of selecting its clients according to their need for financial assistance. It could then concentrate on human deprivation, on the emotional traumas of childhood and the conflicts of family life in all strata of society without having to consider the poor law principles of less eligibility, means test and work enforcement.

Part two

The current issues

Chapter three

Some boundary areas and their problems

Introduction

Though there are a relatively small number of children we do not have the knowledge or resources to help, many of the apparently untreatable and unmanageable teenagers could have been helped earlier in their lives if appropriate assistance had been requested and provided at the right time. Kellmer Pringle[1] has urged us to use knowledge and skills we already possess and points out the consequences of failure to meet children's needs. Rejection and lack of love probably result in anger, hate and lack of concern, outwardly expressed in vandalism, violence and delinquency. Material deprivation leads to impaired family relationships. Lack of stimulation and cultural and linguistic disadvantages lead to impairment of learning capacity. The recognition and giving of praise only for achievement devalues and discourages the under-achievers, and 'under achievement, like envy, seems to feed on itself'. Failure to give practice in role taking and decision making results in limited capacity for exercising and taking responsibility.

In Chapter 2, primary, secondary and tertiary social breakdown have been described and a model has been developed which demonstrates not only the process of social breakdown, but the part various societal agents play in its definition and the prescriptions which follow it. The model has only been developed in relation to schoolchildren, their families and schools, but it is possible to develop it further in relation to other societal institutions.

The present chapter is intended to highlight some of the boundary issues in work with schoolchildren and their families, which serve to obscure just those situations where the education systems are most concerned and involved, and yet often fail to provide the right help at the right time. The Maria Colwell inquiry comments the adage 'too many cooks spoil the broth' may come into the mind of the outside observer. It is inevitable that a considerable number of different agencies and persons will be involved in such cases. What is important is that their respective roles should be clearly defined and that they should not overlap unnecessarily. It is salutory to note how little the recommendations of the Seebohm Committee and subsequent legislation altered the situation in Maria's case.[2]

Of course, as the Committee point out, there was the 'frontier' between East Sussex and Brighton, but in their opinion this was only one explanation for the failure to help Maria.

The following boundary areas have also been selected because they seem to lend credence to the model of social breakdown in that they occur at certain key points (boundary areas) in the process of social breakdown, where the progress towards social breakdown may either be halted or gain in momentum. These are points where the various care-giving agencies, whether preventative, ameliorative, remedial, therapeutic, rehabilitative, custodial or punitive, are most available (or society expects them to be). In Figure 6 (which has been developed and extended from the model by Paley and Thorpe,[3] which they describe as a 'Continuum of Care', designed to prevent, limit or correct juvenile delinquency), the various aspects of 'care' have been outlined, together with an indication of the stage of social breakdown which has been reached by the time such care is available, or has been prescribed. (Thorpe and Paley were, of course, discussing intermediate treatment, which will be discussed in a later section of this chapter.)

As the concept of social breakdown illustrates, society plays its own part in stigmatising or scapegoating children who are in difficulties—and in particular those who appear in court as the result of committing offences which would be regarded as criminal if committed by an adult. Yet at the same time that same society emphasises that such delinquent children are often deprived and in need of care rather than punishment. Recent legislation particularly takes this compassionate approach; while, on the other hand, society simultaneously behaves in an increasingly punitive way towards children as they move nearer to tertiary social breakdown.

The first section on pastoral care and home/school relations explains the ordinary day-to-day care which is, or should be, available to every child of school age. The sections on Educational Priority Areas, community schools and part of the section on special education could be said to cover the *prevention of social breakdown* of children with either physical or emotional handicaps. Counselling, community and youth work and part of special education cover the

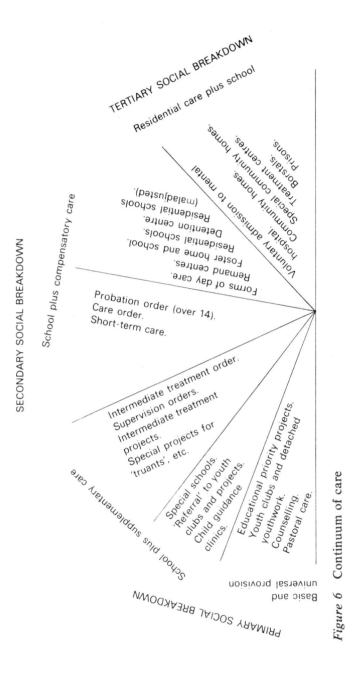

Figure 6 Continuum of care

boundaries between prevention and children at risk of *primary social breakdown*. It is in this area that knowledge and skill is most required so that children can be given appropriate help at the right time and thus prevent further damage. The sections on supervision, truancy and intermediate treatment deal with children who are experiencing *secondary social breakdown* and for whom both school and social work agencies have responsibility (as the health services often do also). Finally, the section on residential care, which includes foster homes, residential schools and community homes, could be said to cover children at the stage of *tertiary social breakdown*. It is the movement into this area and the lack of resources for the care of such children which together form one of the most controversial boundary areas.

While in Figure 6 the boundary areas are presented as if on a continuum so that the full range of caring services for children and their families can be seen in the background, primary, secondary and tertiary social breakdown have been added in an outer segment so as to demonstrate the care-giving services which are (or should be) available at the points of transition. Tutt,[4] in writing of this conflict between care or custody for children in trouble, considers 'that society must make up its mind whether it wants to treat or punish its deprived children'. He points out that the lack of liaison between education and social services departments both at central and local government levels 'makes for inefficiency in the care of children', by causing inappropriate divisions in the services. Some attempts at liaison have since begun but, particularly in relation to non-accidental injury to children, these are barely a beginning. Basically, the services which are intended to provide care for children are still almost separate, as the following section will demonstrate.

1 Pastoral care of schoolchildren and home/school relations

While pastoral care and home/school relations are often regarded as two distinct operations, they could be considered as two sides of a single coin. As has been shown in Chapter 1, the tasks of parents and teachers often overlap and when the two social institutions are functioning effectively they should complement each other. It is an integral aim of school life that all children should receive pastoral care; that is, care and attention must be given to their welfare as well as to their cognitive development. Presumably the somewhat old-fashioned phrase with its parochial implications has its roots in the Christian values of the clergy and church schools of the nineteenth century. This individualised care-giving to parishioners and their families passed into the school system and was probably effective enough where schools were small and served their local communities as did the churches. Indeed, pastoral care in this old-fashioned but 'true' sense is still effective in some small rural schools where the village school, teachers and clergy are an integral part of village community life. The novels of Miss Read are a demonstration of the advantages (and disadvantages!) of such a system. However, with the increase in urbanisation, the developing complexities of the education system, and, in particular, the increase in size of schools and the broadening of the catchment areas they serve, pastoral care in its purest sense began to decline. Tuckwell and Warrior, writing on home and school, had this to say:

> It is typical of our time that increasing lip service is paid to the idea that education is now the community's concern. Schools are increasingly cut off from the people they are supposed to serve and the small neighbourhood school on which primary and secondary education has traditionally been based is disappearing.[5]

Nevertheless, education departments in large urban authorities are endeavouring to maintain community links, particularly in primary schools, and to regenerate them in areas where they have disintegrated (see the section on community schools).

The large comprehensive schools have had much more of a struggle to cater for the individualised welfare of their pupils and organisational structures have been devised to ensure the pastoral care of each child. Marland,[6] the headmaster of a large London comprehensive school, states that pastoral care has a 'central educative purpose in itself'. He stresses that the line between teaching and pastoral care is ill-defined—'the pedagogic concern inevitably has a personal element'—and he defines pastoral care as 'looking after the total care of the pupil'. Pastoral care can be broken down into complementary and separate aims, according to Marland:

(i) to assist the individual to enrich his personal life
(ii) to help prepare the young person for educational choice
(iii) to offer guidance or counselling, helping young people to make their own decisions—by question and so on, and by information where appropriate
(iv) to support the 'subject' teaching
(v) to assist the individual to develop his or her own life style and to respect that of others
(vi) to maintain an orderly atmosphere in which all this is possible.

Organisationally, pastoral care must be part of the main structure of the school, not put in later 'like the plumbing system in a building', as 'this leads to a dislocation between the teaching and the caring'. Marland points out that 'the tutor can only spot the vulnerable pupils if he has the power to do so; this means the tutor having access to knowledge about that pupil and early enough'. The Maria Colwell inquiry illustrates the danger in a situation where even an exceptionally perceptive and sensitive teacher was ineffective because she was not in possession of vital knowledge. 'Knowledge and the mutual respect of having shared some experience together are the core of a tutor's work,' according to Marland.

It seems that there needs to be a good deal of clarity about the role of pastoral care. If it is intended to provide for the total care of a pupil, this seems to imply an unrealisable goal for the school. Another view is that the teacher should identify and respond to stress in an individual child in such a way that the child can contain the anxiety and function in school.

However, even when the structure of the school includes pastoral care of individual pupils as an integral feature, there remain the difficulties connected with inside/outside school relations and communications. The large secondary schools, particularly, frequently have wide catchment areas and, to quote Tuckwell and Warrior again,

> the number of schools locally controlled has diminished. Successive governments since the war have opted for a policy of proportionately fewer but larger schools with a large catchment area. Children today can expect to travel further to their school than their parents. It is not only location and size of schools that set them apart, there seems to be something about institutions which makes for isolation.

Tuckwell and Warrior are not alone in their concern at the growing isolation and isolationism of and in schools. Goffman's work on total institutions is the verification of such a fear.

Reimer,[7] a notable American de-schooler, writes of schools in terms of custodial care and compares them with armies, prisons and asylums, saying that even these total institutions only control some of their inmates. It is Reimer's view that 'school pervades the lives and personalities of their students [pupils] in powerful and insidious ways during their most formative years.' Reimer and other de-schoolers such as Illich are not alone in their concern about the school as a closed system. There is also a developing concern about home/school relations, and serious consideration is increasingly being given to ways in which parents and teachers can work together for the development of their children and pupils. While parent-teacher associations are all too often pragmatic or merely fund-raising organisations, and are frequently dominated by the more articulate middle-class parents, educationists are endeavouring to find ways of involving and interesting parents in the schools' activities. Douglas,[8] in his research on ability and attainment in the primary school, found that middle-class parents take more interest in their children's progress at school and that they become progressively more interested as their children get older, fathers and mothers visiting the schools to discuss their progress; whereas in working-class families he found that among the working classes it was the mothers who were initially interested in their children's education, though this interest seemed to diminish as the children got older. Parental interest in children's education is judged by the teachers in terms of visits to the school, coupled with the use they make of the medical services available. As it is now well proven that children with 'interested' parents pull ahead, there is indeed cause for concern.

(a) Apparent lack of parental interest

Midwinter[9] and others have seen the apparent lack of parental interest in their children's education as of deep concern, but have also pointed out that the problems seem to lie more in the area of relationships and communication with the schools, and that the schools themselves have some responsibility for this. Goodacre[10] writes that 'nearly a generation of parents benefited from compulsory education and the change of philosophy within the education system', while 'along with the shift from a paternalistic system there is increased consumer interest', there is also a 'tradition of parents absolving responsibility to the school' and this tradition, which probably has its roots in the early days when compulsory education was established as a protection for children, may take time and positive action to diminish. These two attitudes often co-exist among parents who are both concerned and interested in their children's education and yet feel helpless and therefore 'uninvolved' in the face of the power of the school.

Goodacre stresses that the parents need to be put back into the picture as to what goes on in school, and points out that teachers are often unaware of the gap for pupils whose educational experience is superior to that of their parents. Parents, too, are often unaware of the stresses for their child at various points in the system. These are usually linked with times of identity crises. Miller[11] particularly deplores the case of adolescents, who he feels are often failed by teachers and parents. Teachers need to recognise that a child has four sets of teachers—parents, peers, school, and other important adults, including the media and folk heroes. Goodacre goes on to stress the stereotyped images which parents and teachers often hold of each other and how difficult it seems for both parties to find opportunities to test out and amend these stereotypes. She adds that current educational methods, too, undermine the authority of the teacher by requiring children to question and enquire and, if they are also confronted by parents who need to flout authority, there are bound to be difficulties. Some of these parents, who are anti-authority, are also delinquent and will not only undervalue but also subtly undermine the values which the child might be learning at school. For such children, the conflict between their involvement at school and at home must be considerable. Saltmarsh, in an article on social work in the school setting, also says:

> Many teachers feel alienated because they feel themselves to be the scapegoats of a society which is charging them with an impossible task of maintaining an authority and setting standards no longer relevant to the children they teach, for these values are given no more than token support at home.[12]

On the other hand, the schooldays of some parents were so dogged by failure and/or humiliation that they avoid going to the children's schools rather than be faced again with the pain. Teachers who have gone from school to college and back to school often forget that for the average parent entering a school means getting in touch with a childish part of themselves again, and that this also involves confronting the uprush of childish feelings which entering a school again arouses. Many of us just shrink, like Alice in Wonderland, to an earlier and regressed childish level, and often behave accordingly.

But there are some parents, often from the families described in Wedge and Prosser's *Born to Fail*,[13] for whom life is such a battle against poverty, poor housing, ill-health and the kind of chronic depression which appears as apathy, that they literally cannot bring themselves to be interested in the schools their children attend.

The development of stereotypes has its roots in confusion, uncertainties and the earlier experiences of both teacher and parents. As was discussed in Chapter 1, there is some overlap of tasks between the school and parents. Inevitably, this must lead to feelings of rivalry between parents and teachers, the parents' feelings of inadequacy and uncertainty perhaps becoming exacerbated by their fears of how much more effective the teachers at school might be; and, even worse, primitive fears of having their children's affection stolen from them. Indeed, as Goodacre points out, one of the tasks of the school seems to be concerned with 'weaning the child away from the highly individualistic outlook of the family and conditioning the child to live with others'—a necessary but painful exercise for the parents. On the other hand, teachers, like everyone else, have a deep need and motivation to do their job and, again because of the overlap of tasks, are often painfully aware that 'my child in my class' really 'belongs to' his or her parents who just do not give a tinker's curse for its education. It seems that this deep and primitive rivalry, as well as real concern for the child, lies at the root of many of the difficulties between school and parents (and not only there: with children in difficulties, teachers and social workers share not only a concern, but also a rivalry to be the good, giving parent who does things right at last). When such rivalry cannot be contained or managed by the parents (or the teachers), then difficulties are bound to occur in home/school relationships. Parents with authority problems stemming from their relationships with their own parents are likely to be in difficulties with other 'authorities', of whom the teacher is a classic example. Goodacre quotes Shipman as stating that there are tendencies in modern educational practice which tend towards rejection of the past as a guide to present or future:

> The increased rate of change also undermines the professional authority of the teacher, because his skills and knowledge may appear to be irrelevant in the modern world.

When a teacher, uncertain of his or her own authority (and/or the authority which society has given him) is involved in a situation of potential conflict with a parent who is anti-authority, then real difficulties are likely to ensue.

A social worker working with just such a mother in a child guidance clinic had tried to help this young woman to 'become' a mother, although she had married at seventeen because she was pregnant, was now separated and had two school-age children. After striking up a friendship with another separated parent with two schoolchildren, they began to cohabit and eventually got an unfurnished flat over a laundrette, in which the mother worked. A baby was born to them and they jogged along well enough, whereas neither family was functioning well before. One day the mother, with enthusiasm, surprised and delighted the social worker by saying she had been to the school the night before. The school had decided to show the children the BBC film on sex education and wanted the parents' approval and involvement in the project. The mother was delighted to be *invited* by the school to participate and tried hard to answer the children's questions at home. The social worker meanwhile helped her to face her own feelings regarding her 'bad' sexuality and enjoy her new-found womanhood enough to accept and answer the questions her children and stepchildren asked about the facts of life.

Schools generally function with middle-class value systems—for which they are often criticised—and this in itself often makes for differences of opinion that at times result in outright failure of communication. Goodacre refers to the linguistic difference between working class and middle-class children as well as the differences in discipline and other cultural values.

(b) General welfare

There are other tasks connected with the welfare of pupils and linking home/school relations, tasks regarding the health of the pupils, remedial education, careers guidance, and ways in which the school itself can link with agencies outside. Various specialist roles for teachers are developing, often with nomenclature linked to similar roles performed by other specialist personnel outside the school. The roles of the school doctor and the school nurse are quite unambiguous and are performed by those specialists, who themselves go into the school. However, in other cases roles are much less clear and this can lead to confusion both inside and outside the school and for parents, who are often unaware of the status (and powers!) of the welfare authorities connected with their children, who give them guidance, advice and on occasion even tell them what to do! While the careers service of the youth employment branch of the education department is a sub-system of the educational system, there is some logic in using the term careers advisory teacher. The remedial teacher also has systemised links with the school psychological service, which itself is also part of the education system. However, roles and functions become much less clear when it comes to a teacher undertaking the welfare function and making links with parents and with social work agencies. While the question of a specialist 'education' social worker will be considered later, there is still much to be said for the execution of two welfare tasks from inside the school system. One of these tasks is the direct link with the families of schoolchildren on basic and simple welfare issues. Looked at in terms of social breakdown, preventive measures might easily be effectively and practically carried out with speed by someone from the school. There is also much to be said for such welfare visits being carried out by a specialist teacher who would make direct links with the home and serve to inform the school, and especially if that teacher were the child's own teacher. Such visits might well be carried out because of minor illness of child or parent, sudden unemployment of a parent, or brief unexplained-absence. If, however, the school has reason to think that in a particular case there was evidence of primary social breakdown, then it would be better to consult the appropriate social work agency (an issue which will be discussed later). If the pupil in question is already having counselling help in school, it might be a matter for the counsellor. Craft[14] writes of the school welfare team highlighting their various roles and delineating a role for the teacher-social worker. This specialist would have knowledge of the social work agencies and methods and would be used by the school as a link with them. It is clear that there is a need for a teacher with specialist knowledge of social services and for some home visiting, a task which requires very different attitudes and skills than those which teaching calls for. However, to call such a person a teacher-social worker seems either to lead to confusion for teachers, parents and social workers and/or to considerable role conflict for the occupant of such a role, whose task performance might at times be at variance with school values, e.g., on truancy. Most of these home/schools liaison teachers, as we might now call them, are qualified teachers but, unlike Craft's teacher-social workers, very few of them have any specific training for this skilled task. Teachers who specialise in welfare functions are usually (though not always) interested in such a role and many of them by now have considerable experience. However, there are increasing requests from such teachers for further training and specialised support.

Green,[15] a London headmaster, writes of the ways in which he and his staff managed to involve the parents of the children in a junior school in a crowded working-class area. New kinds of reports were devised in which parents were asked to write and return comments. Parents were interviewed in school both formally and sometimes informally at the playground gates! There were open days and a parent-teacher association, and parents received letters rather than word-of-mouth messages via their children. Finally the deputy head visited selected parents at home after a written offer of an appointment and having had prior discussions with the class teacher. Of 78 children whose parents were initially considered indifferent or hostile, 43 were progressing or making good progress, even though 35 of their parents remained hostile or indifferent.

While supporting the view of the importance of home/school, parent/teacher links, the National Union of Teachers voiced the following warning:

a good deal of recent discussion about the effects of disadvantage has centered on the role of parents and the suggestion that greater 'parental involvement' in the education of the child and the life of his school is essential, especially for those who are disadvantaged. We believe that there has been much confused thinking on this subject and that there is a need to define much more clearly what is meant by 'parental involvement' and within what framework it should take place.[16]

2 Counselling and social work

School counselling is still a relatively new idea, although the term has been used in the broadest sense for some years and counselling skills have been recognised and described since Socrates! It is only relatively recently that people have been fully employed as full-time counsellors in schools and in the higher-education field. Halmos[17] considers that counsellors have taken over from parsons as the mediators of the faith in human nature, and North[18] writes of the mystique of counselling and refers to them as secular priests. He outlines the range of areas in which a counsellor may concern himself with his client, from academic counselling as an educational process, to the personal and social development of students. He points out the links with psychoanalysis and psychotherapy and adds that this psychotherapeutic ideology (a vulgarisation of the ideas of Freud) has been developed to patch up damaged identities caused by the encroachment of the industrialised world on the private sector of personal and family life. It seems important to mention this mystique and its accompanying attraction and fear for us, because it does go some way towards explaining why the introduction of a counselling service, say into a school, almost always seems to lead to difficulties. Heightened versions of the usual reactions—change, excitement, hostility, resistance, and so on—seem the usual response. Counselling is a vast and important subject and, as North and Halmos indicate, an ideology which is now permeating our daily lives. It is only possible here to make a partial and pragmatic consideration of school counselling and barely to touch on some of the moral issues which are raised by 'interference' in pupils' lives.

Generally speaking, there are three areas of a pupil's school life where counselling help might be of assistance and support. These are, first, *educational guidance*: help with choice of subject, impartial advice, based on a knowledge of the pupil's abilities, aptitudes and limitations. Second, *vocational guidance*: help and advice in choice of career, reassessment of abilities, aptitudes and interests in preparation for higher education or employment. Third, assistance in the area of *personal guidance* in relationship difficulties, with problems at home, with advice and suggestions about broadening social horizons. These three areas may not be causing the pupil such concern that he or she needs to be referred to one of the specialist services outside the school, such as the educational psychologist for educational guidance. It may not yet be time for referral to the youth advisory service. Nor may the pupil be so obviously experiencing such psychological difficulties as to warrant referral to a child guidance clinic, and nor may the pupil and/or family accept such a referral. Yet problems or difficulties in any of these areas might be ameliorated through the use of counselling skills. Counselling *skills* as a helping technique are indeed very similar to casework *skills* in social work.

Jones,[19] in describing what counselling is, writes of rapport, respect for the individual, acceptance, empathy and trust, much as would a social worker when describing the elements of a casework relationship. Like social workers, she also stresses the importance of confidentiality as a demonstration of the respect shown for the individual, as well as in building a relationship of trust between pupil and counsellor. This trusting relationship is the medium through which counselling technique can be effective. However, for counsellors in the school situation, the question of confidentiality is a difficulty. Jones stresses the importance of knowledge of the school setting, of building up relationships which make it possible to demonstrate to the other teachers a professional and responsible attitude: this shows that the counsellor values and respects their expertise and will not undermine *them* to her client and *their* pupil any more than she would betray the client's confidences. Jones was lucky enough to be invited into the school by the head, who acknowledged from the beginning that confidentiality was an integral part of the counselling task: but there are many heads who would find it difficult to allow such departures from their direct control.

So counselling skills are not dissimilar to social work skills. What may be different are the areas of the client/pupil's life in which these skills are used and the setting in which they are practised, which calls for specialist knowledge of the education setting on the part of the counsellor. There seems to be no general agreement as to whether counsellors should offer pupils vocational, educational and personal guidance. Many provide help in all three areas according to the needs of the pupil. Jones herself decided to give counselling assistance in the area of personal guidance only, pointing out that the pastoral case system would take care of the educational guidance and the careers advisors of vocational guidance. This decision was also partly made on grounds of best use of time and of the availability of other teachers with appropriate expertise. There are arguments for all ways of working. Many counsellors, unlike Jones, also have a teaching role and one wonders how this affects their counselling relationships with their clients, whether they actually teach them or not. It may be that this teaching is undertaken for the benefit of other teachers who may be hostile to the specialist role of the counsellor and in order to demystify the counselling role; alternatively, it may be a collusion with a school which is really ambivalent in its attitude towards counselling.

As Jones points out, it is only recently that training for counselling has been developed and many counsellors are untrained and unsupported, though others like herself are trained for marriage guidance. Usually teachers who become counsellors are 'good' with children who have difficulties and are interested in them. Often this means that the teacher is especially friendly and open and makes relationships easily. Teachers who are more comfortable in a non-authoritarian role may gravitate towards becoming counsellors. Nevertheless, almost all school counsellors are trained teachers. While it is not usually expressly stated that they must be teachers, there are subtle pressures to discourage the employment of non-teachers. The teachers' associations, as is well known, take a somewhat narrow view of 'non-specialists' in the school. There are also arguments about the importance of the respect and trust of other teachers towards the counsellor, which is vital for pupils' development. It would be tempting and all too easy (in the classroom) subtly to undermine the delicate and developing relationship between counsellor and client. Counselling must be a voluntary activity and pupils who do not attend cannot be helped by this method. There are also timetabling adaptations which need to be accommodated as pupils who are being counselled may have to be absent from lessons. Nevertheless, there is much to be said for outsiders of all specialisms coming into the schools, as doctors and nurses do.

The role of the counsellor as link person between the school and outside social work and other helping agencies, is obviously of importance and value where the pupil is at risk. It may be that the counsellor can enable a pupil to obtain more specialist help, liaise and at times mediate with other agencies who are also trying to assist him and/or his family. As has already been mentioned, the home/school liaison teacher might have a similar role, and it is important both for the school and for outside social work agencies that such roles should be clearly worked out and explicit. This saves confusion and time and aids essential communication between the school and the caring agencies outside.

A pattern which seems to be developing is that in the junior schools the home/school liaison teacher is the link person, while in the large secondary schools it is the counsellor who undertakes the task, particularly for children considered by the school to be at risk (i.e. prevention of social breakdown).

However, this model detracts quite considerably from the traditional and powerful role of the heads, who have always been the ultimate authority and accountable for everything which happens to the pupils in their care. Saltmarsh[20] points out that 'their autonomy is traditional and often defensive, they are not used to discussing decision making' nor to having it questioned. She is actually discussing relationships between teachers and social workers here, but such views also apply to the question of confidentiality for counselling staff. Heads are in a difficult situation, since they are legally considered as being *in loco parentis* for their pupils. And in society we are apt to think of ourselves as educational experts—after all, we have each been at school. Indeed, there is a parallel in the way we behave when we are at the zoo—we gaze admiringly at some of the animals and yet we simultaneously criticize the whole idea of locking them up!

If we consider the link between counselling and social work as a continuum, the counsellor often seems to stand between the point where the pupil is barely considered to be at risk of social breakdown and the point where he or she is definitely at risk of social breakdown and may need to be referred to an outside care-giving agency. It may be that the counsellor is already in touch with a social worker. It is these kinds of boundary situations which seem to be problematic for counsellor and social worker alike; both of whom are in a way bedevilled by their responsibilities, with the school, on one hand, *in loco parentis* by day and on the other the social worker, who may possibly have a statutory responsibility, and certainly will have if the pupil is subject to a supervision or care order. An example may be useful here. A fourteen-year-old West Indian girl was subject to a supervision order resulting from her being beyond her parents' control. A social worker was in close touch with the family and the girl and was trying to help improve family relationships, which were beginning to pressure the girl into going out at night in order to escape. The girl told the school counsellor (untrained) that she was pregnant and the counsellor told the head. The head insisted that the mother be told. The girl was under age and if she miscarried in school the head would be considered partly responsible. On being told that the girl was subject to a supervision order, the head tried to insist that the social service department should inform the mother. The social worker felt it important that the girl should be able to inform her mother herself. She was also worried that the mother would give the girl a thrashing if told in such a way as to provoke her. The stalemate was broken only when a neighbour told the mother, who *did* thrash the girl, who then ran away but luckily to her social worker. Such incompatibilities of orientation are not easy to resolve without good-will on both sides.

In these kinds of situations real difficulties can arise, often compounded by several factors, all of which can interact and lead to worsening of the situation. This may eventually lead to a situation which the pupil, who is already in trouble, experiences as a tug of war between two parties who are supposed to be trying to help. First, it is unfortunately necessary to repeat that both school systems and social work systems are woefully ignorant about each other's tasks,

responsibilities and organisational structures. Second, this ignorance, coupled with geographic separateness, inevitably leads to
stereotyping, which in turn leads to both parties *behaving* as if the
other were the worst kind of teacher or social worker and an
apparent inability to put such preconceptions to the test. Third, as
has been shown in Chapter 1, the attitudes of social workers and
teachers are likely to be very different. These attitudes, together with
the distinct and separate value systems of schools and social work
agencies, will be considered further in the chapter on the people in
the systems. However, in trying to help a pupil it is of vital
importance for counsellors and social workers to recognise and allow
for these differences of attitude and value system.

In order to try to bring some clarity into this discussion of a
confused situation, an assumption has been made that both
counsellor and social worker are experienced and secure enough
(which virtually means 'trained') to respect and value each other's
professional tasks. Alas, all too frequently, this is not the case. As
has been said, at present too few counsellors are trained and very
often a harassed teacher, inexperienced in the complexities of such a
role, tries to squeeze this in with other duties, having not had the
time or support to think through the differences and subtleties of,
for instance, confidentiality. Unfortunately, too, there are too few
professionally trained social workers in social work agencies and
they, too, are frequently grossly overworked. This leads to in-
securities and defensiveness on both sides even when the responsibilities are clear enough.

However, there is also the anomalous position of the education
welfare service (this will be dealt with in more detail later, in
Chapter 4). Here it must suffice to say that the status and position
of the education welfare service within the education hierarchy
is so unclear, its task is also unclear, and few of its officers are
professionally trained. Many other social workers and teachers
claim (perhaps correctly if a little unfairly) that this makes confusion
worse confounded.

What does seem of critical concern is that the need to try to help
the child *and* the family should not be lost sight of. As Jones has
clearly demonstrated, ways and means can be found to work
together. Since neither the school counsellor nor any social worker
can help a pupil or his family without carefully building a trusting
relationship first, it would seem that this should be regarded as the
first priority. There are many ways of structuring help to such
children and their families. Some children find school a much safer
place in which to seek help. Those who are anti-school would find
help more acceptable outside the school setting. Generally speaking,
parents are better helped outside the school setting and indeed their

children may prefer to keep home and school problems separate, which would seem to imply that this preference needs to be taken into account when considering any intervention. Nevertheless, as Jones demonstrates, interviews with parents about their children (and *with* their child's consent) can be very helpful to all concerned. Saltmarsh points out that there is a distressing assumption in schools that working with children in their families is solely a matter of good personal relationships. This should be viewed as an educational task for social workers and not as a battleground for territorial rights!

The place of counselling within the school structure also raises interesting organisational issues, which ultimately affect both its functioning and that of the school. Schools inevitably have difficulties in relation to combining and balancing the caring and the disciplinary aspects of their function. (Incidentally, they are not alone in this: so do most families, and as has already been mentioned so also do individual teachers and social workers.) Some schools, in effect, try to use the counsellor/counselling unit to resolve disciplinary problems. Disturbed or difficult children, particularly those with behaviour problems, are referred to the counsellor and in some cases virtually turned over to them, as for instance in the case of sanctuaries. While this may make the school a more comfortable place, such policies ultimately encapsulate the counsellor, the unit being seen by pupils as a 'sin bin'; this in turn deterring pupils from voluntarily seeking and using the help available to them.

Jones, now the head of an all-girls' comprehensive school, has changed some of her earlier views regarding the role of the counsellor. She stresses the vital importance of pupil/teacher relationships and the continuity of care. In her school, therefore, the heads of years move up the school with the pupils and continuity of subject teachers, too, is given general priority where appropriate. On the subject of discipline she writes:

When pupils misbehave—and some always will—we have to be
sensitive enough to know whether they are just trying it on,
whether the root cause is in something the school is doing, or
whether they really are disturbed. Most pupils respond well if
expectations of work and behaviour are high, if good work and
behaviour is recognised and praised and unsatisfactory work or
behaviour is disapproved. Caring, as any parent knows,
includes setting limits and showing anger at times. It does not
include being violent, either verbally or physically, for this is a
sure way of setting up a violent reaction in pupils.[21]

For a final and important point, it is necessary to return to the process of social breakdown. If Jordan[22] is right when he points out that the opprobrium presently attached to supplementary benefits is slowly shifting to the social service departments, then counsellors and teachers need to take this into account when considering referral or dealing within the school system with pupils who are already clients of social service departments. Social workers, too, need to take this into account.

Ultimately, the difference between counselling and social work may be of less importance and perhaps more related to the setting in which the activity takes place than any clearly distinguishable features of either. Rose and Marshall in their very comprehensive consideration of this whole area seem to indicate by the title of their book *Counselling and School Social Work*[23] that the two are synonymous. Their research will be discussed in Chapters 4 and 6. In conclusion, what seems to be of prime importance here is that while there are too few care-giving professionals who have the necessary knowledge and skills to help children in difficulty, it is essential that the organisational structures within which they work should not hamper them in their efforts to give appropriate help at the right time. This is clearly one of the areas of most concern for all concerned with children and both more co-operation and more interdisciplinary research is needed.

3 Youth and community service

While youth clubs (and later detached youth services) have long been developed within the voluntary sector, the youth services of the local authority education system have been the neglected Cinderellas of most departments. While, strictly speaking, social education and community service within schools cannot be regarded as part of the youth and community service, the service is perhaps indicative of the growing change of attitudes within the educational system. Services both for young people and by young people within the community were given recognition and encouragement by the Albemarle Report[24] accepted in 1960. Around that time, in addition to a newly constituted youth service, various voluntary organisations began to emerge: the Young Volunteer Force, Task Force and Community Service Volunteers. Social service, often called community education, is now timetabled in the curriculum of many secondary schools. The young volunteers involved undertake practical tasks and various kinds of support (including that of friendship) with disadvantaged sections of the community. The aim of most of these projects is to provide the young volunteer with both social education in the way of life of the community and, at the same time, with an opportunity to serve that community. These voluntary schemes have proved very successful with young people who might have become interested in serving the community in some way later on and have allowed them to become involved sooner than they might have done. They have been less successful in involving the pupils at risk, but such pupils, particularly if they have behaviour problems, are 'a risk' for the community service side of the task. Nevertheless, some interesting experiments are being tried, such as the new Teenage Project in Hammersmith in London, where former clients run a project for teenagers at risk. The voluntary schemes are run by paid volunteer organisers who themselves are often between college and professional education and many of whom go on later to teacher or social work training. The social education side of the projects often leads to some interesting dilemmas for the schools. Obviously, it is important for pupils not only to receive support and guidance while involved in some of the less salubrious areas of society, but also to be able to formulate questions and learn about the causes of such poverty, despair and deprivation. While some large secondary schools have very successfully coped with this in social education departments (where sociology, for instance, can be taught alongside the 'practice'), others have been unable to tackle this side of social education in more than a perfunctory way. Questions about social policy are apt to arouse political arguments and even if the leaders have the appropriate skills (and many of them have not), such political discussions are in danger of causing some comeback from the school managers, who keep a watchful political eye on the school curriculum.

Certainly what these young voluntary workers are doing is trying to prevent or ameliorate a breakdown in social functioning among their target group: they would seem to be working at the primary breakdown end of the process. Could this be defined as social work? Certainly it is often called so both by the schools and by many of the personnel of such voluntary organisations. The nomenclature given to such activities, however, does cause some confusion and uncertainty not only among the volunteers and the recipients of their service, but also among others in the education and social work systems. While few social workers would doubt that such work is both needed and extremely valuable when carried out conscientiously, many would not define it as social work unless the volunteer was working within social work principles and from a social work value base. Some would go even further and not make such a definition unless the volunteers were also using social work skills and social work knowledge or even working from within a base in a social work agency. Of course, the lack of agreed definition as to what is the social work task adds to such confusion, as does the uncertainty among social workers about their 'right' to professionalism, as will be discussed later. Unfortunately this can, and often does, lead to the social work system either taking a 'purist' view or diminishing the value of such work. It is a pity that social workers often take this stance, because individually most would agree there exists a need for such work, and social work principles firmly state that the community should concern itself with its own problems. While an alternative name for such activities might be of some small assistance—perhaps voluntary social service, which is used on occasion—the confusion and resultant tensions will remain while the two systems operate in such a discrete and separate manner. If organisational links were created between the social work system and the schools volunteer services, these could provide the opportunity for education about social work activities as well as possibly improving the quality of the voluntary service offered.

Since 1960 the long-neglected Youth Service itself has been given wider recognition and a much clearer remit for the provision for youth recreation and the prevention of delinquency, although in their overview of the Wincroft Project, Smith, Farrant and Marchant[25] point out that despite the clear need for such a project, first conceived in 1963, it was only started in 1966, delayed primarily by lack of funding. The Youth Service employs community or youth workers in various settings, ranging from the schools themselves—where they often run evening activities—to clubs, youth clubs or community centres. Voluntary and independent organisations have also initiated projects using unattached youth workers or those working from coffee bars, such as those described by Morse, and Goetschius and Tash,[26] and these 'reaching out' activities have also been developed by the education-system-based Youth Service, following their example. Unlike teaching, where only qualified teachers may be employed, the Youth Service employs many unqualified youth workers, a similar situation to that of social work agencies. It is also of interest to note that while a qualified youth worker is not eligible to teach in a school, any qualified teacher is considered qualified to undertake youth work. While at first sight this might seem quite a logical extension of a teacher's duties, further consideration of the youth workers' non-authoritarian role and the methods and skills they use to work with their 'clients' indicates that non-specialised teacher training gives little opportunity to develop such attitudes and skills. This has become even more pronounced since the introduction of the professional youth and community courses, which include the development of a broader range of skills.

It is the Youth Service which theoretically provides a service for all young people (and often their families too) covering basic and universal provision for those experiencing primary social breakdown and working on through to those experiencing secondary social breakdown, by providing additional and compensatory 'care' which may prevent tertiary social breakdown. The Wincroft Project, mentioned earlier, is of particular interest, for it demonstrates most clearly how youth workers selectively tried to fill such gaps in the ordinary provision of services for young people. It is also of interest and note because, as is pointed out by the authors, it was the only service actually located on the high delinquency estate of Wincroft. The aims of the project were twofold: first, to 'work with young people in need of help and assist them in finding a dynamic adjustment to society and thereby among other things to control deliquency'. Second, 'to develop methods of working with difficult young people in an unstructured setting'. The project was concerned 'not merely with adjusting young people to their environment but also with helping them to change it'. It was also concerned with the most difficult young people. The workers selected fifty-four young people whose average age at the beginning of the project was fifteen years, three months. Carefully, and through a variety of means (initially through the opening of a café) and later through the young people themselves, the workers built up and maintained contact with fifty-four boys whom they considered needed additional help. Working within social work principles and using the social work methods—initially primarily groupwork but later primarily casework—the project workers and volunteers were able to achieve some of their aims. The project lasted for two years and when compared at the end with a control group of boys who had not been worked with, fewer of the project boys appeared in court and those that did also had fewer convictions than the boys in the control group. While it would appear that there was a statistically significant difference between the two groups at the end of the evaluation period, with certain aspects of delinquency it proved difficult to weigh the various factors and thus provide a breakdown. However, the project was able to demonstrate improved social performance on the part of the project boys, though in the final analysis of the research there was little evidence that attitudes towards society had actually changed.

During the course of the project some interesting issues began to emerge as regards the relationship of the schools both towards the boys themselves and also towards the project team. At this time Manchester had not yet begun to develop a comprehensive education policy and had a relatively high proportion of its children in selective schooling. Very few of the participant children received selective schooling, and thirty-eight of them had indeed passed through the same school. The authors comment:

Most of the participants left school at the first opportunity. For most of them school was an irrelevance that they swept out of their minds as they swept out of the schoolyard . . . . Neither they nor their parents were closely involved with the process of education and so those most in need of the civilising and socialising influences of education benefited least from attendance at school.

They also comment on the need for the school to be more closely connected with the community and, while expressing regret that the project did not attempt actual co-operation with the schools, they add that plans to enlist further co-operation were partly frustrated. As an example of the difficulty of changing attitudes towards troublesome young people, they refer to a teacher visiting the project with a view to becoming a volunteer who advised the group worker, 'I should get rid of that lad if I were you—he's no good to you'. This was the very lad for whom a football group was being formed and the incident is referred to as an illustration of the contrast between the project's methods and the more orthodox approaches.

The skills that community and youth workers employ are often social work skills, particularly group work skills, but they have also developed community work skills and generally have more knowledge of tenant and neighbourhood groups than the average trained social worker, particularly those who initially trained as caseworkers. Within the community work field there is a continuum of styles and attitudes, mainly influenced by the ideological commitment of the workers and the agencies within which they are based. At one end there are those community workers who see themselves as social workers specialising in the community work method, some of whom actually work within the social work system, although they do not generally undertake statutory duties. The validation by the Central Council for Education and Training in Social Work (CCETSW) of some of the professional community and youth work courses as being able to carry the award of Certificate of Qualification in Social Work (CQSW) has given this sector further recognition. There are also those who see themselves primarily as adult educationists enabling their target group to develop second-chance educational and social opportunities hitherto denied to them, either because they were not able to take advantage of what was offered or because the facilities which were offered were of such poor quality. Finally there are those whose commitment is primarily a political one in that their emphasis is directed towards assisting their target group to change the very system which has denied them the right of equal opportunity and control over resources.

From the point of view of the young people (and their families) the youth and community service is likely to be seen somewhat differently from that of (the rest of) the social work system. This may be partly because the service is part of the education system and also has specific tasks in relation to adolescents. But it may also be in part due to the fact that the youth and community workers have no statutory responsibilities. This seems particularly important (indeed, many youth workers spend a fair proportion of their time aiding teenagers who are in trouble with the law, or in danger of being so) and probably gives the service a distinctly advantageous position in relation to intervention in social breakdown. The workers, too, have been able to develop special skills in relation to work with young people.

An interesting recent development is the employment of community workers within social service departments. These may be workers attached to the area teams, or working as detached workers. They do not have the usual statutory responsibilities of the other social workers, but function solely as community workers, thus being free to intervene at community levels. Many of them also act as community consultants to the rest of the area team, or to the department. It is too early yet to gauge how such appointments are working out, although it is said that in some areas their politically biased activities are causing some concern to the democratically elected representatives.

Milson,[27] writing on the Youth and Community Work Courses, states that despite the siting of most of these courses in colleges of education, 'their skills and attitudes have more in common with social work'. He comments critically on the community school movement, querying the actual numbers there are and pointing out that 'these often merely relate their educational processes within to the community without'. He also quotes a group of community workers approaching a school and 'offering to undertake courses in social education . . . an offer gladly accepted by the staff until they discovered that the programme included elements which encouraged the youngsters to look critically at aspects of their society'. He points out that 'the community and youth staff will be encouraging their students to use non-directive methods rather than imposing discipline or communicating a subject'. Finally, he says that these tutors

> apply community development methods in the training course and to staff-student relationships . . . . They are quicker to scorn the bureaucratic tendencies in the college, whereas their colleagues are more content with a 'theirs not to reason why' approach, since this is more consistent with a teacher's role.

The relationship between youth and community workers and social workers has undergone an interesting and rapid change over the past few years. As has been pointed out, until comparatively recently social workers were primarily trained as caseworkers, which is most simply described as primarily working with individuals and later with families, often using the supportive and insight-giving techniques more familiarly used in psychotherapy. Youth workers on the other hand had become more involved in using group work skills and were also involving themselves in community work. Social caseworkers, as they were often called, began to branch out into using group work skills and community work skills at about the same time as youth workers became more 'professionalised' (i.e., since the Albemarle Report began to take effect) and to consider that some of their clients could use the additional and specialised casework help. As the two kinds of worker began to meet more regularly, for each the stereotypes of the other began to diminish and more realistic relationships began to develop. There was then a period when social workers who knew little of community work and community and youth workers exaggerated the skills of the other, either overvaluing or undervaluing the efficacy of both in situations of social breakdown. This 'honeymoon' period (highs and lows) in their relationship coincided with the establishment of the social service departments, an all-time low period for social workers who not only had to amalgamate organisationally, but also had to learn to work with other types of client problems. Not only did they become concerned with clients who were elderly, mentally ill or children, but they also had additional responsibilities thrust upon them by the 1969 Children and Young Persons Act. Community and youth workers at about this time were also becoming aware of the enormity of the burden of statutory responsibility that the social service departments carry. Since that time and particularly since the employment of community workers in these departments, a much more realistic partnership has developed. Most social workers now learn something of all three social work methods in their training, and youth and community workers are more knowledgeable about work with individuals and families (as casework which now includes a broader range of activities is coming to be called).

What seems to be happening, partly perhaps as the result of this move towards understanding each other, is an estrangement from the schools. This seems to have been further exacerbated by the raising of the school leaving age. Many of these Raising of the School-Leaving Age (ROSLA) children find the community workers' skills and the non-authoritarian nature of their projects much more acceptable to their life-style than the more rigid structure and authoritarian attitudes of their schools. While some attempts have been made to introduce a more democratic style of involvement of pupils in schools, it is peculiarly difficult for adolescent pupils, by their very nature engaged in questioning both authority and standards, to be able to really take advantage of the opportunities offered while they remain within the ordinary school system. Unfortunately, as has already been said, the 1969 Children and Young Persons Act was not fully implemented, nor were the resources made available, particularly for residential care, and these factors, coupled with the somewhat less authoritarian approach of all social workers, have further estranged them from the schools. These crises will be further discussed as they are certainly the most critical in the relationship between schools and social work.

The introduction of school counsellors, particularly where they are trained in the use of non-directive techniques, seems to be beginning to create within the school system an opportunity for working with teenagers who are starting to experience primary social breakdown. If they can form creative links with the community and youth workers who, while working within the education system, usually work outside the school itself, then real opportunities will begin to be provided within the education system.

4 Educational Priority Areas and community schools

The idea of positive discrimination for run-down neighbourhoods (where the people are poor and where the services are often the worst) was first suggested by the Plowden Report.[28] This recommended positive discrimination which should favour schools in those neighbourhoods where children are most handicapped by their home conditions. The extra resources should not only bring the schools in these deprived areas up to standard, but they should be as good as the best in the country: 'So the Plowden Report proposed that these educational priority areas should introduce community schools, in-service training for teachers, attached social work, special equipment, expanded nursery education and research.' Marris and Rein[29] comment, 'these recommendations might have been taken from the prospectus of almost any community school agency in an American city'. Their assessment of the American War on Poverty programme in 1960-4, shows many parallels with some recent British ideas of reform. Marris and Rein refer to the urban aid programme and the community development projects which

seek, by integration of services, by experiment, community involvement and selective concentration . . . to redirect services more productively . . . . At the same time, in creating an administration more responsive to the needs put forward by local groups, they appear more democratic. But they still assign leadership to teacher and social worker, assuming that the interests of professional services and the community are mutual and that self help will reinforce the intentions of the Government.

Marris and Rein's book is an account of the dilemmas which the anti-poverty programme encountered.

Much has already been written about the Educational Priority Area (EPA) programme which was one of the sequelae of the Plowden recommendations and, now that the individual evaluations of some of the projects have been published, the debate continues. While action research is not new, the particular theory which emerged and the style and the structure of the projects, are wholly unique. Six areas were chosen, and although there has been some comment about the political aspects of the choices, they were all areas of social need. The project was directed from Oxford University by Dr A. H. Halsey and the Oxford project team had the task of working out the guidelines for the project. The only rural area selected was the run-down mining area of Dennaby in the West Riding. Three other projects were in the deprived areas of the inner city areas of Birmingham, Liverpool and Deptford in London and the sixth project was in Dundee in Scotland. The ILEA responsible for the Deptford project devised an EPA index by means of which educational priority area schools were highlighted, then ranked in order of priority. The criteria used were the proportion of employed males, supplements of cash from the state, overcrowding of houses, lack of basic amenities, poor school attendance, proportions of handicapped pupils, immigrant children, teacher turnover and pupil turnover.

The aims of the projects were as follows:

1 To raise the educational performance of the children;
2 to improve the morale of the teachers;
3 to increase the involvement of the parents in their children's education;
4 to increase their 'sense of responsibility' for their communities and the people living in them.

The project teams were largely autonomous; they were area based and had their main links with primary education—indeed an essential feature was their individualised and local approach.

The EPA projects, as Halsey[30] says, took the idea of primary community schools from Plowden and 'developed it to the point where they regard it as an essential principle along with that of positive discrimination for educational priority areas'. In all schools

the community school seeks almost to obliterate the boundary between school and the community and to turn the community into a school and the school into a community. It emphasises both teaching and learning roles for all social positions so that children may teach and teachers may learn as well as vice versa parents may do both instead of neither.

Halsey goes on to outline organisational structures and strategies to make their brave new world a reality, pointing out that the nub of it all is to encourage the parent to join the educational process.

It is interesting to note that despite their aims and their links with poverty and social breakdown, only two of the teams specifically included social workers. The Dundee and Deptford projects both had education welfare officers attached to the teams from the beginning, although the work of the Dennaby project (particularly in relation to the multi-purpose Red House education centre) later led to the attachment of a social worker on secondment from the social services department. It is not clear whether any of the education welfare officers were in fact professionally qualified social workers and, while omission of this knowledge is regrettable, it is perhaps also indicative of the lack of respect educationists give to the professional role of social workers. If, as is possible, some of the education welfare officers were in fact not qualified, then it would have been interesting to compare the ways in which they worked and why they chose to make the social work intervention in the way they did. While there is no reason to doubt that as social workers they were unusually knowledgeable and skilled in relation to the education system, there is some indication (particularly in the Scottish project) that the social work described had a somewhat pragmatic bias. There is no way of knowing whether this is a particular aspect of education social work or whether it has to do with the level of skills and expertise of the social workers concerned.

While further evidence was demonstrated regarding the overlap of the tasks of education and social work—indeed, head teachers and project directors seem to have found it difficult to distinguish between the two—it is significant that the project findings were not generally related to this boundary area of overlap. While the work of the social workers in Scotland was included as a chapter in the findings, the work of Lyons[31] in the Deptford project was written up separately and published later. The Dundee social workers had some interesting comments to make:

> While school casework with families in need was for many
> reasons the right place for social workers to start their work in
> E.P.A. schools, with some families it raised problems. Justified
> or not, for many parents the image of the school was one of a
> rigid, critical and authoritarian regime which they regarded
> with a mixture of respect, rejection and fear. When the school

made a gesture of general friendship and non-critical concern, however, the door was open to future relations with families in genuine need . . . . The understanding and tolerance shown to families in social difficulties varied greatly from one school and from one teacher to another. Within any one school one could find the complete range, from active constructive sympathy towards both children and families to undisguised intolerance, not towards the children but towards the parents who appeared feckless and neglectful, or who failed to measure up to what the school regarded as minimum standards . . . again the social workers sometimes found the school system too rigid and inflexible to allow tolerance towards individual children or families . . . . Another obviously different viewpoint arose in the schools' use of corporal punishment. The use of corporal punishment varied very widely from one school and class to another but it was to be found, at least on occasion, in every primary school. To the social workers it was very disappointing to find corporal punishment being used on children from severely disturbed backgrounds.[32]

While the extracts selected from this chapter perhaps give a distinctive bias to the more negative attitudes of the schools, they are nevertheless illustrative of the value conflicts which can and do exist between teachers and social workers who share a genuine concern with the same families. George and Teresa Smith, who were both involved in the Dennaby project (who have subsequently written on community schools and whose work will be cited later), together with the first wardens of the Red House, Geoff and Lynn Poulton, demonstrate in their work that they subscribe to social work values, whether or not they are professionally qualified as social workers.

The EPA teams all found that the crisis time just prior to going to school presented an opportunity for involving families and linking them with the education system. In the Deptford project the two liaison teachers saw their role differently, one as 'selling education to parents', the other (who was more orientated towards a counselling approach) emphasising the need to work with various welfare agencies.

Halsey also comments on the uncertainty and the degree to which the home/school liaison teacher should or need become involved in social work. Ideally, he says,

liaison teaching is primarily concerned with interpreting the aims and methods of education to parents, with awakening their enthusiasm and encouraging them to recognise and play their own part . . . . By contrast the social worker is properly concerned with breakdown; with cases where special problems put families in need of help from the social services . . . . as at Red House where families with children were admitted for short periods in emergencies, such crisis work might be necessary, nevertheless, the liaison teacher's job should be clearly distinguished from social work and his relation to social workers thereby clarified.

Since the EPA projects, which have been the focus of much attention in the education world, the idea of teachers doing home visiting seems to have become more acceptable, but there is still much debate about the advisability of such visits. Some of the objections are rationalisations by teachers who reasonably enough may be anxious about visiting adults (i.e., parents) at home when their training equips them to teach children—at school! Another objection relates to how the children themselves view this linking of home and school. Some children manage to 'survive educationally', coping with two different value systems in two different 'worlds' by keeping them distinct and separate. Home visiting by the teacher should not be undertaken lightly and only exceptionally without the child's knowledge and agreement.

One of the other innovative suggestions arising from the EPA projects is that of Educational Visitors. Halsey describes the educational visitor as having the task 'of raising standards of life by carrying new knowledge and new methods from the frontiers of educational skill in the teaching professions to the family which is remote and unknowing about pedagogical mysteries'. The work of the educational visitor in the Dennaby team was highly successful. During 1971 Mrs Armstrong visited twenty children aged from eighteen months to three years. Initially the visit was intended to examine and improve the educability of the child by working with him at home, but it also proved useful in discussing the child with the mother and in helping her to see herself as important in helping the child to learn. The DHSS in its pamphlet *The Family in Society—Preparation for Parenthood*,[33] acknowledges the considerable interest in such visitors but points out that 'success depends on recruiting highly motivated educational visitors who are knowledgeable about both the theory and practice of learning and sensitive as the best social workers are to the nuances of family relationships'.

The report from the sixth National Conference of Education Home Visitors highlights just how much this small but developing service bridges the education and social work systems. Education visitors are employed by education departments, social service departments and by independent projects; some are volunteers. In some school-based schemes the education visitor is on the staff of the school and therefore is responsible to the head. Project-based schemes, such as those in Birmingham, Liverpool and Southampton, seem to function as community projects, either working as neighbour-hood groups or along community development lines. There appears to be no precise definition of the role or work of educational visitors, although Poulton describes the aims of visiting schemes for women at home with children under five as follows:

They help mothers and fathers to feel that they have an important part to play in their children's development.

They help parents to feel that they have an important part to play in supporting each other in their neighbourhoods.

They introduce home influences to the school and project the school's aims towards the home.

They build up a greater sense of confidence and trust between teachers and parents.

They provide the possibility of closer liaison and understanding between health, education and social services related to families.

They reach out to isolated people on a regular basis, establishing school and neighbourhood links with them.

Some schemes aim to reinforce the capacity of people in neighbourhoods to play a major role in organising and controlling new initiatives.

All the schemes are concerned for the quality of life open to the children and their parents.[34]

Questions on the issues of supervision, support and training for education visitors and their role as agents of social change are likely to present dilemmas to their employing bodies.

Smith and Smith,[35] who were both involved in the Dennaby project, take up the overlap of tasks specifically in relation to community schools. They 'consider that the essential question is how far education in the shape of community schools can become a base for wider community development'. Since the debate about the terms 'community' and 'community development' waxes strong and has inevitable ideological overtones in both social work and education, it is not surprising that the term 'community school' is also interpreted in many different ways. Smith and Smith offer some helpful ideas in relation to the assumptions underlying the EPA projects:

Firstly, 'community' refers to a relatively small area, characterised by a high degree of face-to-face interaction, with some degree of shared value patterns. Second, it implies concern with the total group in any category, rather than a selected sub-group. Schools in E.P.A.s for example, clearly fulfil a creaming function, still formalised in some areas with selective secondary education for a minority; community education, in contrast, aims at the complete group, developing a curriculum relevant to the needs of those likely to remain in E.P.A.s. Third, it emphasises a broad, non-specialist approach to the services of the area; social or individual problems are seen to be the result of a complex set of factors and therefore not best tackled by a series of unco-ordinated and highly specialised agencies. Fourth, for the same reason it emphasises linkage and integration among organisations servicing an area; and fifth, it stresses the importance of participation and development of the community's own institutions on the basis that the community is a viable entity, independent of the administrative structures created to service it. Community development then is the broad process which embodies this approach, rather than the bit of social life that is left over when education, health, social services and the other big battalions have been taken out.

They distinguish five types or models of community schools, some of which have been in existence for almost a century, despite the fashionable contemporary preoccupation with such schools:

1   A school which serves an entire neighbourhood: most primary schools and more and more secondary schools forming 'pyramids' with their feeder primary schools would qualify.
2   A school which shares its premises with the community: this has been a long-standing arrangement, which has expanded as schools have become larger and better equipped. But as the Smiths point out,

> size can conflict with a need to develop links in a relatively small area. Also, which shared buildings may be economically sound . . . both groups may function side by side with comparative autonomy: school content and organisation do not necessarily become more community-orientated or responsive by opening the doors to community run activities for adults.

3   'A school which develops a curriculum of community study, arguing for the social and educational relevancy of local and familiar material.' Eric Midwinter,[36] the Director of the Liverpool E.P.A., is a staunch advocate of this type of community school. While he stresses the value of such ideas as publications, education shops, coffee mornings in schools for parents, the central feature of his kind of community school is the community oriented curriculum. Yet as the Smiths

comment 'the problem remains of ensuring that socially relevant material is used to weaken rather than confirm social divisions'.

4 A school where there is some degree of community control. While such schools are by no means uncommon in the USA, they are an unusual feature in this country. A number of Free Schools have developed along the lines of this model, perhaps the best known being the White Lion Free School in Islington. It is interesting to note that the community boundary drawn round this school is very local indeed. While attempts have been made to introduce community participation on the governing bodies of schools, most notably by the introduction of parent governors, this could not be described as an unqualified success. The recommendations of the Taylor committee clearly state:

> we believe . . . that the school [should be] run with as full an awareness as possible of the wishes and feelings of parents and the local community and, conversely, to ensure that these groups are, in their turn, better informed of the needs of the school and the policies and constraints within which the local education committee operates and the head and other teachers work.[37]

5 A school which seeks to involve itself directly in promoting social change within the local community. As the Smiths point out,

> a basic problem in the development of the school as an agent of social change is the gulf between the way an ordinary school functions and that required for community work. Even in its most progressive form, schooling remains a highly structured activity . . . Community work is at the other end of the spectrum; there is no fixed group of clients, place or time of operation and the type of work may change dramatically as new groups or problems crop up.

They go on to point out the need to pay attention to 'conflicts which emerge as schools attempt to balance their traditional concern for individual children against their new role in community development'.[38] Using their experience in the Dennaby EPA project as illustration, the Smiths describe the work of the Red House as a multi-purpose education centre—which was not in fact developed as a community school—as one possible strategy for change. Their account of how the idea of the Red House was evolved and eventually set up shows community involvement at all levels of possible participation and the essential and gradual localised nature of such a project. Each development led to others: for instance the pre-school play groups to parent groups and other groups; and so eventually to using the various groups to help one another.

Finally the Smiths distinguish four themes which can be described as underlying the work in such a model of a community school: First, there is a clear shift from the educational starting point to social and community work, though from an education perspective . . . . a second theme is linkage—reducing the distance between different age levels and levels of education as well as between education and related social and welfare services . . . a third and related theme is the type of role that this method of working demanded from the team at the centre—one with no clear boundaries but with overlapping functions of teacher, social worker, counsellor, as the situation demanded. There was also the creation of 'intermediate roles', when students, secondary pupils, parents and others adopted teaching positions . . . . The final point and most important is the changing conception of the relationship between school and community. Instead of trying to improve the education process in school by encouraging parental involvement, the direction was reversed; the aim should rather be to strengthen the education resources of home and community.

5 Day special schools and social work

The Isle of Wight Study (Rutter *et al.*)[39] showed that approximately one child in six had a significant degree of handicap (whether intellectual or reading retardation, psychiatric disorder, physical handicap or a combination of these). Anderson,[40] referring to the debate on special education schools or special education for the handicapped child, writes that for 'many people special education still means special schools' and indeed it is this narrow definition that is taken in this section. Nevertheless, the Warnock Committee is currently reviewing the education of physically and mentally handicapped children, taking into account the medical, social and educational aspects of their needs, together with arrangements to prepare them for employment. Anderson considers that a useful approach to special education 'is to think in terms of a continuum of provision ranging from placement of a child in an ordinary class with no modifications, to placement in a highly specialised residential institution'. She outlines several points along this continuum:

1 Ordinary class full time with no extra help.
2 Ordinary class full time with extra help provided.
3 Ordinary class (child's base) part time with child withdrawn part time to 'resource room' or special facility.
4 Special class (base) part time, ordinary class for selected activities only.
5 Special class full time other than for 'social activities' (meals, play time, etc.).
6 Day school (base) formally linked to an ordinary school.
7 Day special school without such links.
8 Boarding special school.
9 Residential hospital school.

Anderson points out that only a minority of children are receiving the special education they require and it will be interesting to learn of the recommendation of the Warnock Committee. They will need to tread a careful path between the separatists, who consider that small units and highly specialised staff and resources are the paramount needs of most seriously handicapped children, and the integrationists, who argue that it is advantageous that all children should, as far as possible, be educated in conditions which resemble those of the society in which they should be encouraged to live and work.

Relationships between special schools and social workers have always been closer than those between 'ordinary' schools and social workers. It has long been recognised that children attending special schools also have special social needs and that both they and their families need additional attention and care in order to prevent social breakdown. It is perhaps likely that the close links between special schools and the medical profession have encouraged a broader frame of reference than a purely educational one. The medical model, while clearly recognising the 'illness' as the basis for remedial social and educational activities, does allow for a team approach (albeit under the general medical direction of the doctor). Both paediatric medicine and child psychiatry have traditionally involved the parents of the child patients and this naturally led to the inclusion of medical and psychiatric social workers as part of the team attached to special schools. There are special schools available for blind and partially sighted children, for deaf children, for the physically handicapped, for delicate children (often asthmatic), for subnormal and severely subnormal and for maladjusted children.

(a) Schools for the physically handicapped

The special schools for the physically handicapped include as pupils children who are spastic or suffering from physical impairment, children who are blind and need to be taught Braille, children who are delicate and need special dietary and open-air exercises, and children who are deaf or hard of hearing and who need to be taught to lip read and/or speak, and/or to handle a deaf aid. Usually such schools have strong links with hospitals whose medical and specialist staff may also have appointments connected with the school so that they can move freely and easily between the health and education systems, thus providing the children and their families with a comprehensive service. Even where the personnel may be different, there are customarily close and open communications which allow knowledge to be passed between the systems. Medical social workers have for many years been able to help the families (particularly the mother) not to be too over-protective and restrictive, a natural tendency with a physically disabled child, and one which might prevent the child from reaching its full potential educationally as well as socially. Some of these schools, particularly in urban areas, have their own social worker, who works as part of the team with the doctor, nurse and the school staff. This is particularly important as there are fewer such children and they often have to travel quite long distances to school, usually by special coaches. This makes it difficult for parents to visit, especially if there are younger children. Parents of handicapped children, particularly mothers, often feel guilty as well as grieved that they have given birth to a damaged child and this may lead to rejection or other disturbed forms of mother/child relationships. It is therefore important for links to be maintained with the home, not only to bring knowledge and information back to the school and to the home (for instance, regarding exercises or diet), but also to monitor and support the mother/child and family relationships. Clearly, it is important for the teachers and social workers alike to understand and appreciate the special treatments that are necessary for particular kinds of handicap: for instance the teaching of Braille and the methods by which a deaf child is taught to speak. For these specialist reasons and because social workers, like teachers and doctors, become interested in particular kinds of handicap and the effect on their families, and knowledgeable and skilled at the social work involved, it is important to allow attachments to particular schools in order that the best service can be given to their children and the children's families. Unfortunately, since the reorganisation of social work services, followed in 1974 by the National Health Service reorganisation, there are signs that these specialisms are being neglected, and this is a pity as these children and their families are more at risk than many others.

In rural areas and in some cases of physical handicap (for instance, deafness from birth), children with physical handicaps are educated in boarding schools, either as weekly or termly boarders. Children in boarding schools are at special risk of becoming estranged from their families, simply because of the geographical distance involved, without taking into account any social reasons which may have led to their being at boarding school. It is very important that social workers should maintain the links between school, child and family and that they should encourage parents to visit, even bring them. It is also important constantly to remind the teachers that the children have families. Boarding schools (particularly state schools) are in real danger of becoming closed institutions. The special situation of social workers and residential schools will be dealt with in a later section.

Looked at in terms of the continuum of social breakdown, the physically handicapped *child* seems appropriately considered in the category of prevention of social breakdown. The education of physically handicapped children is geared to protection and support while maximising their potential towards eventually leading as ordinary an everyday life as possible. Even for children who are seriously handicapped (the blind or the deaf), there is emphasis on the development of compensatory skills to enable them to cope. It is really only the severely physically handicapped who could be regarded as at the stage of primary or even secondary social breakdown. Whereas the blind or post-poliomyelitis child might be considered at risk, the spastic is increasingly stigmatised as he or she gets older and would almost certainly be regarded as experiencing primary or even secondary social breakdown, the latter probably on leaving school. Generally speaking, children who will always need some form of supportive care could be regarded as experiencing primary or secondary social breakdown as, even if they are cared for at home, it is likely there will ultimately come a time when the parents cannot manage to look after them.

(b) Educationally subnormal and severely subnormal schools

Educationally Subnormal (ESN) Schools are special schools for children with intelligence quotients of 50-70 per cent. These schools are smaller and the teachers have special skills and aptitudes even if they are not also trained to teach slow-learning and backward children. Children are referred or recommended to the ESN schools by the school medico-psychological service and the parents do have opportunities to appeal against such a recommendation. Classes are smaller and education is concentrated on essential basic requirements. Unfortunately, ESN schools have attracted considerable opprobrium through the stigma attached to being 'dull' in a fast-moving industrialised society. There is particular dissatisfaction in the West Indian community because a disproportionate number of West Indian children have been categorised as ESN. This may be partly due to the culture shock when such children who have spent early years in the West Indies with grandparents come to the UK to live with parents who are virtually strangers. It may be partly due to the fact that many such children speak *patois* at home and partly because there are indications that many West Indian children seem culturally deprived in this culture. It is also difficult to test (and teach!) such children, our psychological tests being devised for European children. There are many reasons but it could be said that for typical West Indian parents, who are often very education-conscious, it is an even deeper affront to find that their child is ESN than it is for the typical English parent. Specially skilled and sympathetic social work is necessary in order to enable the parents to express their anger and despair while enabling them to help their children themselves.

Many educationalists and others are of the view that specialist social workers should be attached to ESN schools, but there is always the danger that having a special social worker to visit the home is part of the stigma of being at a 'silly school'. On the other hand, a sensitive awareness and genuine interest in the backward is an important feature in such social work. There are arguments on both sides.

Unlike most physically handicapped children, there is considerable stigma attached to ESN education. This may be due to primitive fears of madness, for many people do not differentiate between mental retardation and mental illness. However, the knowledge that there can be no real compensation for backwardness may be another reason. Children attending ESN schools could be considered as experiencing primary social breakdown, and this is given recognition by the optional offer of after-care and special help with employment which they are given.

Schools for the severely subnormal were originally occupation centres and were only handed over to the education system in 1970. The majority of children who go to such schools are Mongol children and their parents have what has been called a lifetime of 'chronic sorrow'. The grief and guilt which accompany having a physically handicapped child are even greater in the case of the parents of the mentally handicapped, since it is unlikely that such a child will ever earn his or her own living. It is also an unremitting pain that such children, looking so abnormal, can never pass for normal, even in a crowd, as some physically handicapped children can. Having such a damaged child seems to spark off more primitive feelings of anger, shame and intense possessive protection, and most families could use social work help, particularly when it is first realised that the child is severely subnormal. Children attending severely subnormal schools are usually 'taught' in very much smaller classes and there is an emphasis on teaching them social and physical skills—sharing, dancing, singing, feeding themselves and so on. Some Severely Subnormal (SSN) schools require such children to be 'toilet trained', though most are tolerant of the not infrequent accidents. However, children who are immobile and doubly incontinent are not usually accepted except in SSN schools which have special care units. Children are admitted to these on a short-term basis, usually on social grounds. Such children and their families are certainly at risk of social breakdown. It is, for instance, likely that at some stage residential care might be necessary for someone who is severely abnormal, although, interestingly, now that the support services are improving and the stigma of mental handicap seems to be diminishing, more of them are being cared for by siblings. There is also a definite trend towards keeping the adult mentally handicapped within the community, through the priorities of 'sheltered' housing plus social work support. This is likely to prevent tertiary social breakdown, and as such facilities increase dilemmas are likely to arise in regard to severely subnormal children at the secondary social breakdown phase. For instance, the Mongol child of an elderly widowed mother in failing health might be able to remain in his or her familiar SSN school if 'hostel' facilities could be provided on a weekly or occasional boarder basis.

(c) Schools for the maladjusted

'Pupils who show evidence of emotional instability or psychological disturbance and require special educational treatment in order to effect their personal, social or educational readjustment' are defined as maladjusted, according to the Underwood Report.[41] However, this is an educational concept rather than the psychiatric diagnosis which usually precedes such a recommendation. Wolff[42] points out that maladjusted children demonstrate a widely differing range of behaviour patterns. She quotes the Underwood Committee on Maladjusted Children, who described such children as

> insecure and unhappy in that they fail in their personal
> relationships . . . at the same time they are not really capable
> of improvement by ordinary discipline . . . . Maladjustment
> does not always show itself in aggressive or troublesome
> conduct; indeed quiet, passive behaviour may overlay deep
> emotional disturbance.

While many children may be diagnosed as suffering from neurotic disturbance and may even be attending child guidance clinics, only a relatively small number are deemed maladjusted—that is, the psychiatrist diagnosing and/or treating them is of the opinion that they need special education. Often the social conditions of the disturbed child, the home environment and family relationships, are the deciding factor in recommending placement in a day maladjusted school. Children with behaviour difficulties whose parents cannot provide them with sufficient care, attention and control; children who are so overly dependent on their parents (usually mothers) that they are unable to function autonomously; children who are phobic at school; children who are so withdrawn that they are unable to relate to teachers and other children; and children with one or both parents suffering from serious mental illness, are all typical examples of children who are considered to need the additional supports of special education.

Child psychiatrists are the only professionals who have the power to recommend that a child be treated as maladjusted. There is a long tradition of the psychiatric team, consisting of psychiatrist, psychologist and psychiatric social worker, contributing to a diagnosis together, and a recommendation of maladjusted placement is rarely made until other forms of treatment have been tried. The psychiatric team usually works from within child guidance clinics, where there are often other experts whose roles are specifically defined for the treatment and 'education' of children who are psychiatrically at risk. Child psychotherapists, for instance, give children intense and individualised treatment, usually on psychoanalytic lines, while remedial or tutorial class teachers may run part-time classes specifically geared to children who may eventually need to attend maladjusted schools. Such remedial teachers are specially trained and their small classes may be within the clinic or, alternatively, may be held at schools outside the clinic. Wherever these classes are situated, they have special links with the psychiatric teams and particularly with the educational psychologist, who usually has a co-ordinating and supportive function in relation to them. When a child is deemed maladjusted and a special school is suggested, the parents do have a right of appeal against such a decision.

In any case there are often such waiting lists for places in schools for the maladjusted that the delay can be used for the parents and child to talk through their feelings about such a placement. Wolff makes the important point that while diagnosing a child as emotionally disturbed may be useful as an aid to furthering understanding of that child's difficulties by parents and teachers, it may also be harmful to treat children under stress as different. The anxieties of adults concerned with such children may be communicated to the child and may undermine his confidence still further. If parents and/or child do not accept the placement in a maladjusted school as positive and hopeful, then the chances of the school being able to achieve its educational tasks are likely to be seriously diminished. It is difficult to 'engage' the learning capacities of a child who is emotionally somewhere else (at home) or is resistant to the values of the school. It is such children who may eventually require placement in boarding schools for the maladjusted.

Teachers and others are often frustrated when a child has been referred to a child guidance clinic, because either they hear 'nothing back' or are only 'told in different words what they said in the original referral'. While it is frustrating for teachers and social workers who refer children to a child guidance clinic not to be told all the details of what goes on there, there are limits and boundaries which must be observed. First, children and their families will not confide their deepest secrets if they feel that the therapeutic team cannot be trusted to respect those secrets. Nor may they be able to function properly if such primitive aspects of themselves flow over into the other more potentially competent ordinary areas of their lives (i.e., school). They need to have a safe but boundaried place to express or act out those fearful parts of themselves that impede their whole developmental processes. Only if the child and family trust the clinic can they be helped. If they do not and/or feel that their private lives are being freely discussed, they will often break off treatment. What is relevant to the school is that, perhaps because of such fantasies, a child cannot get on with certain teachers meanwhile. It is part of the clinic educational psychologist's role to link back to the schools and to give them appropriate advice and support to carry out their task in relation to the child. It is perhaps due to the mystique of counselling that most people in the helping professions are filled with insatiable curiosity about 'what makes people tick' and it is only human to want to know about the 'magic' that might be done at the child guidance clinic! Unfortunately, child guidance clinics have no magical powers. What they have is knowledge, specialist skills, time and sanctuary; that is, an opportunity temporarily to escape from the outside world with safety. Sometimes the child guidance clinics do not know any more than they have been told for quite some time; and sometimes they cannot help very much. At other times, when the children and their families feel safe enough to let down the barriers which they have erected in attempts to contain their psychological difficulties, they can help a great deal.

While referrals to maladjusted schools can only be made by a child psychiatrist, referrals to child guidance clinics may be made by the head and with the agreement of the child's parents and any social agencies involved. This entails discussion and agreement amongst the staff and people concerned about the appropriateness of such a referral. As has been seen in the report of the Maria

Colwell inquiry,[43] such agreement is not always easily reached. The behaviour of Maria Colwell towards the end of her life was consonant with a picture of a child suffering from depression. The Committee gained the impression of a 'withdrawn, quiet, sad little girl, who might metaphorically be said to have turned her face to the wall'. Some members of the Committee thought that she should have been referred to a child psychiatrist. Miss Stevenson disagreed, pointing out that the social worker was already in touch with the family and that her perceptive understanding was adequate in such a situation. Is it likely that the Kepples would have agreed to such a referral, or persevered with attending a child guidance clinic? Child guidance clinics cannot work with absent patients any more than schools can teach absent pupils, and there is no law which compels clinic attendance.

The ability of a family to attend a clinic regularly for treatment may be one factor in recommending maladjusted school placement. Once there the child is seen at regular intervals by the referring child psychiatrist to ensure that such a recommendation is still necessary. The social worker at the clinic may continue to see the family or a social worker attached to the school may take over. Such decisions are usually made on the basis of the needs of the family and the appropriate use of resources (i.e., the social worker's time).

Maladjusted schools usually have their own social worker, who is part of the school team and is frequently to be seen around the school. Each maladjusted school has a part-time psychiatrist, often acting in an advisory and supportive capacity to the staff. Many schools also have a child psychotherapist who will give individual children treatment during school hours. The social worker will work with the families, and the whole team, including the teachers, will pool such appropriate knowledge and information as is necessary to help the child reach his or her potential.

This is obviously a much closer relationship than is usually possible between schools and social workers. It has partly grown up because of the evolution of the child guidance team approach and partly because such schools are small and members of the teams are able to get to know and trust each other. It is difficult to expose one's professional uncertainties and working style to any other professional until one is familiar enough with them as a colleague. Maladjusted schools are potentially able to provide such an environment. Treating disturbed children and their families, who are not infrequently also disturbed, is a very demanding and arduous task, and at times the team in the maladjusted schools are working at the limits of their emotional endurance and understanding, not to mention the limits of their patience! The bonds of trust which should develop provide both supports and constraints for such personnel and thus assist them to carry out their task. Nevertheless, this can mean confronting and discussing such unacceptable and painful feelings as envy, rivalry and hostility, which are often aroused by working with such families.

Children attending child guidance clinics and those who have been deemed maladjusted under the 1944 Education Act could be described as experiencing secondary social breakdown. Many of them come from families which are themselves disturbed and unable to function socially with sufficient competence within our industrial, competitive and pressurised society. Children of parents themselves suffering from mental illness or neurotic difficulties are often maladjusted. Children whose lives had had more than a fair share of deprivation and trauma, fears or poverty, losses, ill-health, or those from one-parent families, are often unable to draw the emotional sustenance from their family background which assists other children who experience the emotional stresses and strains of those psychosocial transitions which Erikson called identity crises.

In their evidence to the Warnock Committee, the Association of Workers for Maladjusted Children (1974) stressed that 'maladjustment is a difficult handicap to understand or have sympathy for . . . the common outward signs are aggressive and socially unacceptable behaviour'. The Association also recommended that further research should be undertaken on educating such children in ordinary schools. An indication of the strong difference of opinion between the separatists and the integrationists can be judged from the response to Mrs Warnock's recent comments at the 1975 Head Masters' Conference, when she put forward the idea of 'an enormous campus, with handicapped children in their own school alongside normal schools'. Three associations concerned with the blind and handicapped people deplored such a statement and added that 'while there is room for difference of opinion as to the pace and extent of change . . . [there is] widespread agreement today that there should now be a major shift towards the education of handicapped children in ordinary schools'.[44]

6 Intermediate treatment

Intermediate treatment is perhaps a better example of good intentions gone awry than any other social policy in relation to children. The concept of intermediate treatment (that is, preventive treatment designed to enable a child to remain at home rather than being treated away from home) was first outlined in the 1968 White Paper *Children in Trouble*;[45] it has nowhere been legally defined and is only ambiguously contained in the 1969 Children and Young Persons Act. Clearly, as outlined, the intermediate treatment issue stands at the boundary between secondary and tertiary social breakdown. The idea behind the concept is to provide the necessary resources to prevent children in trouble of one kind or another from ending up with a longish period of residential care. In order to understand and provide some explanation for such ambiguity, it is necessary to summarise the developments and legislation in relation to children which have occurred since the 1933 Children and Young Persons Act.

The philosophy underlying legislation in relation to children has been shifting towards making it the responsibility of the courts to protect rather than punish. This attitude was first reflected in the 1933 Children and Young Persons Act, which stated that the court 'shall have regard to the welfare of the child or young person', and was given more weight by the Ingleby Committee's proposals which were watered down by the Conservatives in the 1963 Act. This Act also introduced the possibility of financial help as a preventative measure where children were at risk of needing to be taken into care because of the poverty of their families (Section 1). Berlins and Wansell[46] write that the 1963 Act 'only marginally amended the old definition of the 1933 Act by expanding the definition of those children who need it from "care and protection" to "care, protection and control"', which did little to do away with the criminal orientation of helping children in trouble, though the age of criminal responsibility was raised to ten. The Longford Committee and the subsequent Labour Government's White Paper *The Child, The Family and the Young Offender*[47] proposed radical reforms, in particular the raising of the age of criminal responsibility and the setting up of family courts. In 1964 the Kilbrandon Committee had made similar recommendations for Scotland (including the setting-up of juvenile panels) which were later implemented. The White Paper was much criticised, particularly by the magistracy (many of them teachers or head teachers) who, while resenting the curtailment of their powers, also pointed to the shortage of resources. In 1968 a new White Paper, *Children in Trouble*, was produced which, while rejecting earlier suggestions for abolishing juvenile courts, made various compromise alternatives. One of these was the concept of intermediate treatment; another was the establishment of twelve Regional Joint Planning Committees which were to oversee and to plan the provision of places for children and young people in trouble. This paper was also attacked, as was the following Bill, which was bitterly debated and amended in the debates in Parliament. As has already been stated, the final Bill left the age of criminal *responsibility* at ten, although allowing for the possibility of raising the age for criminal *proceedings* gradually. The bill also instituted the new care proceedings, the grounds for which were outlined in an earlier chapter (see pp. 43-4). A new condition was to enable children committed of an 'offence' to be dealt with under 'care' rather than 'criminal' proceedings. In effect the implication of this 'offence' condition of Section 1 means that not only does the offence have to be proved against the child beyond a reasonable doubt, but it must *also* be shown that he is in need of care and control which he is unlikely to get from his parents or family.

The 1969 Act also introduced the idea of new kinds of supervision orders (both for care and criminal proceedings) which would be undertaken by local authority social workers (rather than probation officers).

As the Act was only partially implemented, care proceedings for a child who has committed an offence are relatively unused, as criminal proceedings are much less complex and far more familiar. Apart from being unable to send children directly to an approved school and only being able to recommend residential care, magistrates have the same powers as they had before. However, the Act gave to local authority social work departments power and discretion to place a child under a care order in any residential establishment or to allow the child to remain or return home without further recourse to the court. It is this area where, in effect, power has shifted from magistrates to social workers which is the controversial issue.

Unfortunately the 1969 Children and Young Persons Act was implemented at the same time as the Seebohm reorganisation, and this seriously strained the abilities of the hard-pressed and newly reorganised social work services to cope with their tasks. A comparable change in the education service would be 'going comprehensive' and changing the examination system at the same time!

A particular problem, as has been shown in the section on truancy, is the present division of responsibility of children who truant from school and/or commit a criminal offence. Parents who fail to see that their child attends school are liable to penalty under the 1944 Education Act. Under the 1969 Act, proceedings may be taken by the Education Department under care proceedings Section (e), which states that evidence must be produced that the child is of compulsory school age and is not receiving efficient full-time education suitable to his age, ability and attitude. But *before* the court can make a supervision or care order it is also necessary for evidence to be produced in court that the child is not receiving the necessary care, protection and control—and this requires the presentation of evidence by the social service departments.[48] The government, in its recent review document on the Act, concedes that the situation is confused.[49] But there are often marked differences of philosophy and attitude between the two government departments, and unfortunately such ideological battles are too frequently conducted in and around the court room and are often over particular cases of children most in need of help. Nor are educationalists and magistrates the only ones to oppose the liberal philosophy underlying the 1969 Act. The Society of Conservative Lawyers published a booklet, *Apprentices in Crime*, (1974) pointing out that official statistics show that 25 per cent of all serious crimes are committed by young people under seventeen years of age: 'The 1969 Act assumes that an offender is always in need of care and protection from an environment deprived of physical and emotional support. This is not always so. The depraved child is not necessarily deprived.' They went on to make recommendations which would, if implemented, strengthen the punitive elements in dealings with children brought before the courts.

As Goodacre[50] points out 'when the public education system was established, it was paternalistic in nature'. She goes on to say that 'If it had been successful, there would be less need for it to assume this character', and adds that there is evidence that widening state paternalism on matters of decision on many intimate personal and family activities may be less welcome than is generally supposed. It is as well to remember that the educational philosophy which underlies the legislation in this country is based on the 1944 Education Act which embodies the proposals of a pre-war Committee, a generation and light years away from today's conditions and attitudes.

Under the Children and Young Persons Act 1969, the Regional Planning Committees which were set up have duties and responsibilities to formulate plans for the provision of accommodation for children in the care of local authorities. They also have specific duties to co-ordinate plans for intermediate treatment projects and to encourage the development of new projects.

The development group of the DHSS describes 'intermediate treatment' as follows

(i)   It is a form of treatment for children and young persons *who have been found* to be in need of care and control by a juvenile court [my italics].

(ii)   It is a form of treatment which can only be provided by a requirement which is added to a supervision order.

(iii) It is 'intermediate' in its nature between other measures which either place the child in the care of the local authority or leave him in the care of his parents.

(iv) It is a form of treatment which, within the conditions of the order made by a juvenile court, may be exercised at the discretion of a supervisor. He will have a range of facilities at his disposal, both residential and non-residential . . . .

(v)   As a form of treatment, it is intended to enable a child or young person to develop new and beneficial attitudes and activities which may be continued after his supervision order has ended and, by so doing, help him to develop generally and avoid further trouble.

(vi) The range of facilities available for intermediate treatment in the main will be those which are already being or may be used by other children and young persons who are not subject to supervision orders.[51]

In its notes for the guidance of those responsible for the regional planning of new forms of treatment for children in trouble, the DHSS states:

The Court which makes the supervision order in respect of a child has the power to impose a number of different types of condition. A requirement to submit to treatment for a mental condition. A requirement to reside with a named individual, or an intermediate treatment requirement. An intermediate treatment requirement may entail two different forms of treatment:

(a)   residence at a specified place for a fixed period of not more than three months, beginning within the first year of supervision; or

(b)   temporary residence, attendance or participation for a period or periods totalling not more than one month in each year of supervision.[52]

The court may make it a requirement that either type (a) or type (b) or a combination of both should be followed. The children are not necessarily offenders; they may be subject to supervision as a result of being neglected or in moral danger, for instance. The supervisor of the child should have discretion as to the choice of the intermediate treatment programme and 'his discretion is absolute'. 'The supervisor will be either a local authority or a probation officer' . . . and the finance and administration of such a scheme is to be the local authority named in the supervision order.

Some local social service departments appointed Intermediate Treatment Organisers, whose task varied, but many of them were concerned with stimulating interest in organising intermediate treatment schemes. Some examples will be later described briefly, but first some of the confusion and difficulties in relation to intermediate treatment must be discussed. In 1973 the British

Association of Social Workers' working party (under the chairman-ship of David Haxby) pointed out[53] that while intermediate treatment is ambiguously referred to in Section 12 of the 1969 Act 'it has been gradually realised that it must encompass activities which are not necessarily the subject of "directions given by supervisors" nor even related to children who are subject to statutory supervision'. The working party was of the opinion that 'although there had been quite a lot of talk about "treatment", there had been insufficient discussion or thought about the organisation and administration of intermediate treatment'. In particular they enjoined planning committees to discuss intermediate treatment with education departments who might have a special contribution to make in providing the ninety-day (three-month) facilities. They also made other recommendations, including a suggestion that

areas should develop machinery to enable regular contact between the magistrates on the juvenile panel and the social services department. The policy being followed in (a) giving power to supervisors and (b) the use of supervisor's discretion needs to be clearly understood by all the magistrates and social workers involved.

It seems as if the confusion surrounding intermediate treatment may be another example of the decimated 1969 Act not being able to fulfil, perhaps, either the intentions of the White Paper, *Children in Trouble*, or those of the children's Bill passed by the Labour Government in 1969, but implemented in 1970 by a Conservative Government. Since that time, despite the financial constraints, there has been a steady development of intermediate treatment schemes.

The commentators range from those who argue that the Act's 'lack of specificity' and precision and the unimaginativeness of the Regional Planning Committees has led to a 'mere listing of youth clubs and centres to which young people can be directed', to those who consider that the 'structure is both broad and flexible enough as it permits the use of any approved facility and allows the supervisor a great deal of discretion'. Further, severe critics complain that there is no incentive for either education departments or social service departments to finance schemes which may be used by children who are the financial responsibility of the social services department or, in the case of social services departments, to set up special facilities when some exist already. Voluntary associations, on the other hand, see opportunities for obtaining financial aid for the development of innovative projects, though many of them are less keen on receiving young people under compulsion. Others urge that the DHSS guide seems to suggest that Section 1 of the 1963 Act might be used to finance projects for a child who wishes to continue in an intermediate activity after the period of statutory supervision. Such activities would then need to be described as 'diminishing the need to bring children before a juvenile court'. The use of the 1969 Act in this way will need to be urged positively upon local authorities who to date have often been parsimonious in allocating funds for intermediate treatment.

The government review document welcomes the suggestion that local authorities can spend money on 'intermediate treatment for children in care and children at risk whether or not they are subject to a court order . . . there appears to be no legal barrier to doing [so]'.

Aplin and Bamber[54] point out that there are two basic approaches to the use of intermediate treatment and that they may or may not co-exist. First,

> to provide a variety of flexible measures to deal effectively and appropriately with the manifold acts of delinquency . . . and secondly, to provide a system of effective care for children and young persons . . . . If they choose to do so, social services departments can interpret proceedings widely and set up a fully fledged preventive provision at any stage of the child's life. Where it is seen to be appropriate, the referral of the child for preventive care can be made on an informal basis.

The problem of the compulsive aspect of intermediate treatment is also a dilemma. Prins,[55] writing of the compulsive benevolence of intermediate treatment, points out that not all young people will see the treatment as 'constructive and remedial, not punitive', and Thorpe also points out that supervision orders 'unlike probation orders do not even require the formal consent of the client', nor is the supervisor legally 'obliged to consult with the child on this issue'.

Aplin and Bamber link intermediate treatment with prevention and point out Kellmer Pringle's description of primary, secondary and tertiary prevention. They go on to stress that 'Kellmer Pringle envisages prevention as an enterprise that embraces education and social services'. They quote her definition of secondary prevention as 'to help the families through temporary strain and crisis; to improve, and where necessary, supplement the quality of care and education for children considered "vulnerable" or "at risk" and to prevent the disintegration of the family unit'. The difficulty about such use of intermediate treatment is that the *obligation* both to fund and to direct the intermediate treatment projects is restricted to children who are *already* subject to intermediate treatment and supervision orders under the Children and Young Persons Act 1969.

Aplin and Bamber and Thorpe discuss the question of treatment and its definition particularly in relation to education. Aplin and Bamber are critical of the implications contained in the DHSS pamphlet for their assumption that 'merely by occupying a child, some general change in behaviour and attitudes will result'. They point out the experience of the EPA projects and quote the mass exodus of 400 fourth-year juniors, 15 teachers and various students and parents who spent one day a week throughout the term at the environmental studies centre in Kent about 15 miles from Deptford. This gave disappointing results in terms of the children's academic progress and attitudes to school:

> Social services would appear to be in danger of adopting assumptions that education no longer automatically accepts . . . . Treatment involves a strategy for changing the behaviour and attitudes of an individual . . . . the first essential step is establishing a relationship . . . but definite techniques are involved.

Thorpe writes that the treatment model is based on the 'assumption that something is wrong with somebody who requires treatment to put it right'.

Aplin and Bamber stress that the groupwork counselling service in Bristol is an educational provision but point out that 'there is no precedent for education authorities to set up community based as opposed to school based treatment facilities'. The Bristol project provides a continuing and supportive relationship for a minimum of two years, which takes in the move from junior to secondary school:

> The groupwork counsellor is child centred and in many ways acts as a parent surrogate. The catchment area is community wide and takes in all children in a given age range with social and emotional problems . . . and selection is by a screening procedure . . . the service establishes treatment goals for each individual child . . . the service provides individualised treatment to modify an individual's attitudes and behaviour . . . individual counselling plays an important part . . . the individual is helped to grow . . . improved self regard, the ability to have and to put one's point of view and to consider the other person's point of view . . . [There is] provision for after care.

This flexible approach did not appear to be provided only for children subject to supervision orders.

The DHSS development group consider that intermediate treatment will

> need to be provided for children whose difficulties are not so great that full time supervision and treatment away from home

under a care order are required . . . it is not likely to be adequate for the child whose difficulties of personality are severe or deeply rooted, whose home and family problems are intractable or who has specific mental handicap . . . . Children who are socially deprived can develop a suspicious and mistrustful attitude to those in authority and this may prevent the growth of helpful relationships with adults outside the home.

The Day Centre conceived by the Family Service Unit in Islington is financed under urban aid and through the ILEA. The objectives were: to bridge the gap between education and social work and to assist in cementing close co-operation between the EWS and the social services department in dealing with 'children in trouble'; to attempt to combine education and social work and to provide one agency for a particular category of children and their families; to see whether short-term intervention with the ultimate aim of returning the children to the two particular secondary schools on whose registers they were, though many of them were truanting. This project was featured in a BBC film, *Developments in Social Work*, and noteworthy were the non-authoritarian relationships between staff and children and the children's active participation in running the centre. The staff/children ratio is a generous one—3:10. The children appear to make progress with learning, but it is too soon to evaluate the scheme or to gauge whether they will ever be able to return to school. Indeed, little or no effort is being made to encourage them to do so. Grunsell, who started the Centre in 1971, is quoted by the *Times Educational Supplement* as saying:

In theory . . . these places [are] to get the kids back to school . . . . but the head masters don't really want them back. Fundamentally it's part of a massive hypocrisy. They realize they have created an education system which is quite unsuitable for a significant proportion of the children. Our kids don't want to go back . . . and the gap between the small, happy, loving situation and what the schools can offer is enormous.[56]

Finally, the Rayner Foundation has established an intermediate treatment centre which caters for three separate groups of children, though children may 'progress' from one to the other. There is a day centre for children with educational difficulties (not all truants), where a small group of children are given individualised attention, particularly in reading and number skills, by a teacher. There is an evening centre with a specialist teacher who also teaches the twelve boys who remain for three months while attending their original schools. Only boys from the locality are admitted to the centre and considerable efforts are made to liaise with both local schools and social work agencies. Boys in the hostel are encouraged to visit home for the weekend and maintain and improve relationships with their families. The scheme is financed by the Rayner Foundation, by the ILEA, and by grants from the local social service departments. It is too early yet to evaluate the scheme.

A real difficulty seems to surround the 'compulsory' aspect of intermediate treatment schemes. It is not in the tradition of social work for clients to be 'directed' to attend or even to do anything. Local authority social workers particularly, while they have considerable experience in helping children who have come to terms with having to live apart from their families, are unused to having such directive aspects incorporated into their role. Probation officers, on the other hand, have long come to terms with managing the authoritative aspects of their relationships with their clients (who are given the 'choice' of accepting probation or not) and with tailoring these authoritative aspects of their role to the needs of their clients, many of whom have got into trouble because of just such problems with authority. So far there is little evidence that social workers have been able to use the compulsion aspects of intermediate treatment with appropriate selectivity. This may well be because of the confusion surrounding intermediate treatment and the lack of clarity for magistrates and others providing the facilities, including the supervisory social worker. Another difficulty is the question of actual supervision of the child or young person taking part in a scheme. The social work supervisor is not always actually directly involved in the schemes, and there is some concern that the physical safety of the client and others should be protected adequately. For instance, at the Rayner Foundation, trampolining has become a central feature of the evening group. Yet for some while the trampoline had to remain unused until a trained instructor could be found.

Given some financial impetus and clear directions to both local education and social service departments, it is possible that intermediate schemes could provide a comprehensive range of projects which could prove of real use in providing short-term and ameliorative educational social work help for children at the primary and secondary phase of social breakdown. It is unfortunate that the present emphasis is on financial aid for children subject to supervision orders, as by then it is often too late to help such children by any methods short of full day or residential care.

In a more recent comment Ward describes two distinct approaches to intermediate treatment, one focusing on the child-in-his-living-situation and the other focused exclusively on the child. The 'central concern for the child-in-his-living-situation—his actual performance in those everyday situations in which he is experiencing difficulty—home, school, neighbourhood [is one in which] the worker will become involved in the interplay of the child's coping efforts and the demands of the social environment'. On the other hand, the approach which is exclusively concerned with the individual child focuses 'primarily on the child himself, albeit usually in the context of a group and bearing in mind the pressures of his social environment', Ward favours a shift of emphasis to include more elements of the child-in-his-living-situation approach.[57]

7 Truancy and social work

Truancy and persistent absence from school is one of the most controversial issues on the boundaries not only between education and social work but also between education, social work and the health services (particularly those provided by psychiatrists, paediatricians and general practitioners) and indeed almost everyone concerned with children. Truancy is also one of the most emotive crises; it is not always easy to see why, although truants are seen to be rejecting a social institution valued by society—the school. Certainly the symptom of truancy is a very public one even if it is the only visible evidence of other problems and difficulties. Children out of school are often clearly noticeable, especially if they get into trouble. On the other hand, despite all the efforts, researches and endeavours of the people concerned with truants, there has been singular lack of success in treating and controlling truants and getting them back to their schools. Usually the arousal of such intense feelings is indicative of the existence of some primitive underlying feelings which are not being permitted expression. It may also be that, as with society's attitudes towards adult law breakers, which are intensely ambivalent, so are our feelings similarly stirred up with truants, who are also young. Feelings such as envy of their youth and freedom, feelings of fear and wishes to punish them may co-exist along with secret admiration of their ability to 'get away with it'. It is important that we try to recognise such feelings in ourselves for they will certainly influence the actions we take (or fail to take) in dealing with truants.

As is usual with such boundary problems, truancy is a complex issue and it may be useful to consider, first, the facts about compulsory school attendance and the possible size of the problem; second, the attitudes of some of the people whose roles are directly concerned with the problem; and third, a comment on some of the knowledge available to us on the characteristics of truancy; before going on, finally, to look at the management of truancy and ways of dealing with it.

(a) Compulsory school attendance

First, the facts regarding compulsory school attendance. Free schooling was made possible by the 1870 Education Act. It was partially compulsory by 1880, but only completely compulsory for children of five to fourteen years of age in 1918. The 1944 Act[58] raised the school-leaving age to fifteen, though this was not implemented for some years, and in 1973 the school leaving age was raised to sixteen, despite the expression of considerable concern by some educationists. Indeed the concern continues and there is a small but growing lobby to abolish compulsory education altogether. Compulsory school attendance has implications for all those connected with children of school age:

(i) Parents are bound by law, 'to cause their child to receive efficient full time education . . . either regular attendance at school or otherwise'.

(ii) Schools are expected to provide education according to children's age, ability and aptitude. There has been some discussion as to whether schools on part-time because of teacher shortage are in fact breaking the law.

(iii) Education authorities are expected to enforce school attendance (even the children of travellers—gypsies—are expected to attend 200 days). This responsibility is usually delegated to the Education Welfare Service.

(iv) The police have some duties in connection with children out of school who commit offences. In some areas they have recently rounded up children out of school—a step which caused some controversy!

(v) Social service departments (and others) who have children under their supervision or in their care also have responsibilities to see that these children receive suitable education.

(vi) The medical profession who may have responsibilities in connection with the health (either physical or emotional or both) of schoolchildren are also required to make recommendations about appropriate schooling for these children.

(vii) Schoolchildren themselves are liable to be charged as being in need of care, protection and control if they do not attend school regularly.

(b) Size of the problem

Considering the suspected extent of truancy and the amount of public feeling it engenders, there are surprisingly few reliable figures relating to truancy. Tyerman[59] also alludes to the difficulty of obtaining exact figures and points out that, if those which are available were evenly spread over the whole school population and the school year, they would amount to each child spending half a day per week out of school. He further points out that absence from school varies with age groups, being greater and more consistent in the secondary schools, and also that the lower the stream the lower the attendance. Mitchell[60] in his presidential address to the National Society of Education Welfare Officers, estimated truancy as being as high as 10 per cent.

On 17 January 1974, a one-day survey was carried out by the Association of Education Committees on behalf of the DES. The survey found that only 2·2 per cent of all pupils in middle and secondary schools were absent without lawful reason, although altogether 9·9 per cent of all pupils had been absent on this day, the highest percentage of unjustified absences being amongst the fifteen-year-olds—the ROSLA children. These figures produced storms of criticism when announced in Parliament, MPs arguing— Dr Boyson for instance—that the actual figures were far in excess of the 87,000 claimed by the DES, more like 700,000. There were complaints that the figures were 'superficial and open to discreet rigging by the Heads to protect the image of their schools'.

Marten Shipman of the ILEA's research department agreed that the survey was unreliable to some degree 'because of the condoning of truancy by parents'. Terry Casey of the National Association of Schoolmasters 'questioned the numbers of children who truant after signing the register and pointed out that truancy could well be a safety valve for pupils in a really violent school'.

The *Times Educational Supplement* pointed out that it should be made easier for heads to report both the figures for truancy and violence in school with more candour.

(c) Attitudes towards truancy

Attitudes towards truancy are as individual and varied as the individual truant, and of course they are influenced by age, class and cultural values. Nevertheless, it is useful to consider the attitudes of the groups of people whose role performance involves them in widely differing perspectives towards truancy in particular and school attendance in general.

(i) *The pupil*

Young children starting school are very influenced by the attitudes of their family towards it and this will colour their expectations and fears, too. Starting school is one of the psychosocial crises and often coincides with the identity crisis described by Erikson in Chapter 1. It seems clear enough that starting school, changes of school—particularly from primary to secondary—and even transition from class to class, are stress periods when the patterns of school attendance are liable to breakdown.

The raising of the school-leaving age has meant that pupils who would previously have earned their living and taken on other aspects of the adult role are obliged to stay at school. Many of them are resentful and experience school as restrictive and as neither meeting their needs nor engaging their interests.

This question of schools meeting the needs of pupils is a real dilemma and one in which, since both schools and pupils are apt to blame the other party, it is difficult to see who is failing whom, the schools failing the pupils or the pupils failing to subscribe to the mores of society.

Jones,[61] a qualified teacher and youth worker, writes of the peer groups as 'the most powerful and immediate influence in a child's school life'. He points out that 'schools are often labouring against rejection of authority and acts of defiance against the school as the enemy', and that these are 'seen as a passport into the real world'. The case of Tina Wilson, who eventually committed suicide after a period of absence from school, showed that, while affected by a complexity of influences, she had certainly been affected by bullying at school. Polsky,[62] writing of community schools in the USA, clearly demonstrated the sub-cultural pecking order that flourishes, often unrecognised, in other institutions as well as prisons. Some pupils can be successful as surrogate mothers at home, or working in the street market, in a way they can never achieve at school. (The complex reinforcement of such needs by parents who may be more interested in their own needs is only part of the problem.)

The waiting time for places in special schools, perhaps inevitable, is also a time of uncertainty in which the tenuous commitment to school going can be attenuated. Class and cultural differences certainly lead to alienation from school values, one of which is regular attendance. If Dad doesn't go to work when he feels like a day off, why shouldn't his son go to football too? And much has been written recently about the difficulties experienced by the Moslem communities, whose traditional culture lays down that the education of adolescents entails segregation of the sexes.

Large schools with frequent change from one teacher to another as part of the timetable make it difficult for children, for whom the relationship with the teacher is crucial, to maintain the enthusiasm required for learning and eventually remaining in school. Shortage of staff and frequent changes of teacher also have disastrous consequences on the motivation of some children, again those most vulnerable to change.

(ii) *The parents*

Some of the attitudes of parents towards the *school* have already been discussed; obviously these are relevant to truancy, but there are also specific attitudes towards truancy. It may well be that parents' own attitude to compulsory school attendance linger on, after all it was only the grandparents of today's parents who were first 'protected' by compulsory education. Many parents have mixed feelings about the curtailment of their powers in relation to their children and the assumption of such powers by the state. Doubtless many parents resent the raising of the school-leaving age and would much prefer their children to be independent or earning. Others have serious doubts about the relevance and usefulness of today's schools and their effectiveness in preparing children for adult life. Some parents are also frankly anti-school for various reasons and lose no opportunity for 'getting at' the school. Others just let the school 'get on with it' or frankly do not know or are in fact able to care that their children are not in school. Other parents keep their children at home to help with household chores and still others collude with anxious children who are afraid to leave home and/or to go to school. Finally, some parents keep their children at home for 'moral' support for themselves or others. For example, Penny's mother was as frightened as Penny that Granny would die while they were both out. Mother was the sole wage earner, so Penny carried the anxiety, and incidentally the responsibility for them all, and stayed at home from school.

Most parents are uncertain at times whether to 'excuse' their child from school because they complain of feeling ill, and some write notes of excuse on occasion which are patently untrue. Many parents feel inadequate about putting pen to paper and so avoid it, and some homes are devoid of pens or paper. Notes of excuse forged by children are difficult to detect from the childlike notes which some parents write. And of course communications sent via the child from school to home and vice versa are always in jeopardy of failing to arrive.

(iii) *The teachers*

Teachers, and particularly head teachers, are publicly confronted by their failure in their task when schoolchildren truant. It is not possible to teach children who are not in school and their feelings about this failure must colour their attitudes towards truants. *Head teachers* are responsible for the children in their school, for the curriculum and for the organisation and management of their school. The truancy figures of the school are therefore a reflection on their competence and they inevitably react accordingly. Some heads blame others: parents for conniving with children, the Education Welfare Service for failing to get the children to school, the social service departments for colluding with children out of school. The school head is in a very public and invidious position as regards truancy and it is not surprising therefore that he/she is sometimes reactionary and punitive. Many of them have real concern lest the occasional truancy becomes an entrenched and chronic pattern. They are also worried about the possible contagion effect, particularly amongst secondary schoolchildren. A head told the author, 'I don't want deep casework when my girls are out of school—there isn't time. I want them back in school where they should be learning.' The lack of knowledge about the causes of truancy and the ineffectiveness of the treatment of truancy does nothing to prove or disprove whether occasional truancy does inevitably become chronic, nor whether there is a contagion effect.

Fitzherbert has some useful comments to make about teachers' views of truancy,

> Educators with a background in theories of learning and socialisation favour the acquisition of good social habits and basic skills. Bad school attendance is just another 'habit' which can develop if no pressure to prevent it is put on a child and its family. In the child's interests Education Welfare Officers may approve of the use of a certain amount of coercion to get him to school.[63]

Other teachers have varying attitudes though most of them feel helpless to prevent or control truancy. Some frankly feel relieved when a child who is disrupting the class, or is backward or unable to learn, or aggressive and cheeky to them, inciting others to be the same, stays out of school. The group dynamics between teachers and their classes may very well keep some children in school and encourage others to truant: we do not know.

Some teachers, particularly the younger and perhaps more radical seriously doubt whether the schools or the school curriculum engage the children's interest enough for them to be taught. They also wonder whether the hierarchical and organisational structure itself does not make the child feel so powerless and ineffective that he or she may just give up.

Kellmer Pringle[64] writes that 'schools have for far too long over-emphasized the place of cognitive abilities and under-estimated

139

the importance of motivation'. She stresses the importance of the teacher

> as a bridge builder, between the child's world and the community at large . . . and to preserve or rekindle the curiosity and joy in learning shown by the young child, which stand in such stark contrast to the frustrated boredom of not a few secondary school pupils.

Many teachers know all too well they are failing in this task, and though the responsibility is not by any means all theirs, truancy sparks off guilt about failure in all of us.

Jones also writes:

> I remember as a teacher in a very difficult class of youngsters thinking, 'I've got to survive; if anyone goes under it's not going to be me'. I remember a whole range of techniques I used to maintain my own authority as a teacher in the classroom, and the forms of defence I used to protect myself, and not to help the disturbed child in the face of hostile aggressive behaviour.[65]

(iv) (a) Social workers in social service departments

Most social workers are deeply concerned about underprivileged members of society and are not only engaged in trying to help them to function more effectively and gain access to rights and resources to which they are entitled, but are also committed to changing society so as to make these rights a reality and to secure a redistribution of resources. However, social workers are not immune from feelings endemic in society and are no less stirred by the emotive aspects of truancy than anyone else. Social workers are expected to have the capacity to empathise with their clients. Indeed, they are trained to develop and use such skills in order to help their clients. Jones points out that school counsellors also need empathy: 'sympathy is self-centred rather than client centred'. They are also expected to become involved, but not over-involved, with their clients; empathy and an honest discussion of the realities and reactions to the client's behaviour are part of social work. This has implications for social workers working with truants. Whatever their private feelings about the suitability and effectiveness of the school—and social workers share many of the criticisms currently being levelled at schools—they are acting as the agents of society when children are placed under their supervision by the court, and they cannot collude with the child against the law without jeopardising still further that child's trust and faith in authority. Whether or not they agree with the raising of the school-leaving age, and many social workers (and teachers) are of the opinion that the introduction of it was ill-timed and misjudged, they are doing no service to their under-age clients if they encourage them or even help them to find employment. While it is essential to the social worker and the client not to compromise the social worker's own integrity, it should be perfectly possible to say to a client: 'School may not be the best school for you—but staying away won't solve your problems either. If it can't be changed, let's see how we can help you get the best out of what's available in the time you have left.' It must be said that in their quite appropriate wishes to change the system, particularly in the case of a rigid and old-fashioned school, some young social workers have indulged their own anti-authority attitudes, or have even colluded with truants. This is not to say that they should not try to find ways to assist the schools, and in particular the teachers, to change the schools in ways which would make them more relevant to the post-school lives of their pupils. They could begin by discussing truants who are under supervision or care orders with the teachers of the class they ought to be attending.

(iv) (b) Education welfare officers

The role of the education social worker is at present specifically related to truancy and will be discussed in more detail in the chapter on education social work. Currently the Education Welfare Service is becoming overwhelmed with the paper work in connection with truancy as well as with the social work with the truants. There are various forms which have to be filled in in relation to truancy, but the one by which the school 'alerts' the Education Welfare Service to the fact that the child is out of school is the key one. At present the education welfare officer is required to visit all the families of children who have been reported for absence, and there are many complaints from the schools and others about delays. The numbers involved are often far more than the understaffed service can cope with, and in many cases the children are merely ill and have not notified the school, or may even be in care without the school having yet been informed. Systems whereby schools notify the Education Welfare Service need to be considered jointly and frequently reviewed, not only so that unnecessary paper work can be avoided, but also so that the schools and the Education Welfare Service accept this as a shared responsibility, instead of complaining about each other as they frequently do at present. Plowden recommended that education welfare officers should be able to visit truants selectively, which would enable them to pay more attention to the reasons underlying the truancy. Indeed, although most of the education welfare officers are untrained, many of the experienced officers have a good deal of useful pragmatic knowledge about the patterns and process of truancy, particularly in relation to illicit employment, which could be of considerable use to their better-trained colleagues. Although the attitudes of education welfare officers towards truancy tend to be authoritarian and paternalistic rather than guided by the more professional social work attitudes of empathy, acceptance and so on, they are not averse to actively encouraging attendance by a child by taking him to school themselves, as do some other social workers. Unfortunately their lack of training and knowledge does also make them less discriminating and there are accounts of phobic children being carried into school. Education welfare officers are also often expected to undertake 'sweeps', that is, to visit areas like street markets which are likely to employ children under age, and also to visit places of attraction to children out of school, such as amusement arcades. Most other social workers would regard such sweeps as a job for the police rather than for social workers. Indeed many social workers (and others) would question the appropriateness of the attitude which undertakes such sweeps, as it seems to indicate that the problem is merely to get the child into school and then all will be well.

(v) *Youth and community workers*

Youth workers, particularly detached youth workers, are often the most closely in touch with the truants who have been failed by their schools as well as by society. It is they who may come into contact with the truants who are in the phase between primary and secondary social breakdown. Too often they have to stand helplessly by while the pupil inevitably moves into delinquency, appearances in court and then tertiary social breakdown. They have not the resources or the powers to provide any alternatives, although, often they are the only bridging people in the supportive professions who have the opportunity and the trust to build helping relationships with the truants.

(vi) *Police*

There is some doubt whether the police have a role in relation to truancy *per se*. Their task is the prevention of crime. While the Juvenile Bureau does have the discretion to decide whether to caution a child found guilty of a criminal offence or proceed with a charge, there is some doubt about the legal basis of current interest in truancy. Certainly children out of school may be at risk of becoming delinquent, although some of them have been bona fide reasons for being away. It is a difficult role for the police, and the ambiguity of having a dual role, part law enforcement agents for society, part acting as a preventive social agency in respect of juveniles, compounds the situation. This is especially difficult where the juvenile denies committing an offence and the parents are 'unco-operative'.

(vii) Others

(a) *Doctors*   It is important to mention briefly the difficult position in which doctors find themselves in relation to truancy. Clearly, general practitioners can, and often do, give medical certificates in support of a child staying off school; but it is difficult to gauge when a genuine illness becomes unnecessarily protracted either as a result of a child's anxiety or because of vested parental interests.

Child psychiatrists are in an even more difficult situation. Clearly a child has been referred to them because of emotional problems, only one aspect of which may be difficulties about going to school. Many psychiatrists consider that a brief respite from the pressure to attend school is necessary in order to allow the child to engage in treatment with a therapist, so that the difficulties which lie at the root of the problem can be discovered and worked on together and in confidence. In such situations it is not easy for the psychiatrist to make clear the reasons for such a recommendation without breaching the confidential aspects of the case and thus perhaps jeopardising the treatment.

(b) *Educational administrators and the inspectorate*   Educational administrators play a powerful role in the organisation and structure of the school service. Some of the senior officers and the inspectorate have been teachers themselves. Nevertheless, there is a natural tendency for administrators to adopt the pattern of proportional rather than creative justice in relation to truancy. Stevenson (writing of the supplementary Benefits Commission)[66] describes proportional justice as 'fairness between individuals in society'. Social workers she describes as being concerned with creative justice, which 'is concerned with uniqueness and therefore with differential needs of individuals'. Inevitably there are sometimes conflicts between the two.

(d) Knowledge about truancy

Kahn and Nursten,[67] writing on school refusal and school phobia as a psychosocial problem, distinguish between truancy, school withdrawal and school phobia:

A truant is usually absent from school with or without his
parents' or the school's permission.
School withdrawal is when the parents openly encourage the
child to stay away from school.
School phobics are children who seem to suffer from intense
and irrational fears. These fears may be centred on activities at
school and are often connected with games or PT, but they may
shift from one focus to another. Or they may take the form of
recurrent physical symptoms for which no adequate cause can
be found and which also changes focus.

Nursten and Kahn point out that the conflict may be predominantly in the child, in the family (most often in the mother), in
both child and family. Often such symptoms reveal themselves at
stress points—the identity crisis outlined in Chapter 1. Nursten and
Kahn indicate that referral of school phobics to child guidance
clinics is the appropriate measure. A child guidance case may
illustrate. Janice, aged five, had just started school. She was an only
child and lived with her parents and her grandparents. Her mother
could not get her to stay at school and often did not manage to get
her to leave home. On investigation it was discovered that the
mother herself had been a school refuser, after being evacuated with
her own mother during the war, Janice's maternal grandfather
remaining in London. Mother and grandmother returned to London
after grandfather had been injured in the blitz, to find that he was
having an affair with someone else. The grandparents never sorted
this out but lived in silent hostility for the next twenty years! The
mother married a weak and timid man who moved in with the
family, whom the mother had been unable to leave. Treatment
consisted of the social worker trying to help the mother to become
less dependent on her own mother, and to support her to get Janice
to school and to leave her there.

Tyerman points out the difficulties in distinguishing between
truants and children alleged to be suffering from school phobia and
those who are withdrawn from school. He adds that in social terms
absence from school is twice as high in children of unskilled workers
as in children with parents in professional occupations. The hard
core of the problem are children who average a day's absence or
more each week. Many such cases result in prosecutions, though
there has been a decline in prosecutions since the 1969 Children and
Young Persons Act. Families often keep their children off school,
and in some families the normal reaction to domestic crises is to
keep the eldest daughter at home.

Tyerman also found that truancy by a child is generally a warning
that he may have emotional problems and/or may be developing

delinquent tendencies: 'At least half the children who play truant are maladjusted and one in two commit other offences.'

School-phobic children are generally considered to be children who are either depressed or suffering from severe separation anxiety (the fear of parting from their mothers, or mother substitute), though some writers consider they are pathologically frightened of school. Tyerman himself is of the opinion that there is little justification or agreement for use of the term school phobia, which has been mainly used in the case of anxious, frightened children referred to child guidance clinics. It is, he points out, 'easier to feel sorry for children who are obviously frightened and parents who are worried'. Children classed as truants 'come from homes where education is regarded as a burden, who are on bad terms with their parents who either condone their child's truancy or treat it lightly. Most truants are unhappy at home or school and some are unhappy at both'. At school fear of punishment, ridicule and constant frustration are features.

Pritchard[68] worked with a sample of fifty-five children from the caseloads of the education welfare Officers in a large Yorkshire county borough. The mean age of the children was nine years ten months and they were selected from the hard core of the caseloads (i.e., those seen at least four times in the previous three months). Using Wolff's Behaviour Inventory, he found that the children could be clearly differentiated into three groups: children scoring on Truancy and two or more items were called the *truant group* (19); children scoring on the item School Refusal and two or more other items were designated the *school-phobic group* (22); the other children (14) fell into neither category. The truants scored significantly higher on stealing, over-aggressiveness, wandering off, destructiveness; the school phobics were more over-active. Pritchard comments that over-dependence, sleeping and eating difficulties were not just confined to school-phobic children. He also points out that surprisingly only twelve children in the study had been seen by other agencies. He comments on why various other agencies connected with the children, for instance general practitioners and health visitors, did not recognise the degree of the children's disturbed behaviour and gives some possible explanations. He adds that not all teachers accept that they have a major responsibility for detecting and referring the emotionally disturbed child. Pritchard outlines the statutory sanctions by the Education Welfare Office, which were taken for the three groups as follows: school phobics 64, truants 37, others 7. Finally, Pritchard comments on the number of school-phobic children who were prosecuted. He attributes this to two factors: school phobics are described as committing social suicide by rejecting the education so rightly valued by society; second, factors in the child's family may have led to a sense of frustration on the part of the education welfare officer who failed to understand the collusive elements between parents and child so typical of school phobics.

(e) Management of truancy

School-phobic children are usually referred to child guidance clinics and though drug treatment may be used to diminish their anxiety, more often attempts are made to involve them and their families in psychotherapy to try together to discover the cause of the children's fears and to help them confront and contain them and get back to school. Sometimes the former is achieved but getting the children back to school is much more difficult. A change of school can help, as this provides the child with an emotional face-saver which may allow him or her to muster enough psychic strength to return to school. Some school-phobic children are given home tuition for limited periods to tide them over or to enable them to keep up work for examinations. These are usually children who have become phobic of the clinic and so cannot attend there either. Some children are provided with tuition at the clinic and other children are admitted part-time to a tutorial class which is smaller and much more flexible, and this may become either a permanent solution or act as a half-way stage to helping them back to school. Children for whom none of these solutions work may be admitted to a residential school for the maladjusted or even to a psychiatric unit. There are one or two adolescent units which not only give children residential psychiatric treatment but also provide tuition. Nevertheless, this treatment of school-phobic children and young people is often long-term and all too frequently, even when apparently successful, the children relapse or develop neurotic symptoms.

Truants, children who refuse to go to school, are increasing in numbers, and it is with these children, often criticised as anti-social and delinquent, that the education system is failing. There are many imaginative innovations developing both inside the school system and outside it. But what is needed is some honest and vigorous attention to which kinds of school fail what sort of child, and which children truant from which school.

Some schools now have *open classes*, often much smaller than usual and run on more democratic lines, where the children can be involved in the choice of their 'lessons' and activities. They are frequently housed in a small 'outbuilding'. Other schools have opened *sanctuaries*, run by one or two teachers, for children who cannot cope with ordinary classes. These are usually for children who could be described as incipient school phobics, and they too seem to do better when the classes are kept small and in one fixed place, and staffed by a permanent teacher who also gives individual tuition. There are also *Education Guidance Centres*, which are intended should act as short-term educational assessment centres for children to enable them to remain within the education system but give them an opportunity to have individual attention and expert assessment from educational psychologists and specialist teachers and help with their school difficulties.

Outside the school system other *centres* are increasingly being set up by social service departments, to which teachers may be attached, or by voluntary agencies and settlements such as the *Intermediate Treatment Centres* for the ESN described in a previous section. Some *Adventure playgrounds* attract truants during school hours as well as after school and during the holidays. The adventure playground leaders are then in some conflict as to whether to allow the children to stay or send them away, knowing that outside there will be more risk of their committing offences. Some adventure playgrounds, too, are now beginning to have teachers attached to them. *Free schools*, as will be seen later, also have some success in attracting and helping truants whom the school system has failed.

There are several significant features about these alternative ways of managing truants. In nearly all cases the 'school substitute' is situated outside the school premises or at least in un-schoollike buildings. The classes are small, the teachers are permanent and the teaching methods democratic. The teacher pupil ratios are generous, usually about 1:10. All these factors, coupled with their apparent success, as well as the fact that there is little evidence that children at these temporary centres will ever get back into their ordinary schools, have led to even more defensiveness on the part of more traditional educationalists and, from some, to denouncement and hostility towards these new centres and the 'free school' attitude which they are said to employ. Perhaps as a final comment (though by no means a conclusion to this thorny issue), it is useful to quote Goldschmied who, speaking at the inaugural meeting in 1976 of the Social Work in Education Special Interest Group of the British Association of Social Workers (BASW) described a co-operative approach as follows:

> Learning can take place where there exists some positive
> relationship between teacher and taught. Social work in a
> non-attendance context must focus itself on creating or
> mending a relationship between school and child; child and
> school; parents and school; school and parents. If the parents
> will not let the child go to school then their relationship with
> the child must be looked at; if one parent condones absence

and the other does not, the relationship between them becomes the issue. If the child is regarded as the client, it should not take long to discover which of the relationships in question are right and which are wrong.[69]

8 Suspensions and exclusions from school

Children who are suspended or excluded from school are a small but significant group of children, though the numbers are thought to be increasing. Usually such action is only taken as a last resort, every effort being made to keep a child in school or to negotiate a temporary but agreed absence with the child and his or her family. Children who are suspended from school are required to stay off school for a definite and time-fixed period. Quite frequently this is merely a few days—a 'cooling off' period to allow the child and his family to take stock and a fresh look at the child's attitude towards and behaviour in school. Sometimes a child or young person may be suspended for a few weeks or even until the end of term. Children who are excluded from school are often waiting to be admitted to another school (often a special school or residential school), and may be in the process of being assessed for special treatment.

When children are suspended or excluded, it is usually for violent or very disturbed behaviour, assault on a child or teacher, or for disobedience. Legally the head has the right to suspend or exclude a child from school, but this must be reported to the managers/governors, to whom the parents have a right of appeal. Only the managers/governors have the right to expel a child, and an interesting dilemma arises when the head who has recommended suspension or exclusion is also a governor. Should heads, as 'interested' parties, also be able to exercise their right to vote?

There seem to have been very few attempts to study suspended or excluded children *per se* although, as is later shown, many of these children are already likely to be attending child guidance or adolescent clinics and/or may also be attending special schools; some may be already under supervision or care orders. Nevertheless, whether or not the child and family are in touch with a social work agency or are referred to one, seems to be very much a question of chance. Stritch and Crunk[70] in the USA studied children suspended from school and their families, and found that indefinitely suspending a child from school results in counter-productive negative judgments, feelings and behaviour on the part of the family towards the suspending school and to the school system in general. They studied groups of children suspended from school in New Orleans: those suspended and referred to the visiting teacher (education welfare officer), those suspended and not referred, and, for comparison, those referred but not suspended. They found that the typical child who was suspended (and not referred) was the black adolescent boy somewhat less academically bright than his school peers, whose social background was characterised by greater family disorganisation. Most suspensions took place in the early part of the school year.

They point out that the suspended child is for a time totally isolated from the experiences of school and peers and the family is effectively cut off from the education system until such time as the child is readmitted to school. Children who are excluded from school are usually either violently aggressive or apparently unmanageable in the school setting. Occasionally children who may be amenable for periods and then suddenly have unpredictable and violent outbursts may be excluded from school. York, Heron and Wolff[71] studied forty-one children who were excluded from Edinburgh schools and found that an act of aggressive or disruptive behaviour always precipitated the exclusion and often the behaviour was also dangerous, and in every case, it was the culmination of incidents—vicious attacks on other children, throwing objects in the classroom (a glass and lighted firework were quoted) and intolerable outbursts of temper. Many of the children also stole, but this was not the reason for the exclusion. There were twice as many exclusions in the winter when opportunities for outdoor play are restricted, and more exclusions took place in the middle third of the term. The children came from primary and secondary schools and thirteen of them were already attending special schools of some kind; thirty-four of them were boys. Generally the children were of lower intelligence than average, their reading ability was also backward, some were very behind. The children had a formidable repertoire of symptoms: aggressive and anti-social symptoms predominated and 34 children had 5 or more symptoms; 15 of them had already appeared in court; 17 were psychiatrically assessed as having conduct disorders; other psychiatric diagnoses included mixed behaviour disorder, hyper-syndrome, depressive stress and childhood psychosis. The children were extraordinarily aggressive and delinquent, though on the whole in good physical health. Most of them came from social class IV or V (unskilled manual). Only 22 of the children were living with both natural parents, and particular discord was noted in 16 of those. Many of the parents had physical illnesses and very striking was the incidence of psychiatric and sociopathic disorders, only 7 of the 34 children seen in the hospital department having parents without evidence of psychiatric or personality disorders. When the children were followed up three years later, only 4 out of the 25 children still at school were living at home and attending ordinary schools; 19

were in psychiatric hospitals, residential schools or children's homes.

As can be seen from this research, most of the children excluded from school were already in touch with psychiatric and social work agencies. Unfortunately Caplan[72] found that in a crisis situation normal problem-solving mechanisms fail to function for a period and that when they regain their effectiveness the resolution of the crisis may produce an adaptive or a maladaptive solution. He also found that such a situation is an opportunity for growth, like the life crises which Erikson discussed, and that appropriate help given for short periods may enable the crisis situation to be used to promote improved social functioning. Since suspension or exclusion from school are likely to prove a crisis situation for both the child and his family, it might well be worth making an immediate referral for follow-up by a social work agency. It would be worth monitoring such an experiment to find out (a) how many children and their families are already in touch with social work agencies and whether they were thought to be progressing, and (b) whether the provision of short-term intensive help with the focal problem of the suspension produced favourable results.

9 Residential school establishments

Residential care is one of the most important, controversial and neglected of the boundary areas between social work and education. It is important because schoolchildren in need of education and care away from their homes are among the most vulnerable and damaged children, whose deprivation is often demonstrated in the form of anti-social behaviour and delinquency. Important too, because if these children are given the right kind of education and care then there is some hope that the tertiary social breakdown which they are beginning to experience can be ameliorated. If it cannot then these are the children who are likely to become the parents of another generation of children at grave risk, if only because they are deprived of access to resources which should be available to them. This area is controversial because, as has already been mentioned, residential care is one of the most striking aspects of society, one where the conflicts between care or custody, punishment or therapy, need to be contained within one institution which itself contains children whose individual and experiential history and problems often have their roots in those very areas. Just as within any family whose social functioning capacity is good enough there needs to be a creative tension between care and control, so does there need to be something similar in schools or residential centres for children. Yet these residential establishments are among the most neglected areas of both education and social work. Residential schools and centres have long been starved of resources (although some of them do have fine buildings and equipment, they are rarely purpose-built) and they are most often situated in the heart of rural areas, which means that the children's contact with their families is attenuated if not minimised. While the staff of such schools and centres have the most demanding jobs in both the education and social work systems, they have consistently been undervalued, undertrained, and underpaid, whether as teachers or social workers. Since the 1969 Children and Young Persons Act came into force on 1 January 1971, whereby all approved schools were translated (even if they were not exactly transformed) into Community Homes, some considerable attempts have been made to remedy some of this neglect. Nevertheless, prior to that time and apart from the really creative and innovative use of the control/therapy tension in establishments run by independent organisations, many residential establishments of all kinds merely resulted in reinforcing for the children all the worst aspects of their previous lives. Yet the average cost of keeping a child in a residential establishment was £68.00 per week in 1975-6.

As Tutt points out:

Society must decide whether it wants to treat or punish its deprived children . . . schools are openly criticised by the media, at one moment for being excessively punitive, and the next for being too permissive. Staff react to this uncertainty by ineffectually maintaining the status quo, and rejecting experimentation and innovation in case it leads to undesirable publicity.[73]

Too often it has been mere chance that a child has been admitted to one kind of residential establishment rather than another. As Tutt himself points out, residential provision comes under the aegis of three different systems: schools for the maladjusted are under the education system, adolescent psychiatric provision is under the National Health Service and the community homes (formerly approved schools) under social services. While things seem to have improved slightly since 1969, little real progress has been made.

(a) Assessment and admission

As was shown in the chapter on social breakdown, children may be admitted to residential establishments on grounds which may be educational, social or psychiatric. Thus, providing the parents agree, children may be admitted to residential *schools* on either educational or social grounds regardless of whether they have been through the courts and adjudged to be in need of residential 'care'. They may be recommended residential education by a doctor, either on health grounds (as, for instance, in the case of asthmatic children who frequently improve both their health and their educational potential when at small boarding schools near the sea and away from their 'over-anxious' parents), or emotional grounds (as for maladjusted children whose parents cannot either control or care for them because of their own difficulties).

Yet many of these children (or others like them) may also first appear in court either because they have committed an offence or because they have been considered to be in need of care by the social service system or the education system (because of non-attendance at school). Such children may become subject to a supervision order or a care order and even be admitted to the same schools. Before such drastic action is taken, however, these children are made subject to an interim care order and admitted to an assessment centre or remand home (depending on their age) where they are carefully assessed by a team of professional experts. Such assessment usually takes the form of careful observation of their behaviour and capacity for relationships (by the residential staff), assessment of their educational attainments (by the teachers), of their educational needs and potential (by the psychologist), of their emotional strengths and vulnerabilities (by the psychiatrist), and a social worker also assesses the social functioning and potential of the child in his or her family situation (including the housing and financial situation). These aspects are then combined into a comprehensive report and recommendation to the juvenile court. When the child returns there the magistrates may give an absolute or conditional discharge, fix a fine or make the child subject to a supervision order or care order. For boys under fourteen they may order them to go to an attendance centre for a certain number of hours each week, and those over fourteen may be sent to a detention centre for up to six months for a 'short, sharp shock' intended to inculcate in them a wish to change their ways. Juveniles over fifteen but under twenty-one, they may send to Borstal and in certain cases younger children may also be sent to Borstal. Since 1971, however, there has been a good deal of concern expressed over children who have been 'certified as unruly' and admitted to prisons, at least until secure provision has been found for them. Children made subject to supervision orders remain at home and they and their families are supported and befriended either by probation officers or social workers of the local authority social service department (the arrangements as to which social workers may be involved are usually local ones agreed by the probation and social services committees and often dependent on availability of staff). Children who are made subject to care orders (in 1974 there were 95,867 of them) may be admitted to foster homes or family group homes, from whence they go out to ordinary schools, or they may be admitted to residential care of some kind. A great deal has been written about foster care but in essence the aim is that a child, by being attached to a substitute family, should be enabled to live as ordinary a life as is possible. Foster parents usually have long-established links with local schools and the transition is accomplished as carefully as possible. While these children are living away from their homes, the tasks of school and foster home are distinct. Foster care is often the vital last hope for the child of being able to maintain or recreate an opportunity for social functioning. However, those children who, after careful assessment and passing through the courts, are admitted to residential schools, community homes, subnormality or psychiatric hospitals, could be described as experiencing tertiary social breakdown. A similar term could be applied to those children admitted to Special Treatment Centres (for children who are difficult to contain in ordinary community homes) and to young people admitted to Borstals or prisons.

Children admitted via the courts, who have been assessed by the very comprehensive team approach, theoretically have a greater opportunity of being admitted to a residential establishment which is equipped to meet their needs and enhance their potential. Children who are admitted to residential schools via the educational system are also assessed but usually with a bias on assessment by professionals within that system (i.e., teachers and psychologists, school medical officers and education social workers) although their reports may be passed on to other professionals who may later become involved with the child. Inevitably such reports give weighting to the *educational* aspects of the child's needs and often are inclined to minimise both the importance of the family and its strengths and potential for change, given appropriate help. On the other hand, children admitted to residential schools, hospitals or psychiatric centres following assessment by medical teams are usually assessed by professionals within that system, which in their turn give weighting to the *disease* aspects of the child, whether assessed in medical or psychiatric terms. In the case of assessment by child guidance teams of professionals, this varies depending on whether the child guidance clinic is based within the health service system or the education system. In cases where the recommendation is made by a team based within the education system, such recommendations are almost always accepted without question, indeed quite often the child guidance team is part of the school medical service and performs such assessment as part of its overall function. If, however, the assessment is made by a hospital-based team, then the recommendation is usually vetted and approved by the education system personnel. While such approval is nearly always forthcoming, education authorities wish to preserve their power to decide to which residential institution a child should actually be admitted. Indeed they keep an approved and inspected list of private schools and homes other than those they maintain as part of their own system. While at first sight both on grounds of cost and of maintenance of standards of such institutions this may seem reasonable, in practice anomalies and difficulties can occur. Such institutions and homes are inspected and approved by inspectors either of the local authority education system or from the DES (unless they provide predominantly nursing care, in which case they would be inspected by DHSS inspectors) and again their criteria are likely to be education-biased. Also for professionals working with the child and his family, who after all must agree before such a placement can be made, it is difficult to guarantee where a child may be sent and thus make the transition from home to school as smooth as possible. While children who have been thus assessed in any one of the three ways might even end up in the same residential school, the process of assessment is very difficult and inevitably affects the way in which both the child and his or her family see themselves and the residential establishment. Very little work seems to have been done to compare and contrast these differing 'processing experiences' and their effect on the eventual outcome of the child's capacity for social functioning.

(b) Residential establishments

By far the majority of children who end up in residential establishments are admitted to community homes after being made subject to care orders. Since 1971 these are run either by independent organisations or by local authority social service departments and the children in them are all placed there and paid for by the social service departments responsible for their care. In a residential *school* the bias is towards the *educational* aspects of care and the organisational structure reflects the usual school organisational structure; the head at the top of a hierarchical model flanked by teachers, with other care staff (still usually called child-care staff) in a secondary role and the visiting experts (psychiatrists and social workers) as advisers and consultants to the head and teaching staff. In the other residential settings things are different. In the residential institutions run on the medical model, such as psychiatric centres or subnormality hospitals, the bias is towards *medical* care, including therapy and nursing, with a division of responsibility as between doctors and nurses, though the doctor has ultimate medico-legal responsibility. In such a model it is the teachers and social workers who, though usually present, are tangential to the main task.

With the introduction of community homes it was the intention to provide a caring community which would provide *care and treatment in a planned environment.* Indeed the DHSS brought out a pamphlet of just that name,[74] in which they state that their aim is 'to provide community homes whose scope is such that a child's entire needs may be provided for within the treatment programme offered by the home to which he goes'. The emphasis, then, is intended to be on a therapeutic approach to care, while it is recognised that for certain children control is also essential and the importance of education is recognised. In describing how the child's needs might be met, the pamphlet continues:

> For healthy development it is important not only that a child's basic physical needs should be met adequately but also that he should experience satisfying personal relationships, both with adults and with other children, and should have the opportunity for satisfactory identifications. It is through this experience that a child can grow up with a realisation of his own worth. He needs the underlying sense of security that it gives if he is to learn to cope with his impulses, to be able to postpone immediate gratification and to develop self-discipline. A child must feel safe enough to make mistakes and to be able to learn from them without due anxiety; he has to be helped to appreciate the needs and feelings of others and to learn to share and to give and thus acquire habits of socially acceptable behaviour. He needs opportunity to acquire skill in making choices and must be encouraged to develop a concept of right and wrong. A growing ability to communicate with others and an increasing sense of satisfaction through achievement are fundamental to healthy development.

The 1969 Act, which was never fully implemented, was based on the recommendations of the White Paper *Children in Trouble*, in which the expressed intention was that

> local authorities will be responsible for developing a comprehensive system of residential care and treatment for children received or committed into their care who are not boarded out with foster parents . . . a considerable variety of provision will be needed within this system, which will be described for legal purposes as the public system of community homes for children and young persons. The needs of the great majority of children will be met by homes which, as now, will care for them as nearly as possible in the same way as a good family, making use of the education, health and other services which are generally available. Even in the long term, however,

there will remain a substantial minority of children whose needs cannot be met in this way. There will thus be a continuing need for some establishments providing education and treatment on the premises. In some cases this will be with the limited aim of preparing for an early return to the use of the normal services. In others the first priority will be a therapeutic approach to social education. Some of these children, particularly those whose behaviour is most difficult, will also need control in secure conditions, or very specialised forms of treatment.

Thus the intention so clearly expressed in the above paragraph was that there should be a variety of residential establishments available, which co-ordinated together and working co-operatively should provide a range of facilities, care and control so as to meet the needs of the range of children and their needs. Sadly this does not appear to have even begun to happen and, indeed, as was indicated in the section on intermediate treatment, the 1969 Act itself has been subject to severe disrepute, perhaps particularly from teachers and magistrates.

While some of the reasons for the relative failure to provide a comprehensive residential care service for all children in need have already been mentioned, notably the failure to implement the whole Act and the lack of communication and liaison between the various systems involved, there are other reasons also. Many of the buildings are inadequate for adaptation to such new tasks. They were often geographically isolated and with the various local government and departmental reorganisations became even more cut off organisationally from their previous support systems. Community homes often lacked all kinds of resources but, particularly, adequate and trained staff, although considerable attempts (which will be discussed in the next section) have been and are being made to remedy this situation.

(c) Staffing and training for residential work

In 1970 the CCETSW set up a working party to discuss training for residential work. This was one of the first tasks which the Council undertook and it has produced two reports, one a consultative document[75] which set out the issues and made various recommendations and which produced a storm of reactions, many of them critical and not a few based on an inadequate reading of the Council's intentions. The working party distinguished between several models of residential care: 'the provision of refuge, providing correction, as an agent of socialisation, as an opportunity for therapeutic intervention or as a place for terminal care'. While the first and the last models do not appear to have much relevance for children of school age, the other three models do, and indeed, as the report of the working party goes on to state, entail differences in the relationship between the staff and residents:

> Frequently conflicts arise between the model adopted by the workers and that adopted by certain influential sections of public opinion . . . such conflicts usually centering around the degree of control necessary to protect the client and the public and the degree of freedom and self expression to be made available in a therapeutic or rehabilitative programme.

The working party were at pains to distinguish between residential centres: they were after all asked to recommend a training for residential workers and their terms of reference only included residential establishments within the social work system. This perforce led not only to the exclusion of the prison service (including Borstals, remand centres and detention centres, though not after-care hostels) but also residential schools (though not the approved schools which were to become community homes), and in addition did not include long-stay hospitals such as those for the subnormal (although hostels and after-care homes for the disabled were included). This somewhat anomalous position implied that the models considered in the previous paragraphs were not taken into account, although both the special residential schools and the long stay hospitals employ care assistants who may be variously described as child-care workers or assistant nurses. As has already been discussed, the position of these workers in the hierarchy of such institutions is relatively low. It is interesting to note here that as in so many other areas where the boundary issues are highlighted, it is the voluntary or independent organisations which have firmly confronted the dilemmas of these different models and have developed models where the tasks and responsibilities are both clearly defined and more democratic (though this will be further discussed later in the section on tasks).

The CCETSW working party came out with a definition of residential social work as a 'method of social work in which a team of workers operates together with a group of residents to create a living environment designed to enhance the functioning of individual residents in the context of their total environment'. When considered solely in relation to schoolchildren and their needs this definition (which is after all designed for *all* groups of people needing residential care) may seem somewhat clumsy and convoluted. Nevertheless, it does demonstrate an underlying social work philosophy, which is that the clients' (in this case the residents') needs should be paramount. It stresses the value of the team approach to enhance the residents' strengths and potential. The definition also stresses the importance of the social context in which the residential living environment is situated. But the most important aspect of the definition is that the residential establishment should be designed to enhance the functioning of the individual residents. Put like this, and substituting children for residents, there is little to which those who accept the philosophy of the White Paper could take exception. Many social workers might disagree that residential work *is* a social work method, preferring to describe it as a setting in which the various social work methods may be practised by the residential and fieldwork social workers. While the first discussion document from which this definition has been taken was hotly debated and not infrequently misunderstood, the working party continued its deliberations and its final recommendations contain some significant shifts of opinion. Most notably, while the original document considered residential work as 'welfare work'—which was clearly destined to continue the second-class status of the work—the new report[76] came out with the firm declaration (as evidenced by its title) that 'residential work is part of social work'. The eventual recommended qualification has been integrated with a modular training programme which covers many other aspects of social service (as distinct from social work), including residential work, day care and home-help organisers, who all take a core programme and particular modules specific both to the professional tasks and to the omissions in any earlier training they may have received. The qualification will be the certificate in social service. Significantly, too, since this document has been published, many professional social work courses which award the CQSW have options in residential social work.

(d) The residential task

The CCETSW definition of the residential task has already been discussed, but this is a generic definition intended to cover the whole of social work practice within such residential establishments. Beedell,[77] in writing of residential work specifically with children, develops a model in relation to the provision for children's needs. He suggests that residential work for children 'takes over a more or less substantial part of responsibility for "parenting"'. In defining this he seems to take substantially the same line as the socialisation model for families adopted in the first chapter. He goes on to describe the essential characteristics of such parenting, and how these may be provided as a resocialisation experience in residential care. As he points out, the staff in residential establishments 'hope to be able to provide not only good ordinary experience for their charges but also some good extraordinary experience'.

Beedell describes seven aspects of residential experience: *holding*, which enables children to maintain their personal identity; *acceptance* of the individual at a deeper individualised level such as to enable the child to feel safe enough to risk his/her whole self by testing out behaviour; *experience of care, comfort and control*; *nurturing* in all ways; *living in a small group*; the development of personal *integrity*; and *therapy*. The last two he admits are difficult to distinguish from each other. He writes of 'educational integrity provision' as including

admission of the whole child to the unit; protection from the pressure of 'others' with recognition of 'others' as 'egos' in their own right; opportunities for reflection and expression as ways of confirming one's ideas of oneself and testing one's wholeness; recognition of fragile learning points . . . . At the growing points of learning what is brought from the past is more uncertain, anxiety is higher and therefore the consequent achievement and rewards if we succeed are more satisfying and the consequent pain if we fail more intense. There is a conflict here which every educator and/or therapist has to face. It helps if the adult faces this conflict in himself fairly and squarely.

Beedell divides the therapy as endeavouring to meet four areas of need: 'exploratory ego building (thus making up for past deprivations)'; 'remedial ego building'; 'personality resolution and integration'; and 'primary experience (which makes good substantial gaps in the child's earlier life)'.

In the final chapter of his helpful book, Beedell considers issues in relation to setting residential work within the context of education and social work. He describes the 'characteristics of work in a life space situation' and has developed a useful diagram which is reproduced here as Figure 7.

Beedell, too, points out the area of overlap between education and social work, the different social contexts and the different underlying value systems. Although Figure 7 is specifically related to residential work with schoolchildren, in many ways it reflects and complements in microcosm Figure 4 in Chapter 1. While the two larger ovals in Figure 7 indicate that social work and education are carried out in the main separately and distinctly, there is an area of overlap and this overlap has been widely discussed in this book. Beedell, however, distinguishes two areas within this general overlap where social work and education not only intermingle but are often difficult to distinguish from each other: specialised interview situations and life-space situations. The *specialised interview situations*, which are shown at the top of the diagram, he describes as including:

159

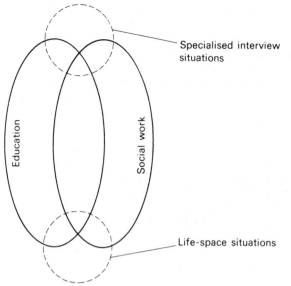

Specialised interview situations

Education

Social work

Life-space situations

Figure 7   Education and social work
(Source: Christopher Beedell, *Residential Life with Children*,
Routledge & Kegan Paul, 1970)

all the contexts in which the worker carries on his relationship
with the client mainly (though not necessarily entirely) in one to
one interview situations. This area covers much social casework,
specialised therapy and diagnosis; some remedial teaching,
much psychological testing; vocational guidance, etc.; and what
may broadly be termed 'counselling'.

Beedell was of course writing mainly in relation to children in care,
hence the individuals and families, or casework, bias to this
description of social work intervention. He goes on to quote Clare
Winnicott, who describes the psychosocial nature of such a relationship thus: 'It is indirect—in fact its value lies here, that it can
influence ordinary living but is not strictly a part of the living.' The
lower circle, that described as *life-space situations*, Beedell considers
is part of ordinary life although a specialised part: 'In such
counselling situations worker and client are specially insulated from
the rest of life by privacy, time limits and certain sets of social
expectation, in order to carry on a fairly well defined task.' This area
covers residential work of all kinds, certain types of group therapy
and assessment or remedial teaching and a number of other
situations such as youth club or community centre work. Beedell
comments:

Perhaps the most clear differentiation between education and social work is that education is mainly concerned with the normal pattern of achievement (with transmitting a culture and all that this implies) and social work with the casualties, misfits or deviants from the usual pattern. Schools are organised on the assumption that at least 90% of their population are not seriously delinquent or maladjusted, etc. Though the preventive services of Children's Departments [Beedell was writing in 1970] have wide 'educational' power to make available such advice, guidance and assistance as may promote the welfare of children.

The next phrase of the sentence, 'by diminishing the need to receive children or keep them in care', makes it clear that these are designed to catch potential casualties.

Beedell concludes that the professional position of the residential worker is such that

he must operate sometimes within the value system of education, sometimes within that of social work, sometimes in a common area. He must be able to shift, in appropriate circumstances, from a largely reality determined set course to an unconsciously determined follow-where-it-leads depth exploration or to a combination of these. He must at one time uphold and exemplify conventional value systems, at another agree to regard these for the moment as merely convenient assumptions.

While Beedell, writing prior to the implementation of the 1969 Children and Young Persons Act, has given a vivid picture of residential life with children, Tutt, whose work has been in community homes which were former approved schools, is particularly scathing about the central conflict regarding their function being located in society itself:

Society's need is for institutions in which to place members whose behaviour deviates from cultural norms to a degree where society is no longer able to tolerate it. The residential institution therefore acts as a social control, guaranteeing that the extremes of behaviour are removed from society thus re-establishing the equilibrium.

While Tutt appears to include institutions within his definition of social control, this in no way detracts from his argument that at the same time community homes are required to be therapeutic, in the sense that the staff, by fostering close and understanding relationships with the children, are expected to remedy the deprivations and psychological illnesses which led to the child's admission to the home. Tutt points out that 'the dilemma is one of custody versus rehabilitation and punishment versus treatment'. He goes on to consider that effectiveness of residential treatment can be measured in four ways: custodial effectiveness (i.e., the limiting of absconding); rehabilitation success rates; detrimental punitive effectiveness; and treatment effectiveness. He finds that residential treatment fails to achieve its objectives because they are unclear and muddled. It is often expected to carry out two diametrically opposed tasks and as long as such confusion exists, it is doomed to failure.

The review document on the 1969 Act does not really grasp the nettle:

Despite heavy investment and increased demands, the numbers actually accommodated in these community homes have not risen. Some authorities providing homes have not clearly defined the roles and functions of those homes and have allowed the heads to exercise a discretion on admission that goes beyond a necessary professional discretion.[78]

Part three

The people in the system

Chapter four

Education social work: definition of tasks and an educational dilemma

The development of education social work

At the present time (1977) education social work is predominantly the responsibility of the Education Welfare Service, which in most authorities is part of the education system. A growing body of professional social work opinion seems to indicate that social work practice carried out specifically in relation to schools could be considered as a specialism within social work, and though there are specific issues (to be considered later), such a specialism merits further development. While the title of the service, Education Welfare, is perhaps indicative of the somewhat old-fashioned image of the service, there are movements within the Service itself which would like to up-date this image and to bring it in line with modern social work philosophy and practice.

The service began with the appointment of school attendance visitors, soon after the 1870 Education Act established School Boards. By 1876, about half the child population was going to school and by 1880 education was virtually compulsory. It is perhaps indicative of the ambivalence with which the public views the Education Welfare Service that even today an education welfare officer is frequently alluded to as 'the School Board man', although the title became that of School Enquiry Officer. In 1903, and later in the 1933 Children and Young Persons Act, employment regulations were introduced in order to protect schoolchildren from the exploitation of employers and their parents (the days of the industrial revolution were not far in the past). The enforcement of these employment regulations was usually delegated to the school enquiry officers. Today these regulations—often local authority by-laws—involve detailed complexities, with specific regulations not only as to age and hours of work (e.g., a child under thirteen may not be employed) but also as to the type of work which may be undertaken at what age. As a BBC *Man Alive* programme demonstrated ('Child Labour', 17 July 1974), children, parents and employers alike are often genuinely ignorant of such laws and they are regularly disregarded. In 1907 free school meals were supplied to children in need and in 1908 the Children's Charter not only provided medical inspection but a host of other welfare functions. Tasks in connection with these new regulations were added to the role of the school enquiry officer.

Other Education Acts in 1918 and 1921 added to or consolidated the duties of the school enquiry officer, as did the 1933 Children and Young Persons Act. It was not until the 1944 Education Act, however, that credence was given to the 'welfare' tasks of their role. The school enquiry service became the Education Welfare Service under this Act. In London the tasks of school attendance and employment and those of school meals and medical inspection had evolved separately, carried out by the voluntary care committee ladies (originally the Feeding Committee). These ladies were usually the caring, crusading middle-class philanthropists who initiated so many social reforms in the late nineteenth and early twentieth centuries. The care committees were 'serviced' by a paid organiser whose task was to co-ordinate the service. The 1944 Act stated that

the local education authorities have a duty to contribute to the spiritual, mental and physical development of the community by ensuring that education shall be available to meet the needs of the population of their area; they must provide for medical inspection of pupils—free medical treatment where necessary— free meals and other facilities where appropriate.[1]

Education authorities were charged with the responsibility to provide 'necessary clothing' to enable children to take advantage of schooling. This is usually interpreted as outer clothing and footwear. The Act also laid a very definitive duty on the parents of each child of school age: 'to cause him to receive efficient full-time education suitable to his age, ability and aptitude, either by regular attendance at school or otherwise'. It clarified and laid down actions connected with parents who neglected or failed in their duty to see that their child was being educated efficiently and appropriately (Sections 37 and 39). The Act appeared to envisage a partnership and a shared responsibility between parents and education authorities (Section 36). By 1950 the execution of these welfare responsibilities, including school attendance, had fallen to the Education Welfare Service.

There is little doubt that despite the enthusiasm and exceptional hard work of the education welfare officers, their service is now old-fashioned and hampered by its clerical responsibilities. The Education Welfare Service has virtually been ignored and neglected by the employing education system; it has been treated as a Cinderella service by the schools and too often with contempt by other social work agencies. This is a distressing state of affairs when it is considered that the task of the Education Welfare Service is to provide bridges and links between the schools and the families of the schoolchildren they serve. A detailed discussion of the tasks of the education social workers will follow later.

Education social work has evolved and developed in isolation not only from social work, but also from teaching. Some of the reasons may be as follows:

(i) Education social workers (whatever they may have been called) have always been employed by the education authorities, whose primary task is the development of education. In this they are somewhat analogous to medical social workers, who have also emerged in a setting (the hospital) whose primary task is curing the sick, not social work. However, the medical profession, though often ambivalent towards the medical social workers, has given them support and contributed greatly in their training. Perhaps because of this medical social workers, unlike education welfare officers, have been able to make links across to their colleagues in other settings. It may also be due to the fact that these social workers were predominantly middle-class and women.

(ii) School enquiry officers were usually men, often of limited educational background themselves; they saw their task in rather more restricted and authoritarian ways—to 'get kids into school' rather than to look for the reasons underlying why they were not going. Many school enquiry officers were retired police officers (as indeed are a significant proportion of education welfare officers today), warm-hearted and concerned as they were, but still giving priority to the authoritarian aspects of their role.

(iii) Between the wars social work in this country became caught up in what Woodroofe called 'the psychiatric deluge'. This happened to a lesser extent than in the USA, but nevertheless social workers became over-preoccupied with the 'inner worlds' of their clients and less concerned about the conditions in which they lived. It took the rediscovery of poverty in the 1950s before social workers again turned their full attention to the community and social aspects of child care and began to give due attention to the conditions in which many children lived, as well as to their emotional distress.

(iv) Paradoxically, the war accentuated the developing child-centredness of our society. Evacuation and its sequelae alerted everyone concerned with children to their distress, but the problems were seen as firmly in the child. There was a burgeoning of knowledge and understanding but the focus on preventive and remedial action tended to be focused on the child as distinct from his

167

or her family. In the education system it is only recently that the far-sightedness of writers such as Clegg and Megson and the work of the EPA teams have turned attention outwards again, back into the community. The interdisciplinary work of the National Children's Bureau has also brought a sharing of what was often compartmentalised knowledge available to only one discipline.

(v) As in social work, the teachers, too, dealt with the new knowledge and attitudes by turning their attention inwards and preoccupying themselves with the 9 a.m. to 4 p.m. lives of schoolchildren. This turning inwards was perhaps exacerbated by educational 'advances', particularly 'going comprehensive', which was more than enough to preoccupy them.

(vi) Somehow the knowledge explosion which followed the war did not reach the Education Welfare Service in any significant way. The teachers did not see themselves as needing to be involved in the families of the children they taught. Most of them were trained in colleges of education where their professional role was both exclusive and isolated: the overwhelming need for more teachers following the post-war birth 'bulge' was of paramount importance. Teachers now have much cause to regret this exclusive preoccupation.

(vii) Social workers were also preoccupied with the developing aspects of their role. Apart from the probation service, which was in a special position *vis à vis* the courts, social workers had not really been confronted with statutory duties. The responsibilities given to them by the 1948 Children and Young Persons Act led to the children's departments becoming preoccupied first with the provision of substitute care; and following the 1963 Children and Young Persons Act, with preventing those family situations which might lead to children being taken into care. The 1959 Mental Health Act, too, led them to become preoccupied with these new aspects and with the integration of the caring and control aspects of their role.

(viii) As will be discussed later, both teachers and social workers have become preoccupied with professionalism and recognition of their status, and ideas of sharing with the low-status education welfare service must have been dismissed as jeopardising their cause.

(ix) Lastly, the Education Welfare Service itself did not begin to clamour for much-needed training (or recognition). One reason for this was the much smaller numbers involved. Plowden calculated 2,000 distributed between 159 authorities. Since the deterioration of conditions in the inner cities and the increase of truancy and violence in the schools, there has been an increase in the staffing in the Education Welfare Service. For the first time young graduates and those who regard higher education and training as a right rather than a privilege have joined the Education Welfare Service, and requests for training and recognition have led to some recognition of the service. Recently teachers, social workers and others, too, have become aware of the Education Welfare Service, though all too often only to use it as a whipping-boy for the social problems (particularly truancy) which are endemic to our society.

Both the Newsom Committee[2] and the Plowden Committee[3] made recommendations about liaison between schools, the former recommending teacher/youth leader posts and the latter teacher/social worker posts, and Plowden recognised the value and importance of the work of the Education Welfare Service, commenting on the link between primary schools and social workers and prophesying that the need for such links would increase in the years to come. With typical percipience, Plowden also commented on the deployment of trained manpower in the social services, remarking succinctly, 'It is clear all is not well', but recognised, too, that the Seebohm Committee on local authority and allied personal social services was currently also sitting. Plowden went on:

> Relations between schools and social services should be improved, there is the problem of the teachers' own knowledge and in their capacity to identify social problems and to be aware of services to help children . . . . There are problems between schools and other services—the ability and willingness to keep each other adequately informed; and there is the broader problem, the schools' contact with their pupils' own homes.

The Report further points out that in primary schools 'welfare cases are usually handled by the Head Teacher and that class teachers have little contact with social workers about pupils who are being helped by outside agencies'. Teachers and social workers alike would say this is still often the case.

Fitzherbert writes:

> While an explicit welfare commitment may be a necessary condition for making the school a truly caring place for all children, it is not a sufficient one. An overdeveloped sense of responsibility for the welfare of children in a head teacher can be of limited effectiveness, unless it is coupled with the ability to share his load with others, outside professionals as well as fellow teachers.[4]

She goes on to describe some of the views of the most dedicated head teachers, whose commitment to the welfare of their pupils (whether inside or outside school) is unquestionable and whose leadership in such matters is higher personalised and therefore difficult to delegate.

It would also seem that heads and other educational administrators do not always appreciate the importance and value of direct communication between people who *actually know* the child and his or her family; in any case, as Plowden points out 'the Head teacher himself is not always informed'. Plowden concluded by recommending that

the school social worker or a social worker closely collaborating with the school needs to be clear about his powers to act on truancy, on additional forms of guidance, supervision and help he may be asked to provide . . . . He must be known to the teachers in the schools he serves and be accepted by them as a colleague. The size of his caseload must be controlled . . . . If some or all of this work is to be carried out by the present Education Welfare Officers who in view of the shortage of professionally trained social workers are similarly equipped to undertake this work, then their caseload should be pruned of other duties; routine investigation of attendance work would have to be carried out selectively so that they would have time for more social work activity.

The Seebohm Committee[5] took up the theme of school social work, making a number of comments and touching on the question of counselling services in schools as part of the education system and the establishment of a special post inside the schools with special responsibility for liaison with outside social services. The task of the Seebohm Committee was to recommend the reorganisation of the social services, and it was their view that some social work in schools should be the responsibility of the local social services departments, which they also recommended for child guidance services; however, they recognised school attendance as a possible problem area, as was the provision for children with special educational needs.

When the Conservative Government implemented the recommendations of the Seebohm Committee in 1970, they did not make specific recommendations regarding either the Education Welfare or the Child Guidance Services. The Lincoln Ralphs Committee which was set up to consider the role of the Education Welfare Service and reported in 1973,[6] came out with the straightforward recommendation that the service should be a social work service, and some of the Committee's findings will be discussed in the next section. However, their findings regarding organisation, staffing and clarity of function revealed a confusing picture. In about forty-five authorities, education welfare officers report to senior staff in an education welfare section, most others report direct to senior education staff. About 50 per cent of heads allow education welfare officers direct access to teachers, whereas the other half require them to report directly to them. The wide range of staff employed reflects the different attitudes within the education system to home/school liaison. The Ralphs Committee also found that in 1971 only 1·5 per cent of the 2,310 filled posts in the service had a social work qualification and only 12 per cent were undertaking in-service or day-release training. Further, they noted that 85 per cent of the staff were in fact over thirty-five years old and 65 per cent of them had more than five years' experience. A recent article by Davis,[7] based on a survey, outlines four typical organisational models, as set out in Table 5. Davis points out that the discrepancies in relation to the ratios of education welfare officers to pupils vary from 1:6,900, the highest in his survey, to 1:2,400, the lowest.

TABLE 5   *Some models of the education welfare service*

I School population 116,900	*II School population 101,000*
1 Principal education welfare officer	1 Chief education welfare officer
5 Area education welfare officers	4 Divisional education welfare officers
11 Senior education welfare officers	8 Area education welfare officers
5 Court officers	1 Employment officer
51 Education welfare officers	41 Education welfare officers
4 Trainee education welfare officers	
III School population 61,100	*IV School population 42,600*
1 Principal education welfare officer	1 Chief education welfare officer
1 Deputy principal education welfare officer	2 Area education welfare officers
5 Senior education welfare officers	16 Education welfare officers
17 Education welfare officers	

SOURCE: Leonard Davis, *Community Care,* 18 February 1976.

Certainly the recommendations of the Ralphs Committee have begun to prove a considerable morale booster to the service. Since 1973 there has been enthusiasm among education welfare officers to undertake social work training and many have in fact done so, particularly on the Phase III social work courses at polytechnics.[8] Unfortunately, the shortage of places on professional social work courses and the limited educational backgrounds of some of the education welfare officers themselves have caused some setbacks, but the enthusiasm to become a fully professional social work service remains. Local authorities, too, have increased their establishments and introduced or stepped up secondment policies for training. During the past couple of years the CCETSW has also begun to promote interest in social work in the education setting and has actively encouraged interested colleges and universities to set aside 'options' for education social workers as they do for probation officers. The 1976 Conference of the Education Welfare Officers' National Association agreed to amalgamate with other associations (including that of the chief education welfare officers) by an overwhelming majority. The new association will be known as the National Association of Education Social Workers.

It is, however, worth mentioning that in the USA school social work has long been recognised as part of social work and this has naturally led to organisational differences and developments, some of which may yet spread to this country. Costin,[10] in making a plea for the reappraisal of assumptions concerning school social work, links the beginnings of school social work with industrialisation and compulsory school attendance. In the USA social workers in the settlement houses concerned themselves with the *relevance* of education to the child's present and future:

> Early definitions of school social work defined two phases of work. Firstly, interpreting to the school the child's out-of-school life; supplementing the teacher's knowledge of the child . . . so that she may be able to teach the whole child . . . . Secondly, the visiting teacher interprets to the parents the demands of the school and explains the particular difficulties and needs of the child.

(It is interesting that in the USA the school social worker has his or her origins as a visiting teacher. It is possible that this may develop here also.) By the 1920s the visiting teachers were firmly in the social work system and in the 1930s though retaining their name, they were avoiding the law-enforcement duties and the broad social environment and concentrating on casework within the school; indeed, they were gently chided for so doing by two well-known social work teachers, Charlotte Towle and Anthea Reynolds. During the 1940s and the 1950s school social work as a specialism within social casework was beginning to be clearly recognised:

> In short it involves helping the child take responsibility for that part of his problem that is appropriately his, helping his parents to feel the same concern felt by the school's personnel for the child's disequilibrium in school, helping parents and children utilise existing community agencies if the needs of the child can best be met this way, and helping the schools to individualise the child.[11]

Group work, too, was being used in the schools though the predominant form of social work was casework with the child and for the parents.

However, interest was beginning to develop in collaborating with other school personnel and during the 1950s attention began to be focused on deleterious school conditions. Costin quotes Taber as writing:

we tend to rob children of their individuality, their most precious possession . . . . Although we recognise the importance of adapting an educational programme to individual needs . . . we still have a tendency to provide education on a mass production and assembly line basis . . . . Our confusion and vaccillation over discipline are contagious to children . . . despite strides . . . made in developing parent teacher associations, there are still too many schools in which parents and teachers only have a nodding acquaintance.[12]

Such comments might well be written today by some of the radical educationalists in this country. There is a prevailing myth (which seems to be substantiated as regards education social work so far) that what happens in the USA tends to be reproduced ten years later in this country, suitably amended for our culture.

Tasks, location and an organisational basis for education social work

The dilemmas connected with the definition and boundaries between the tasks of education and social work form the basis of this book. At present, as has been shown, the statutory tasks connected with social work with children and their families are divided between the education and social service departments of the local authorities. Other tasks which are acknowledged to be social work tasks in relation to schoolchildren and their families are carried out in a more random way, according to the social work agency to which the family gets referral. While there is a problem in defining a task (or tasks) for education social work, there are really three separate areas which need consideration, although they are all linked. In our social policy related to children there has been a gradual shift towards caring for, rather than punishing children who commit what would be criminal offences if committed by adults. The 1969 Children and Young Persons Act (because of the incomplete implementation of a carefully integrated children's bill) has resulted in a situation which was not intended by either of the two major political parties. As has already been pointed out, society itself is divided about whether such children should be punished or not. All social policy related to children is subject to legislation and this implies not only 'power politics' between central and local government, but also political struggles and bargains at every level. As the community development projects have amply demonstrated, both education and social work are highly political activities and it is in the political arena that the vital decisions are made, not in the schools or social work departments.

Nevertheless, the three aspects of decisions related to establishing a basis for and defining the tasks of education social work and the priorities which are accorded to the allocation of resources, can be very much influenced by local activities and by the attitudes and views of the people concerned. First, there is the question of whether there are *discrete tasks* in connection with social work in connection with schoolchildren. Second, if there are such tasks, there is the question of the location of a functional base from which such tasks might be carried out. Third, there is the *organisational basis* on which such a service might operate; that is, of which system, the education system or the social work system, should education social work form a part.

(a) A task for education social work

The current tasks of the Education Welfare Service vary slightly from authority to authority but until recently have not been outlined anywhere with real clarity. Indeed, this is a reflection of the neglect and apathy with which the idea of setting up an Education Welfare Service has been received. In 1965 the ILEA commissioned Bedford College to investigate its welfare services for children and make proposals for their reorganisation. These proposals were never formally published, but were generally assumed to have involved changes of departmental boundaries and responsibilities between health and education which were politically unacceptable. This was two years after the LCC children's departments were transferred to the London boroughs, in the reorganisation of metropolitan London. Following an internal working party (under the then Assistant Education Officer, Mr W. R. Braide), the authority decided to amalgamate the school enquiry service and the school care organisers into a new-look Education Welfare Service. Again there seemed to be political implications in that the impending reorganisation of the London boroughs' social work services into social service departments was imminent. Unlike any other metropolitan area, the education services and the social services of Inner London are still quite separate and this is the focus of grave misgivings, political and otherwise. Furthermore, even within the ILEA itself, the social work with schools is separated into three areas. While these appear distinct within the ILEA, to those outside, particularly social workers, the divisions appear to have been left delineated for historical reasons rather than the needs of London schoolchildren. Social workers (formerly psychiatric social workers) working in the child guidance clinics and schools for the maladjusted, are in the Chief School Medical Officer's department and are all professionally trained. There are also social workers working with handicapped children (blind, deaf and physically handicapped). The largest section is the Education Welfare Service itself, established just prior to the social service departments. Nevertheless, only the new Education Welfare Service made an attempt to clarify its aims. Clegg and Megson write somewhat euphemistically of full co-operation with social services departments and of 'its function [being] seen as complementary to social services'.[13] Such was the intention. If in practice things did not quite work out that way, then this might be explained by the overwhelming reorganisational events of 1971, compounded by the social problems typical of any big city. The ILEA Education Welfare Service set out to assist the schools as follows:

1 By helping to link home and school.
2 By bringing to light incipient social distress of which absence from school may be one of the early signs.
3 By ensuring that parents are fully aware of the benefits to which they are entitled under the Education Acts or which may be obtainable through other social work agencies.
4 By ensuring that the authority's statutory duties in respect of school attendance and welfare benefits are carried out in accordance with good social work practice.
5 By setting out to establish proper channels of communication between schools and the borough social services departments and other agencies in the welfare field.[14]

While the Education Welfare Service units outside Inner London were not bedevilled by the complications of the split as between the ILEA and the Inner London boroughs, nor did they receive the advantages which accrued from the organisational attention given within London. Indeed, they did not begin to come in from what could be described as the professional cold until the report of the Ralphs Committee in 1973.

As has been already mentioned, during 1970 the Local Government Training Board set up a working party under Dr Lincoln Ralphs (now Sir T. Lincoln Ralphs) to consider the role and training of education welfare officers.[15] The committee reported in 1973 and in 1974 produced its training recommendations. The working party found the tasks of the education welfare service related to several functional areas:

1 school attendance	7 free meals
2 handicapped children	8 maintenance (i.e., education
3 court proceedings	grants)
4 transport (to and	9 placement of children
from school)	10 child neglect
5 clothing	11 extra distant pupils
6 child employment	12 nursery education

They came to the conclusion that the tasks of the Education Welfare Service were primarily of a social work nature and made recommendations that staff should be trained as professional social workers, but with specific additional knowledge and skills to enable them to practise in an educational setting. This additional knowledge was specified as educational theory of practice, sociology of education, educational law and administration and the education of children with special needs. The working party saw the future tasks of the education welfare officer as developing in two specific areas:

1   those which education welfare officers already shared with educational and medical specialists; for instance
    (i)   assessment, treatment and after-care of handicapped children;
    (ii) greater assistance to the schools in helping them to meet more effectively the social needs of the individuals and the community within which the school is based;
    (iii) greater support to the teacher dealing with these problems experienced collectively or individually by the children.
2   the need to expand current activities to a wider range of children by
    (i)   advising on schooling, particularly at transfer stages in the child's educational career;
    (ii) assessing the social needs of younger children in order to assist heads to select children for places in primary schools and classes.

Thus the envisaged role and function of the education welfare officer would seem to overlap not only with the social workers in social service departments but also with the tasks of the education visitor as described by Halsey[16] and others.

It may well be that when the expanded programme for the under-fives is sufficiently developed, there will be a need for someone with both education and social work expertise to make recommendations as regards an appropriate choice between day care, nursery school, nursery class or pre-school playgroup for a particular child. At present the young children in most need (i.e., those in inner cities) are increasingly lucky to obtain a place in any of these, let alone have a choice. Indeed, it is in this vital area of family stress that the educational cuts are most stringent.

One of the most useful definitions of the task of education social work has been made by Lyons[17] in her report on her work in the Deptford EPA project with primary schools. Lyons, an education welfare officer in the ILEA, was seconded by the Authority to work in the project team, and she acted as a community-based social worker ancillary to the existing education and social services (the project was primarily conducted before the Seebohm reorganisation). Lyons's task was to service three of the project's infant schools. She began defining her task in relation to the aims of the EPA projects and in particular to those of the director of the Deptford project (Charles Betty). Lyons disagrees with Halsey, who writes that social workers are only concerned with social breakdown, expressing the view that this is too narrow a definition, particularly as regards the potential of education social work. The local and reformulated aims of his/her role and task were, she said, based on the following assumptions and questions:

(i) School is a universal experience—the potential work load of an education social worker is the whole school population. Is there any difference between those children identified by teachers as raising problems in school and those whom a social worker might identify as 'at risk' socially?

(ii) A child's home circumstances and the relationship between the home and the school has some significance in the child's adaptation to and progress in the educational environment (see Green's findings). What are the home circumstances and the home/school relationships like, and can a social worker do anything to enable some improvement to take place in either or both, if necessary?

(iii) Comparatively few teachers have had the personal experience of the social services and/or professional contact with social workers. Their understanding of the structure of the social services and methods of social work and perception of the role of the social worker may therefore be limited. Can an education social worker, by being readily available to teachers, improve the amount of information available to them and thus their understanding of this area of work?

(iv) Although all social workers have had experience of the educational environment themselves, they sometimes fail to acknowledge the important part which school plays in the lives of children with whose families they are working.

Can the education social worker encourage closer contact between teachers and social workers in general in the interests of the children and families with whom they are both concerned?

(v) Little has been written about the functioning of an education social worker—in fact it is hardly a recognised sub-division of social work. Could the project's social worker's action be documented to provide further information about the relationships between parents, teachers and social workers and details about the possible scope of work of an education social worker in particular?

Within this broad aim of contributing to attempts to enable children to take full advantage of their educational opportunities, the projects social worker's aims were finally defined as

(a) to increase home/school contact and understanding or otherwise enable parents to participate more fully in their children's education.

(b) to examine further the relationship between education, social work and the school, and to illustrate ways in which a social worker can assist in the assessment and solution of problems experienced in E.P.A. schools.

Lyons worked with only specific infants schools and for the time limit of the project (1968-71) unfortunately she was not carrying out the usual statutory duties of an education welfare officer and, partly because the project was developing and partly because of the uniqueness of her role, there was an inevitable delay in referrals. The 184 referrals Lyons classified as follows:

29% Social problems (housing or financial difficulties)
29% Behaviour problems (varying from aggressive to withdrawn)
19% Educational problems (needing special education, poor progress and also cases of lack of contact between home and school)
13% Medical problems (child's need for medical treatment and possible failure to receive it)
10% Attendance problems (poor attendance and/or persistent lateness).

Lyons writes in conclusion that

education social workers should not only perform existing functions under the Education Act more effectively . . . but also place greater emphasis on the consultation aspects of their role in relation to school staff, and their availability to discuss and deal with a wider range of problems than those usually referred. Finally, the importance of their liaison role both between home and school and with colleagues in a wider community.

Lyons, thus, effectively subsumes the tasks of the education visitor within the role of education social worker.

Fitzherbert,[18] writing of her work with the Immigrant/Home School Action research project in Ealing, also conducted in primary schools, expressed similar views to Lyons. She also pointed out that

teachers could hardly be expected to take on whole families, yet this is what is needed. To focus only on the child in school means in many cases healing the symptoms rather than the cause of the problem. All student teachers should be taught two basic skills: how to recognise social deprivation in their pupils and how to refer children whose problems frequently become apparent in the classroom first. At the same time social workers should include teachers in their planning for families known to them.

Fitzherbert also pointed out that in many ways it is more acceptable and less stigmatising for families in difficulties if they are visited by someone from the school: 'It is not such an admission of failure to let the school know you are in trouble'.

In October 1973, in response to a request from the government, BASW set up a working party 'to explore the relationship between social work services and schools, to consider how social work services can best be provided and how the administration of educational and social services can best be correlated'.

The working party outlined the need for social work help in relation to behavioural problems and listed the help available in relation to material aid, welfare rights and benefits. As has been mentioned already, they also referred specifically to truancy, and described the current organisation as divided between an education welfare service and the social service departments. While describing the role of counselling and recognising the importance of such a role, they did comment on the inside/outside school conflict for such a person and pointed out that this was both the role of teaching and social work coverage. They stressed the need to 'straddle both camps'.

The working party particularly stressed the need for co-operation between schools and social work agencies over children with special needs, and BASW have now set up a special interest group on social work within the education system.

The people in the system

At the invitation of the ILEA, during late 1972 and early 1973 I was social work consultant to an organisation and methods review of the Education Welfare Service. My task was to provide guidelines on the professional functions for the education welfare officers in each grade and to make recommendations regarding their workloads. During the course of the review I formed the opinion that not only was there a social work content in the role and function of the Education Welfare Service, but (subject to the introduction of professionally trained social work staff and certain other conditions) the Education Welfare Service nationally has considerable scope as an early-warning system and service for children at risk.[19]

In the area of primary social breakdown (i.e., for children at risk), there does seem to be a role for a specialist social worker in close touch with the schools, having easy access to information, the people in the education system, and, of course, to schoolchildren and their families. The tasks such a worker might carry out would be as follows:

1 Consultation with school staff. Plowden, Lyons and others have made out a clear case for such a role to be undertaken by a social worker.
2 Particularised support and consultation, possibly supervision (in the social work sense) of the school counsellor or home/school liaison teacher.
3 In conjunction with school staff and school psychological and medical service, running 'social work surgeries' based in schools themselves. Families might be referred by any members of the school team—or could refer themselves.
4 Informing parents of their rights and responsibilities and the welfare facilities under the Education Acts, particularly in relation to child guidance, special education, suspensions, non-attendance, free dinners, clothing, etc.
5 Prophylactic and 'crisis' work with children and their families at risk.
6 General advice and consultation on home/school relations because of particularised knowledge of the social conditions of the area which the school serves.
7 Advice, liaison and consultation with local social work agencies about school policy and organisation.
8 Whether or not the education welfare officer might also undertake statutory duties in connection with compulsory education would, of course, depend on the organisational basis of the service.

It is perhaps interesting to note here that a recent government review document recommended in principle the suggestion 'that in cases where the main cause of concern is a child's failure to attend school, the education welfare service should be able to be designated supervisor'.[20]

Recent work in the USA has indicated the possibility of further important tasks for the education social worker, particularly in connection with school/community relations. Costin writes:

the schools' purpose is to provide a life setting for teaching and learning and the attainment of competence. Social work's *obligation* [my italics] is to help make the school a rich and stimulating environment for children and young people in which they can prepare themselves for the world in which they have to live.[21]

She gives as an instance the ways in which social workers 'can assume active responsibility for consultation with administrators and teachers in the *formulation of school policy as that directly affects the welfare of the pupils* . . [and] . . . renewed attention . . . to liaise among home, school and community'. According to Costin, the largest groups—that is, the groups towards which education social workers might direct their attention—are the pre-school children, neglected and deprived children and the deprived middle classes.

Bielecki also points out the opportunities which school social workers have for engaging and involving teenagers in secondary schools:

The social worker with his training in assessment of behaviour and interpersonal relationships skills can serve as a neutral, non-authoritarian observer, who can assess the tone and feeling of the high school community [secondary school], its needs, and the possible solution to the problem by listening to, observing and interacting with students and faculty [pupils, staff] and administrators. With the skills in mediation necessary for parent-child conflicts, the social worker can become a liaison between students and faculty or administration.[22]

While there are particular difficulties in the USA in relation to racial problems, there are also similar issues at stake here, including lack of communication between Western culturally oriented schools and the predominantly immigrant communities that some of them serve. For instance, it is possible that some of the inflexible positions taken up both by schools and by parents of adolescent Asian girls might have been mediated and resolved more easily through the early intervention of education social workers. Indeed, Cheetham,[23] in writing of social work with immigrants, describes just such a situation where the social worker (agency unspecified) was eventually able to bring about a happy resolution.

Certainly there is a clear *role* for a boundary worker (or perhaps workers) between schools and the communities, though whether or not that boundary worker should be a social worker is a matter of debate. From the results of a recent research project which they conducted in relation to secondary schools in Lancashire, Rose, Marshall et al.[24] conclude that there is a specialist role for social work in connection with schools. Over a period of four years (from 1965 onwards) an eventual total of ten social workers were attached to four secondary schools, with two 'control' schools carrying out social work with children referred to them by the school staff as maladjusted or delinquent. It is perhaps important to note (as the authors themselves comment) that the area had somewhat restricted social services. The research findings clearly show that the social workers were successful in reducing the levels of delinquency and poor attendance. Not only was this no mean achievement, but the research design employed to assess the results is one of the few successful attempts actually to evaluate the usefulness of social work intervention.

Much of the 'social work' carried out by the workers in Rose and Marshall's study varied considerably despite the intention of the research that the work should be mainly 'casework'. The reasons for such variety are multiple and indeed indicative of the problems of undertaking any interventive work in this boundary area. The 'social work' intervention seemed as much dictated by the role the 'social worker' was expected to carry out in the school as by the 'needs' of the children referred. While these roles were naturally influenced by the organisation of the school and especially by the attitude and style of the head, they are also likely to have been influenced by the backgrounds of the workers, which were varied. Only two, in fact, were already social workers (in the sense of being professionally trained as such), two were teacher/social workers (that is, trained teachers who had done social work as their main subject at college), one was a community worker, one a group worker and the others were not trained in social work. This variety itself is interesting and not atypical of the backgrounds of the people who work in the boundary area, but it provides little clarification as to what is teaching and what is social work. Indeed much of the work undertaken by these 'social workers' could and would be described as counselling or even pastoral care, and thus the research seems to provide further evidence of the overlap between education and social work.

(b) The functional location base of social work in connection with schools

A central question of the functional location base of school social work is whether the service should be carried out from within a school, which organisationally dovetails with the school system, or whether the service should be area based. A school-based service might centre on a school, or more likely a group of schools, for instance a secondary school (increasingly likely to be comprehensive) and its group of primary schools. The alternative model is an area-based service, a similar model to the reorganised social service departments, and indeed in many cases co-terminous with their boundaries. The *school-based* service would have the following advantages:

1 The social worker would have easy access to all educational records.

2 He or she would be known to the staff, would be acceptable to them and could easily liaise and consult with them.

3 He or she would have easy opportunity to get to know the child in school.

4 The service could easily focus on the individual child, particularly within the school setting.

5 He or she would also have easy opportunity for contact with parents informally.

6 He or she would be seen by the children and their families as being directly connected with the school. This would, of course, have advantages and disadvantages, but either would be preferable to the social worker being seen as totally unconnected to the school.

7 As with the medical social worker in hospitals, the education social worker would require and quickly acquire specialist knowledge in relation to the setting in which he or she worked (i.e., the school), which would be of advantage to both the setting and the clients.

8 Problems related to school attendance could be immediately considered and screened as regards patterns of non-attendance or the current difficulties of the school climate.

Should the social work be *area based* there would be the following advantages:

1 The possibility of relationships being established with whole families, which would avoid duplication of social workers.

2 Easy links could be made with other social work agencies in the area.

3 The social worker would have knowledge and easy access to the local resources available to children and their families.

4 In the case of primary schools who serve the children and their families local to the school, there would also be easy links with the schools.

5 Knowledge of the demography and social conditions of the area would be easily obtained.

6 Problems related to school attendance could be seen as part of sub-cultural 'norms', family patterns, or the failure of the school to perform its educational tasks appropriately.

7 The social worker could easily keep in touch with developments in social work practice.

As can be seen, there are at present advantages and disadvantages in connection with both models. If the social worker is based within the school or a group of schools, there is a danger of the social worker becoming too identified and integral with the school system. This might result in the workers failing to be effective in their boundary functions—that of building bridges between the school and the families of the schoolchildren, between the community and the school, and between the school and other social work agencies. There is also the possibility that *some* families in difficulties would perceive them as part of the school and so would decline offers and overtures made to them. Further, the social workers would not be able to work with all the schoolchildren in the family or with the *family* problems (as envisaged by the Seebohm Report). On the other hand, social workers who were area based would be unlikely to form good relationships with the school staff, partly because there would be so many social workers connected with the school. This would probably lead to continuation of the present ignorance and misunderstanding on both sides about the role and function of teachers and of social workers. It would almost certainly preclude the possibility of the development of a consultative role *vis à vis* the school staff (unless the social worker were to be specifically appointed to undertake such tasks).

In either case the secondary schools as currently placed are often at a disadvantage because of the wide catchment area they serve. Should the social workers be school based, the area they would need to cover would be so diffuse as to prevent the development of any coherent knowledge of the demography and social conditions of the area. Should they be area based, it is unlikely that they would even be familiar with the secondary schools that the children in the family attend. This would also probably be the case for special schools. The developing practice of appointing school counsellors in secondary schools would go some way to meet these difficulties but, if, as Miller[25] urges, adolescence offers the opportunity of a second chance to the disturbed young person, then it is crucial that help should be quickly available to the adolescent in difficulties. As has already been said, adolescence is one of the crucial identity crises, and it is often possible to help the adolescent free himself or herself from a disturbed or troubled family background, where it may not be possible to help the family as a whole.

Various models are already functioning. The BASW working party report that in Glasgow teams of education social workers from the social service departments are *attached* to secondary schools and their feeder primary schools. In the research project conducted by Rose and Marshall in Lancashire, the service was school based, although the research was carried out during the period just prior to and just after the foundation of social service departments, and in an area which had a comparatively underdeveloped children's department. In Coventry the social services department has appointed special school-based liaison officers. The ILEA school health service has appointed school social workers to the physically handicapped schools, who are appointed by the London boroughs and seconded back to these schools for 75 per cent of their time, being based in the special service area teams, where they spend the other 25 per cent of their time. The ILEA Education Welfare Service has its own area-based teams, but are also experimenting with some school-based projects. What seems to be of the utmost importance is that all these experiments should be monitored and assessed and it may well be that different models are appropriate in different areas, perhaps according to size and the organisation of the school system.

Nevertheless, the issue of whether education social work should be area or school based is meaningless unless there are enough social workers to staff such a service, regardless of where they are based. As Davis showed in his survey, at present some education welfare officers service up to ten or more schools and very few schools indeed (and those mostly special schools) have a full-time social worker appointed to undertake the social work for that school. Many education welfare officers talk of 'not being able to bring all the work out of a school' and come to dread the referrals from the teachers, which are part of their role and function. As the BASW working document[26] states, 'the real question is how can we afford *not* to have a school social work service, not how can we afford to have one'.

Unfortunately the working of the 1969 Children and Young Persons Act has not improved relationships between schools and social workers of any kind, and has certainly resulted in further tensions between social service departments and the Education Welfare Service. Nevertheless, alongside this is the gradual development of joint projects between teachers and social workers. There is also an increased interest and awareness in each other's work, particularly among the young (and perhaps more radical) teachers and social workers, as is evidenced by their membership of organisations like the Child Poverty Action Group.

Finally, there is the question of the best organisational basis for a system to promote and maintain efficient administration and accountability in such a service.

(c) The organisational basis of the education welfare service

Since 1970 there has been much debate about the organisational and administrative base of the Education Welfare Service. This has incidentally brought the service to the attention of social workers and teachers and others. In 1972 the government asked the views of various interested parties as to the best organisational base for an Education Welfare Service. They pointed out the two aspects of its task—carrying out the statutory functions of the education department in relation to school attendance, and various other duties such as assessing claims for free school meals and clothing entitlement, education maintenance allowances and assistance with the cost of clothing, etc. They also pointed out the supportive social work which the education welfare officers give to schoolchildren and their families. The government distinguished between the assignment of duties to local authority committees, which is determined by statute, and the responsibilities with regard to attendance at schools and the allocation of duties to staff, which is not.

The two associations concerned with the Education Welfare Service (the National Association of Chief Education Welfare Officers and the National Association of Education Welfare Officers), while stressing the social work nature of their task and their need for training, have stated that they would prefer to remain within the education system. Naturally the Association of Education Committees have stated a similar preference. So far the recommendations of the various teachers' organisations have not been made public. BASW set up the working party which produced the working document, from which quotations have already been made, and which asked for reactions and views so that final recommendations could be made to the government.

It is difficult to see the organisational issues clearly, as they often are obscured by the inadequacies of the service both in quality and quantity and confused by the other issues already discussed.

The advantages for education social work of remaining within the education system are:

1 Close organisational links with educational administration.
2 Close organisational links with the school.
3 Being seen by schoolchildren and their families as part of the school system.
4 Schoolchildren and their families also having some choice

regarding the social work agency with which they become involved.

5 Opportunities for informal consultation and referral at the stage of primary breakdown.

6 Exclusive focus on the task—social work with children and their families—and therefore no danger of this specialism being neglected.

7 Opportunities for negotiation between the two systems as to which 'style' of intervention might be more appropriate.

8 Close organisational links with educational resources, tutorial classes, home teachers, special schools, etc.

Most personnel in the education system (including the education welfare officers themselves) want this form of organisation at present.

The advantages for education social work being transferred to the social work departments are:

1 Close organisational links with other statutory social work for children and their families.

2 Close organisational links with community homes.

3 Close organisational links with available social work resources, day care, foster parents, etc.

4 Close organisational links with local authority social workers and access to their greater professional and training facilities.

5 The current division of statutory responsibilities in relation to schoolchildren and their families would be avoided—would be in accordance with the recommendations and philosophy of the Seebohm Committee: that social work with the family problems should be the responsibility of one department so children of the same family who are in different schools could be dealt with by the same social worker.

6 The service would not be seen as part of the school service.

7 The resulting organisational links would provide a better career structure for social workers in that they could more easily move between different sub-systems within the system.

Most professionally trained social workers seem to think this is ultimately advisable.

As in the question of the location of the functional base of education social work, there are serious disadvantages to both models. Should education social work remain in the education system as at present, the division between aspects of social work with children and their families would be retained. There are also serious doubts as to the 'good-will' of the education system towards the service, particularly in these days of economic stringency and because of the long history of neglect. There is also the very real danger of the education social worker becoming too identified with the schools, to the detriment of serving the community and home/ school relations.

During the past few years there has been considerable debate as to whether the social work connected with education (i.e., schools) should be totally incorporated within the social service departments. Indeed at the time of their inauguration a number of authorities made such a change in their organisation. This caused much concern and anger to many educationalists and seems to have proved premature and ill-thought-out. Several of these authorities when amalgamated with others in 1974 reverted to the more traditional pattern of organisation. In only three does the Social Services department provide a full social work service to schools. There is also currently much concern that the social service departments are beset with problems related to their social work tasks in relation to areas of the population other than children and their families, since they also have statutory functions to carry out in relation to the mentally ill, the elderly and the disabled. Many educationalists (and others) are of the opinion that, even if children were referred earlier in the process of social breakdown, the help they need would not be available because the social service departments are virtually running a crisis service because of lack of trained staff and resources. There are also criticisms of the monolithic structure of social service departments and the struggles with bureaucracy. However, the latter criticism could also be levelled at social work within the education system.

The real crux of the matter is the question of accountability. As the BASW working party state:

> part of the schools' task is to establish social control [see also Chapter 1] and it is difficult to differentiate what is being done for the sake of the individual and what is being done for the sake of the institution. The controlling aspect of school is demonstrated by the hierarchical system which exists in most schools. The head teacher has almost total power . . . and to share power is to weaken the ability to improve control . . . . The head teacher frequently spends much of his time defining the boundaries of the institution, controlling what comes in and what goes out.[27]

Saltmarsh[28] also raises this issue, pointing out that heads often find the conflict inherent in situations where differences of opinion arise between social workers and heads hard to tolerate; such is the tradition of their autonomy and accountability. The BASW working party points out that 'society wants things this way as it needs to be assured that all is under control at school . . . and that the head "is personally responsible"'. Such a 'collusion between social and institutional pressures has little to do with the interests of the individual child'.

Linked with the question of accountability is that of confidentiality. A traditional social work principle is that information given to social workers by their clients should not be passed on without their permission and agreement. Of recent years social workers have increasingly found themselves in some dilemmas regarding such confidentiality, which in any case has never been given the legal protection that is afforded to doctors and lawyers. Perhaps particularly since the rapid increase in their statutory powers, social workers have become more confused over defining the circumstances and criteria when such 'secrets' may (or must) be passed on to others. More recently particular concern has been expressed over the ready availability of information within the social service departments. However, anxiety over non-accidental injury to children has served to obscure some of this concern, without giving equally clear leads to social workers, who have been traditionally encouraged to build up trusting relationships with their clients, on the understanding that what passes between them is confidential. Nevertheless, despite this uncertainty, professional social workers would not lightly allow themselves to work in situations where the values of another system (i.e., that of education) should govern both when and to whom confidential information should be passed on. This thorny issue will be discussed further in the next chapter.

In some ways, as has already been pointed out, education social workers working alongside teachers are in a similar position to that of medical social workers in the hospital setting. Indeed, the traditional powers of the head are not dissimilar to those society has also accorded to the doctor, although recently the powers of the doctor have begun to diminish. Medical social workers, too, have been involved in a long struggle to establish their autonomy and freedom to practise according to their own value systems, which may also be at variance with that of the doctors at times. Since April 1974 while remaining located in the hospitals and given the 'protection of service' they are actually employed by the social service departments and are therefore organisationally part of the local authority system. It is too soon yet to see how this double accountability (for the doctor still has the ultimate authority for the patient in hospital) will work out, though there are conflicting criticisms both ways and these have been exacerbated by the departure of some medical social workers because of the level of salary scale offered to them by their new employers. Certainly Seebohm seemed to envisage a similar arrangement for education social work. What seems more important is that an effective and professional service should be provided in relation to schoolchildren and their families and that the decisions regarding organisational issues should be made on the grounds of carefully evaluated effectiveness, not on those of political expediency or economy.

A recent statement by the Under-secretary of State at the DES appears to suggest that the DES and the DHSS now accept that the Education Welfare Service should not be incorporated into the social service departments: 'It is now apparent that the decision has been made on the separate existence of an education welfare service'. The president of the National Association of Chief Education Welfare Officers said:

> I firmly believe that as a profession we were fortunate—that the service of education was fortunate, and that ultimately the children being educated were fortunate—that the education service survived the Seebohm concept of an all-embracing social work agency.[29]

Chapter five

Teachers and social workers

Introduction

While this section will focus predominantly on the 'professionals' within the system, it is also important to see teachers and social workers within the context of the other people in the system. These others, while always important, particularly the administrative staff, can at times outweigh the professionals either in numerical terms (as happens frequently within the social work system) or in terms of power (as can happen within both systems, particularly the education system, where professional decisions are often overruled). The question of the professional's somewhat uneasy co-existence within the bureaucratic systems of the local education and social service departments will be considered later, but it is important to consider the conflicts of professional and political values which seem to be arising all too frequently within local authority structures and are likely to increase as a result of the hardening of financial arteries which is the current economic situation. Perhaps partly because of the difficulties surrounding the definition of the educational and social work tasks, but also because of the political nature of both education and social work (as discussed in the first chapter), the balance of power between elected representatives and professionals regarding the execution of practice and decision making seems to be a much more delicate and potentially conflictual exercise than within other local authority departments.

The Tyndale enquiry revealed the power of the local politicians in relation to events at the school.[1] While education in London is idiosyncratic in its organisation because of the existence of the ILEA, it is clear that throughout the country the elected members and particularly those who are school managers wield a great deal of power, far more than either the administrative staff or professional teachers. The position of school managers was considered by the

Taylor Committee.[2] In the case of the enquiry into the death of Steven Meurs,[3] the inadequacy of resources and the apparent lack of recognition of this fact by the elected representatives, seems to have been a considerable factor. Yet it was to the failure of communications among the departments that the cause of his death was largely attributed.

It is important to recognise at the outset that one of the crucial differences between the education and the social work systems is their different approach to the recruitment of the professionals who perform the central tasks of the two services. The state education system, albeit at the insistence of the teachers' unions and associations, has since 1970 only employed qualified teachers in the schools. At that time a number of teachers, notably those 'qualified' by being graduates in their subject, were blanketed in. This has on the whole protected standards, though to a lesser extent the employment prospects for teachers in the late 1970s and early 1980s. However, it has also restricted the development of innovations which might involve the use of non-teachers, even other professionals such as social workers. This exclusiveness, too, seems to have led in part to a degree of elitism in some establishments such as residential special schools, where the teachers are considered of higher status than the other staff, such as the residential child care social workers. However, in social service departments particularly, no such exclusiveness exists. While some departments employ predominantly qualified social workers plus a few trainees (unqualified social workers on short-term contract prior to going on professional training courses), others employ many unqualified social workers, sometimes up to more than half their social work establishment. Some of these are teachers—and their numbers are likely to increase as the result ot teacher unemployment. While the senior and management staff may be predominantly highly skilled and professionally qualified, much of the day-to-day work with clients is carried out either by unqualified staff or by those who have only qualified very recently. Indeed, one of the major criticisms of the social service departments following the Seebohm reorganisation is that there are too many chiefs and not enough indians. This situation seems to be beginning to improve, anyway in areas where adequate resources enabled shrewd training policies to be formulated during the period of rapid expansion from 1970 to 1975, but there are other authorities where the difficulties outlined seem destined to continue, until perhaps the supply of trained social workers, coupled with economic restrictions, squeezes them out of the urban areas where they predominantly seem to cluster. In the present economic uncertainty it is hard to predict the future level of trained social workers.

Bureaucracy

By far the majority of 'non-professional' personnel employed in both the education and the social service systems are administrators. In both systems the administrative personnel may or may not be professionally qualified, though in the case of social service departments there was a recommendation in the Seebohm Report that Directors of Social Services should be professionally qualified social workers whenever possible. While the 'managers' in both systems (heads and the inspectorate in the case of education, and area directors and social service advisers in the case of social service departments) are professionals, generally speaking the purely administrative personnel are not. Both teachers and social workers most frequently work in large bureaucratic organisations in which they co-exist somewhat uncomfortably, side by side with the administrators, who are both trained within and used to local authority structures, with their chain of accountability being passed 'upwards' to the democratically elected representatives. In such structures, with their carefully controlled areas of discretion and the inevitable limitation of autonomy, the logement of two developing professions presents an uneasy partnership. Cooper[4] writes: 'Conflict or accommodation between social work values and skills and managerial values and methods will be worked out in a local government setting and there is no escape.' The Tyndale enquiry has brought to the surface the uneasy rumblings of a similar nature within the education system.

Bureaucratic rules and authority, according to Toren,[5] are often seen as infringing upon the professional's freedom to apply his knowledge and skills according to his judgment and convictions. Toren considers both social work and teaching as semi-professions. The argument for such a definition will be considered later, but she points out that semi-professionalism

> denotes that the profession does not rest on a firm theoretical knowledge base; the period of training is relatively short; the members cannot claim a monopoly of exclusive skills and the special area of their competence is less well defined than as compared with fully fledged professions.

She describes such a semi-professional state as heteronomy and points out that such members are guided from without by administrative rules and superiors in the hierarchy as well as by internalised professionalised norms from within. However, Toren also points out that '*direct* supervision in semi-professionals is always carried out by senior ex-professionals who have risen from the ranks'—e.g., the head or the senior or principal social worker. Toren's argument also reveals that teachers and social workers are not controlled to the same degree in the performance of all their tasks. Indeed, it is in administrative matters rather than in the direct execution of their professional contacts with their pupils and clients that they are subject to such differential zoning of control. She further points out that social work is identified in the minds of the public as a feminine profession and that the recent entrants into the profession from the lower social strata may have had a negative influence on the profession's prestige. While this may be a dubious argument and perhaps more applicable to the USA, about which Toren was writing, it could be similarly applied to the teaching profession.

Finally, Toren points out that one of the main features of 'bureaucratic organisations is that the work of its members is directed by a set of universalistic rules and generalised procedures' which 'can only be maintained if the work is specific and routine'. The human relations professions do not readily lend themselves to such routinisation without putting into jeopardy the value system on which their professional philosophy is based.

Professionalism

While Toren, writing of social workers, and Lortie,[6] writing of teachers, are referring to American social work and school systems, there seem to be many similarities with their English counterparts. Lortie locates certain issues which must be resolved in all occupations:

1 How favourably the occupation relates to the employment market.
2 The nature of the knowledge and skill possessed by the members of that occupation.
3 The relation established to the political authorities.
4 The extent to which those performing similar activities influence the careers of members of the occupation.

He describes the socialisation of teachers as an incomplete sub-culture, and points out the importance placed by many of the established professions on an internalised professional conscience: 'Established professions take few chances with newcomers; [they] are subjected to years of scrutiny.' He adds: 'the system of supervising beginning teachers does not suggest a precise instrument of work socialisation through which professional colleagues engage in on the spot assistance to the newcomer'.

Etzioni[7] considers that both teaching and social work are semi-professions, pointing out that while the 'basis of professional authority is knowledge', the 'relationship between administrative and professional authority' is affected by the kind of knowledge the professional has:

Pure professional organisations are primarily devoted to the creation and application of knowledge, their professionals are usually protected in their work by the guarantee of privileged communication and they are often concerned with matters of life and death. Semi-professional organisations are more concerned with communication and to a lesser extent the application of knowledge; their professionals are less likely to be guaranteed the right of privileged communications and they are rarely directly concerned with matters of life and death.

When professional authority is based on shorter training, involves values other than life or death and covers the communication of knowledge, then it is related to the administrative structure in a different way. The semi-professional has less autonomy and is more subject to discretion and supervision from higher ranks (e.g., heads and senior social workers) and also such semi-professionals often have skills and personality traits more compatible with such organisations, although they are not without strain. Such organisations are 'run more frequently by the semi-professionals themselves rather than by others'. Toren writes of semi-professionalism and social work and quotes Carr Saunders's differentiation of four major types of profession:

1 the established professions, their practice based on theoretical study (law, medicine);
2 the new professions (engineering, chemistry, accounting);
3 the semi-professions who replace theoretical knowledge with technical skill (teaching, social work, nursing);
4 the would-be professions which require neither theoretical study nor the acquisition of exact techniques but rather familiarity with modern practice in business administration (hospital managers, sales managers).[8]

Greenwood gives a model of professionalism consisting of five components:

1 a basis of systematic theory;
2 authority recognised by the clientele of the professional group;
3 broader community sanction and approval of this authority;
4 a code of ethics regulating relationships of professionals with clients and colleagues;
5 a professional culture sustained by formal professional associations.[9]

Toren, in writing of social work as a semi-profession, points out that social work possesses some of these attributes but also comments that different observers come to different conclusions. Both professions lack the basis of a systematic theory which is acknowledged as exclusive to them. Indeed much of the knowledge base relevant to *both* professions comes from the social sciences, in particular psychology and sociology. On the other hand, both professions have a developing *practice* theory in relation to their 'technical' skills.

Before considering Greenwood's second and third points it is necessary to consider the question of authority. While Etzioni *et al.* consider the possession of knowledge as one of the factors on which the public recognition of authority is based, they also point out the lack of unique and exclusive knowledge in either teaching or social work. Foren and Bailey,[10] in writing of authority in relation to social casework, differentiate several meanings of the word 'authority'. They point out that while power and authority are closely connected, they are nevertheless distinct. The aspect of the power of teachers and social workers in relation to the definition of social breakdown has been discussed (in Chapter 2), but the basis of their authority has not been considered. Foren and Bailey write of a kind of 'authority which implies the right to be obeyed or to be believed'. In this sense, authority is taken to mean that a person possessing such authority is recognised by general consensus to have some degree of coercive power, as long as it is kept within the limits of popular toleration; and this is rarely challenged. They also describe another kind of authority: 'to an actor, whose personal achievements and ability have marked him out as an expert'. This expertise is conferred by some form of accreditation and is 'usually maintained by respect for the intellectual or other personal qualities of the expert and by occasional demonstrations of his powers'. It would seem then that teachers and social workers have both forms of authority; but Foren and Bailey go on to describe another aspect of authority and that is the acceptor's perception of the source of that authority. This, of course, is also bound up with the crucial issue of teachers and social workers as agents of social control. At the present time it would appear that it is the acceptor's perception of the authority which is changing. The professional associations of both teachers and social workers are much preoccupied with professional codes of conduct and are considering formalised procedures whereby miscreants can be 'struck off' for certain malpractices, as can doctors and lawyers. At present the final responsibility for regulating the relationships with such professionals and their clients rests with the employing bodies. The National Union of Teachers (NUT) do provide a *Handbook of School Administration*[11] which offers guidance and basic facts relating to administrative practices, especially concerning common problems such as corporal punishment and exclusion from school. BASW too have compiled a *Code of Ethics*[12] and have recently been concerned with safeguarding both the standards of the profession and the rights of its members. The existence of such professional organisations as the NUT, BASW and the Association of Schoolmasters and Schoolmistresses are an indication that a professional culture, such as Greenwood describes, does indeed exist. However, it also appears that these organisations are at present preoccupied with what might be described as primary issues of definition, mainly connected with the exclusiveness of the profession. Both teachers and social workers seem divided about just how unionised they want to become, although is appears that the unionisation movement does seem to be gathering momentum. In social work especially there is a significant body of opinion which thinks that social workers are too preoccupied with developing their 'progress' towards professionalisation and that this is not only at the expense of the service they provide, but also increases the social distance between them and their clients. This approach also discourages the enhancement of self-help groups amongst clients. Finally, in the development of the professional associations it would seem that the hierarchical structures are being perpetuated while the power is being dispersed; for instance, there are separate organisations for headmasters and headmistresses and as between the public and private sectors of education, and also for the directors of social service departments.

While many of the concurrent uncertainties in both teaching and social work may stem from other sources, in particular the current economic stringencies, some undoubtedly seem to be due to their semi-professional status. As has been stated, both are uncertain about the definition of their professional areas of competence and task and about their authority and the public sanction for it. While social workers, in particular, have been given more and more statutory duties and responsibilities, it is generally recognised that they have not been given the necessary additional resources necessary to carry out these extra duties. Both systems have been subject to massive reorganisation resulting from legislative changes in response to political issues related to equalising educational opportunities and the redistribution of resources. While many of these changes have presented challenges and opportunities, some of which have been grasped, they have followed in quick succession and have often been carried out for reasons of political expediency rather than being both based and timed by reflective response to the need for change.

Perhaps the most notable current issue is the apparent public mistrust of teachers and social workers, to the detriment of their credibility. It would seem that their expertise is being both devalued and diminished. Social work in particular has been subjected to a series of public or semi-public inquiries resulting from the death of clients, many of them children. Since the inquiry into the care and supervision provided in relation to Maria Colwell, there have been a number of others, mostly concerned with the death from neglect or non-accidental injury of young children, in which social workers' expertise has been called into question and criticised.

The Chairman of the Tyndale enquiry was specifically required by his terms of reference 'to conduct a Public Inquiry into the teaching, organisation and management of the William Tyndale Junior and Infants Schools'. While in no way wishing to criticise the subsequent report, which was not only meticulous in its thoroughness, but also scrupulous in attempting to differentiate between what might be described as professional judgments regarding educational methods and the behaviour of the professionals concerned, one might wish to query whether a lawyer (albeit a distinguished one) would automatically be the best person to carry out such an inquiry. It is true that the chairman was assisted by two advisors (one of whom was himself a head teacher), but it would be a service to possible future inquiries if some of these issues could be debated. With regard to social work, it could not be said that all the inquiries have been documented with the elaborate care and consideration which the Tyndale chairman lent to his task. While it is undeniable that when failures in services do occur some inquiries should be undertaken, and that both social workers and teachers should, of course, be accountable for their actions, it is open to doubt and to debate whether the methods chosen to consider such issues have been the appropriate ones. It is also open to question whether a public inquiry conducted under conditions customarily prevailing in a court of law (for instance, the adversary model), but not subject to a court's constraints, is the appropriate way to ascertain the facts.

Another issue is the 'trial by media' aspect of such situations, whereby delicate and distressing situations involving very vulnerable people are highlighted, oversimplified and widely publicised; and where the professionals concerned—endeavouring to protect their clients, and, according to their principles, refusing to disclose or discuss private matters which they consider should be confidential— are made to appear unsympathetic, bigoted and even uncaring. While there is no doubt that many social workers (possibly teachers also) are inept at dealing with the media, there is also no doubt that many media personnel are more interested in a good story than in the vital issues which are at stake: they are not concerned to protect the interests of the vulnerable individuals caught up in the situation. Neither teachers nor social workers are used to the unpopular public image which they see being foisted on them at the present time, and see themselves as being turned into scapegoats by a materialistic society. Both professions regard themselves as among the caring professions and to be pilloried in this way leaves them confused and vulnerable. For such professions, whose commitment and concern have played a traditional part in their evolution, this is a painful experience and may play some part in their disavowal of each other's expertise. It is perhaps worth commenting wrily that there do not seem to have been public inquiries related to the professional performance of some of the more established professions, such as medicine or the law.

In sum, it would seem that both teachers and social workers could be described as moving towards professionalism, although how important such progress is seems to be open to debate.

Values

As could be seen in Figure 3, the body of values affects professional attitudes towards people, and these, together with ways of understanding, influence the interventive or teaching repertoire used to carry out the tasks.

Meyer, Litwak and Warren[13] describe an interesting comparison of teachers and social workers in relation to occupational and class differences in social values which was carried out in the USA but has been replicated by the Crafts[14] in this country. Meyer et al. suggest that the historical emergences of professions may reflect the multiplicity of values in any society, rather than the more traditional sociological classification of professions in terms of reflecting the social class system. They also point out that the nature of the work setting produces value differences, and go on to state that 'teachers usually deal with groups whereas social workers usually deal directly with single people'. Second, that

the teacher works with children and adolescents where there is a clear status difference, coupled with an important social mandate to inculcate knowledge and socialise 'the client' and that this mandate carries considerable social backing for a one way influence to change . . . the caseworker frequently deals with the adult . . . the relationship has considerably less coercion built into it; success is mainly based on persuasion.

There are also differences in that the supervision received by the teacher is usually from the head and has a clearly evaluative function, whereas the caseworker is usually supervised by a social worker of more colleagal status. Third, the degree of specialisation differs within each profession. Subject teachers have distinctive knowledge and skills which cannot easily be transferred to other subjects. Fourth, with compulsory education for all children the teaching profession cannot afford such stringent selection procedures as for social work. Finally, according to Meyer et al., teaching and social work appear to start from different premises and to have different goals. The social worker is involved in changing personality, interpersonal relations and conditions of living, while the teacher tends to be concerned mainly with transmitting a body of information of 'culture' that does not necessarily assume that the person or his situation must be changed.

While all these points are arguable, if only because Meyer *et al.* take a rather narrower definition of the aims and goals of social work than is taken earlier in this book, the research does attempt to differentiate between the value bases of the two professions.

Meyer and his colleagues stress five values:

1 *Individual v. system goals*

While a primary social value in our society centres on individual worth, the contrasting idea is that the goals of the group or the state are pre-eminent. Social and cultural norms are traditionally stressed in the school curriculum, while social workers have concentrated more on minimising the psychic tensions of individuals (as associated with psychoanalytically based doctrines).

2 *Individual responsibility v. group responsibility*

Perhaps paradoxically, social work has a strong tradition asserting the responsibility of the group for the welfare of individual members. In contrast, the teacher does not directly confront this issue, but tends to emphasise the individual's achievements. The single adult/child status relationship and the hierarchical context of the school tend to heighten this, whereas the colleagal context of social work tends to support the idea of collective responsibility.

3 *Security-satisfaction v. struggle-suffering-denial*

In their practice, social workers are usually concerned with deprived clients and therefore stress the importance of satisfying the basic psycho-biological needs. The teacher, on the other hand, faces a group of children whose impulses and needs must be disciplined in order to permit the transmission of knowledge to a class. There is therefore less reason for the teacher to question the value of the puritan ethic that discipline, control and denial are character-building.

4 *Innovation-change v. traditionalism*

Social work has a heritage of social reform and this need for change is likely to be reinforced by exposure to deviant social groups. In contrast, school teaching, in its role as preserver and transmitter of culture, stresses continuity and conservation; and this is reinforced by exposure to ignorant but non-deviant children.

5 *Interdependence v. individual autonomy*
Social work views the autonomy of the individual as limited, stressing the dependence on others, of families on surrounding conditions, and of one undesirable condition upon another. Both the tasks of the teacher and the work setting would encourage the sense that the person himself is capable of determining his own destiny.

Meyer *et al.* outline four other value dimensions which are not used in this research: personal liberty v. society control; relativism-secularism v. absolutism-sacredness; changeable human nature v. inherent human nature-fatalism; diversity-heterogenity v. consensus-homogeneity-conformity. They also made a comparison between project schools, where compensatory and remedial programmes (similar to the EPA projects) were in force and those schools which were functioning in the usual way. They found that the values of the teachers in the non-project schools were similar to social work values; though when the study was repeated later this difference was not substantiated and the values of all the teachers were nearer to those of social workers.

While this study was carried out in the USA some twelve years ago and since that time there have clearly been changes in the value systems of both teachers and social workers, it is worth recording here as it represents one of the few attempts to compare the values of the two professions. British social workers might insist that one of the present conflicts within the profession is the extent to which they are expected to stress social and cultural norms at the expense of the individual. Many would also argue that in the past the preoccupation of social workers with minimising psychic tensions within individuals have led the profession to neglect the social reform aspects of social work. Community workers, in particular, frequently voice the opinion that the caseworkers' preoccupations with psychoanalytic ideology led to them merely patching up the sores of society with sticking plaster rather than initiating more radical changes. Teachers, on the other hand, are beginning to complain more and more frequently that they are expected to concentrate on system goals at the expense of individual children or those children from sub-cultures for whom the goals of the state are often either irrelevant or deleterious. Keddie, for example, writing on the myth of cultural deprivation, points out that

it is not clear of what culture these families and their children can be deprived, since no group can be deprived of its own culture . . . . Culturally deprived children then come from homes where mainstream values do not prevail, and are therefore less educable than other children . . . . The argument is that it is the school's function to transmit the mainstream values of society and that the failure of children to acquire these values lies in their lack of educability. Thus their failure in school is located in the home, the pre-school environment, and not within the nature and organisation of the school which 'processes' the children into achievement rates. This individualisation of failure rests on a concept of mainstream culture that is by definition, in the use of indices such as income, occupation, education, etc., a minority culture, the culture of the middle class which is then said to stand for 'society at large'.[15]

Teachers, too, are beginning to become involved in social reform and also to consider that such activities are or should become part of their role. This in turn brings them closer to social workers; but also to confrontation with them in some situations, for instance those where their differing attitudes stemming from other values as regards personal liberty v. societal control might indicate alternate means, although the goals might be similar. Many of the conflicts around children who are at risk or even being neglected centre on these values and the differing emphasis placed on them. Correspondingly, particularly since the 1948 Children's Act, which gave social workers the power and responsibility to work with deprived children, they have yet managed to maintain some semblance of client self-determination within the relationship. In some measure the efforts on the part of social workers to maintain an authoritative relationship with the children in their care, while having the minimum of social distance between them, may have also affected the teachers, who appear to have been becoming increasingly dissatisfied with the social distance between themselves and their pupils. There is a shift in society generally and perhaps particularly among teachers towards the social work values relating to an individual's right to a minimum level of security-satisfaction. Yet this awareness of needs and preoccupation with rights to minimum standards is not without its effect on teachers. It leads to painful awareness which may not only make it difficult for them to carry out tasks which are part of their role, but may also encourage rivalry with social workers. Street,[16] writing of educators and social workers, points out that 'teachers suddenly attentive to the cultural and social deprivations of their inner city [pupils] may sometimes be the worse for it; they may lower standards and love their pupils rather than teach them'. The head of an EPA school commented:

While I see and am concerned about the deprivations of some of the children in my school, I have decided that my job is to try to teach the children; it's the only chance some of them will get—and it's what I am trained and paid to do.

Teachers, therefore, while paying attention to the world of the child outside the school situation, must focus on the educational tasks of the school. The crucial dilemmas centre on the definition of the educational tasks.

Even the teacher's role as preserver and transmitter of culture is being questioned. Midwinter,[17] now director of a teachers' centre, comments that 'schools are agents of affirmation, not change agents; they merely rubber stamp an inevitability'. He goes on to stress the need for the schools' inclusion in the community and to develop broadly social goals rather than narrowly academic ones. Though others would argue along with the Tyndale teachers that schools are change agents, many teachers would agree with his suggestion that the teacher should become a social explorer rather than a social custodian of outmoded social mores. Paradoxically, just at a time when there is a concern among teachers about large bureaucratic structures and their resistance to change (i.e., comprehensive schools merely reinforcing traditional divisive social systems), most social workers have been reorganised within large social service departments which are already demonstrating the typical resistance to change which seems inevitable in such large bureaucratic structures. Finally, while the values of social workers seem to have been reinforced following their development of group work among their clients and by their links with and incursions into community work, there are also some indications that teachers, too, are beginning to question their commitment to the value of promoting individual autonomy. Particularly those teachers who are concerned with secondary children in special educational projects such as truancy centres and sanctuaries are beginning to place value on developing interdependence within the group.

As has been mentioned, Craft and Craft undertook in this country a research study similar to that of Meyer *et al.* They administered a questionnaire to a small self-selected sample of teachers and social workers attending a course on home, school and welfare and published their results in 1971. Their findings were related to five areas, and while acknowledging the limitations of their small pilot study they considered them worth further exploration:

1 *General:* Both sub-groups agreed that teaching and social work overlap but the social workers in particular perceived some distinctiveness of role between the two.
2 *Operational techniques:* Both sub-groups agreed that teaching and social work might equally include both

authoritative and permissive elements, but each saw teaching as involving slightly more structure.

3 *Social functions:* Both sub-groups agreed that teaching and social work are agencies of social control but teachers thought social work was the more important. Both sub-groups regarded the needs of the individual as possibly more important than those of society and both tended to see social work as more individual-orientated than teaching.

4 *Role orientation:* Both sub-groups agreed that teachers have the more specific role of the two but social workers tended to see *both* roles as more specific and well-defined than did the teachers. Both sub-groups agreed that teaching and social work include both instrumental and expressive elements. If anything the social workers saw their own role as a shade more instrumental than teaching.

5 *Policy issues:* Both sub-groups favoured a degree of inter-professional training and they *particularly* favoured closer working relations in the field. Both agreed on the importance of home background information in teaching, on the importance of social factors in the education process and on the value of more elaborate school welfare provision. But social workers were surprisingly less keen on close parent-teacher relations.

Fitzherbert,[18] in a book written with the aim of educating the teacher to become the conductor of the welfare orchestra, discusses the thorny question of confidentiality. She quotes a ministerial paper on child-care services in Scotland:

This [the passing on of confidential information], individual members of respective professions must solve for themselves bearing in mind the ethical standards of their profession. A general principle might be that information essential to the understanding, treatment and welfare of a child should be passed, but only to other professionals who are involved in his care, for example, social workers and teachers.

How can it be that the principle of confidentiality is so often considered to be an overriding obstacle to successful communications between professions? It seems that it is not the principle itself, which is flexible enough, but the way in which it is used by professionals . . . which causes difficulty. It can be invoked not so much to protect the interests of clients as to provide a convenient smokescreen behind which to hide from interference or criticism . . . . It is not difficult to show that many people who plead the confidentiality principle as a reason for not sharing information—often in the genuine belief that it is an unbreachable ethical code—are either deceiving themselves or being deceived if they believe that any medical or psychological information is ever entirely confidential. The confidentiality principle is regularly breached between people who trust each other.

BASW's *Code of Ethics* states that the social worker

recognises that information clearly entrusted for one purpose should not be used for another purpose without sanction. He respects the privacy of clients and confidential information about clients gained in his relationship with them or others. He will divulge such information only with the consent of the client (or informant) except: where there is clear evidence of serious danger to the client, worker, other persons or the community: in other circumstances judged exceptional, on the basis of professional consideration and consultation.

Whereas it could be argued that there might be some dilemma and differences regarding the definitions of 'serious danger', as guidelines these are clear enough.

Street (writing of the USA), in seeking explanations of the lack of interest of the school and social work systems in each other's activities, described them in terms of sibling rivalry, although pointing out that as a sociologist he had enough status anxieties of his own! He quotes W. I. Thomas and points out that this classical social workish criticism of schools has as much if not more relevance in 1967 as it did when it was written in 1931. Again this was written of the American scene but it still has a depressingly apposite relevance to some British schools:

While in the present condition of society there is no point at which the prevention of delinquency and the socialisation of the family can be undertaken so successfully as in the school, the school itself has very grave defects of character and the question of its adaptation to the welfare of the child involves at the same time the question of change and reform in the school itself . . . . The average school . . . works on the assumption of uniformity of personality and presents the same materials and plans in the same order to all. The assumption is that children react in the same way to the same influences regardless of their personal traits or social past . . . . The fact that the school work is detached from activity and not related to the plan-forming and creative faculty explains its failure to interest the child . . . . The school presents indispensable information, a technique for handling problems such as reading, writing and ciphering and presents the solution of the innumerable problems which are already solved and which it is unnecessary to solve again. But the school works injuriously on personality development and creative tendencies. By presenting the whole body of cultural values in a planless way, planless so far as . . . personal development is concerned, it tends to thwart and delay the expression of plan-making tendencies of children until physiological maturity approaches and the energetic, plan-forming creative period is passed . . . . Clinicians and caseworkers who handle successfully difficult children taken from the schools report that the schools tend to accentuate rather than obviate the difficult features.

Street also found that the differences in theory between the education and social work professions were being reduced and was sympathetic to what he described as an occupational disease, in that teachers facing large groups of children for six hours a day are likely to induce a concern for order and discipline as paramount virtues for survival. The teachers' necessary concern for a complexity of pedagogic tasks present them with so many problems that, according to Street, they cannot possibly be attentive to the full range of characteristics of a large number of students. As has already been mentioned, such a concern might divert the teachers too far from the curriculum or from attention to the pupils' learning progress. Street goes on to mention the crises of resources and expectations in the inner city schools, and also the political and moral aspects of these, particularly as regards equality, compensatory action and racial integration. He comments on the middle-class character of the school, which can itself be deleterious to some children and certainly favours 'conventional children who come to school with the language, skills, motivation, demeanor and general cultural preparation generally expected by the school'. Such criticisms are frequently expressed by both teachers and social workers in relation to inner city schools in this country, and the areas which they might be expected to serve. Street also writes of innovations which are applied mechanically and of the failure to research the character and results of the new practices.

Rose and Marshall,[19] who came across similar attitudes in their research, comment on the considerable emphasis placed upon the need for counsellors to be teachers, but add that research findings and their own experience with teacher-trained and non-teacher trained

> point to there being no difference in acceptance or effectiveness. It is impossible to believe that a worker whose role is based upon interpersonal understanding could not make a reasonably good attempt to understand the teacher's problems as well as those of their clients.

In their opinion, the working situations and the professional attitudes and feelings of the teacher, including those of professional solidarity, inevitably influence their attitudes:

> For him the school is a small society, and as in other small societies, it tends to be in-turning and exclusive. A person who does not teach often seems to him to be on to a good thing: she is not tied down to teaching schedules and heavy loads of marking, she gets out and about, and is much more master of her own time.

While there have been genuine attempts to research the various compensatory programmes such as the EPAs of the ILEA children in special difficulties schemes, the quality of such research has been variable and because of the highly political nature of the subject has sometimes been distorted by its presentation.

Goodacre[20] carried out a three-year enquiry to (1) investigate the nature and extent of the task of teaching infants to read (particularly in areas where little assistance could be expected from the children's homes), and (2) to study the reading readiness, attainment and progress of children in relation to their individual attributes, home circumstances and school conditions. Goodacre, as has already been mentioned, sees the teacher's role as classifier, instructor and socialiser. She found that students reach a peak of growing insight into the teacher's role in their second year of training but tend to become more traditional as entry into the reality of the classroom becomes more imminent. Goodacre conducted her research by means of questionnaires and rating forms with 100 infant schools in London, with the following results. She found that generally teachers considered that the home background of the children was important, particularly the provision of suitable reading material and the type of atmosphere in which it was taken for granted by the parents and child that reading was a desirable skill to be acquired. Teachers varied as to how they categorised their pupils in relation to their home backgrounds. A 'good' home tended to be described as one which facilitate the teacher's task of instruction for participation in the formal learning situation and also for the acceptance of the teacher's role in it. Older or more authoritarian types of teachers were more likely to categorise pupils in terms of good or poor homes. Contacts with parents seldom existed beyond meetings on school premises. Few schools had parent-teacher organisations and few teachers visited the homes. One in three parents were not seen by the teachers at school even at the beginning of the child's schooling.

Teachers made their judgments on the basis of attendance and lateness, conversations with the child, class news, observations of personal belongings, the type and quality of the child's clothing, particularly underclothing, and also on whether parents bought or borrowed the child's reading book. They also used paternal occupation as a criterion for assessing the pupil's home background but were least reliable in their assessments in the lowest social levels. Teachers' inferences regarding pupils whose parents follow different types of occupation revealed their lack of knowledge regarding the gradients of status in the manual classes. They had a tendency to stress the power and responsibility of occupations which in the past were related to educational mobility and hence intellectual capacity. This also led them to think that socially homogeneous groups were also intellectually similar. School organisation rather than the social area appeared to be the effective factor influencing the teachers' ratings of individual pupils. Class teachers of infants schools found their greatest satisfaction in relationships with the children rather than adults (colleagues or parents), their major dissatisfactions being the low status accorded to infant teachers by the community. They saw themselves as cheerful, conscientious and adaptable but lacking in ambition, originality, confidence and foresight. While infant teachers generally attach considerable importance to environmental factors, the way they reacted was more likely to be related to their own basic personalities. It was the more authoritarian teacher who tended to have an unfavourable attitude towards pupils' home backgrounds, particularly in relation to parents. Generally the head's personality and attitudes did not appear to have any direct bearing on the pupils' reading attainments, except in relation to schools in lower-working-class areas, and indirectly as regards their attitudes to homes and to staff morale. The findings of this research were affected by the organisation of the schools. In infants schools, teachers have only two years to get to know the pupils. Infant philosophy is more pervasive throughout the school. The differences which existed as a result of the teacher's position in the school seemed to be more a question of degree, for instance more heads mentioned the attendance of parents at open days. The teacher's own social-class origin appeared to have little effect on the findings. Goodacre makes the general comment that 'teachers were often unable to express themselves convincingly and logically and that the heads who were most anxious about their status in the community were also those who were most pessimistic about the school's ability to influence pupils' values'.

Training

Lees and Lees,[21] writing of social work and teacher training, pointed out the areas of similarity, notably in the social sciences, which had resulted from changes in teacher training. They pointed out the increasing preoccupation of both teaching and social work with 'aspiring to foster closer links with the community and to develop community resources'. They list the EPAs, school counsellors, parent-teacher associations and the community school movement in education and the setting up of neighbourhood advice centres, community development projects and the appointment of community workers to local authority social service departments in social work. Despite this overlap of preoccupation and areas of knowledge, they comment on the lack of personal contact and conclude that some shared training, particularly in the social sciences, might have desirable results. However, they also caution that the differences between the two roles would make a merging of training inappropriate.

They also recommend interprofessional seminars for qualified teachers and social workers and recently there has been mutual interest from teachers and social workers in such seminars. Jones,[22] a headmistress speaking on schools and welfare agencies at a conference organised by NACRO, pointed out the need for teachers and social workers to have a much clearer idea about both the similarities and differences between the ways in which they work:

> To the social worker the teacher may appear to be interfering, controlling, manipulative, over involved, hasty to act, unable to listen properly, blind to obvious cries for help given out by the child, possessive, judgemental and unreasonable. To the teacher the social worker may appear to be too young and inexperienced, naive, gullible, easily manipulated, slow to act, impossible to contact on the telephone, elusive and therefore defensive, ignorant of what the pupil is really like, inneffectual, soft, on the child's side.

Her admission that schools are not as all-powerful as they are believed to be, that society expects them to make good failures which have occurred elsewhere and that schools cannot do it, provoked a storm of comment from the press, much of it critical, some of it sympathetic.

Teacher training

While teachers in the private sector of education have a time-honoured place in society, it is only since the establishment of the state system of education during the nineteenth century that the role of the school teacher in the public sector reveals a struggle for status and recognition. Hurt's[23] lively account of the first educational administrators' attempts to resolve the battle for power in the classroom as between the state and the church, which hitherto had undisputed power, gives an indication of the historical roots of the tight political hold on schools and indeed on teacher training which still exists today: 'From time immemorial, those who were literate did not labour and those who were illiterate performed the menial tasks of a society that maintained the well-being of a privileged few.' The fear was that training the much-needed teachers in a state education system was 'fraught with danger . . . since children of the labouring classes were to be trained in submission to their superiors it follows that education was not intended to be a means whereby they could elevate themselves in society'.

The jealous attempts by both state and church to maintain the current *status quo* seem to have had a considerable effect on teacher training. The training colleges gradually established by the church, state and private institutions evolved outside the universities in an attempt to concede to the preservation of an elitist system. This in turn led to the much-criticised binary system of higher education whereby there are 'independent' universities and the publicly controlled polytechnics and colleges of education. Some attempt to bridge the binary system in teacher training was made by the establishment and linkage of colleges of education with the university institutes of education by the formation of the Area Training Organisations. Since it has become compulsory for all teachers to have an approved training in teaching, and university graduates, those who hitherto were assumed fit to teach by virtue of their degrees, must also take a postgraduate certificate of education. The B.Ed., an honours qualification awarded to the certificated teacher after a fourth year of study, was introduced in an attempt to provide some parity with the postgraduate qualified teachers.

After the war the increased need for teachers resulting from the increased birth rate led to a rapid expansion in teacher training. There is a body of opinion which regrets the emphasis on expansion of places and the resultant neglect of the style and quality of teacher training. Since the White Paper ironically entitled *A Framework for Expansion*, the teacher-training places have been drastically cut. At the time of writing (1977) the colleges of education are beset by the reorganisational issues connected with these cuts and the accompanying direction to diversify their courses to include students who are not committed, even nominally, to becoming teachers. This situation has led to a somewhat undignified scramble on the part of the colleges to look towards fresh fields, and in particular to turn their attention to developments in social work (including youth and community work). It is sad that the general change of emphasis towards the community has been hastened by such urgent economic necessity, for it seems inevitable that the new courses hastily assembled may result from the needs to preserve departments and prevent redundancies of staff, rather than from carefully planned innovatory courses based on the genuine and shared developing interests in community needs.

Nevertheless, there are also serious attempts, perhaps particularly in the universities, to re-evaluate teacher training. Leeds University Institute of Education conducted a survey of teachers in the schools within its area training organisation, circulating a random sample of approximately half the primary, secondary and middle schools.[24] Their questionnaire covered four major areas of concern, the required entry qualifications; the nature of the teacher training course; teaching practice; and the probationary year. The results were as follows:

(a) Entry qualifications for teacher education

At present the minimum qualification for entry to a college of education is normally 5 G.C.E. 'O' levels or passes at Grade 1 in C.S.E. . . . . While many of the teachers regarded these minimum standards as about right, there were also many who regarded them as too low.

(b) Teacher education course

Typically the three year course at a college of education includes, in addition to teaching practice in schools, a course or courses in education . . . . [This] is primarily concerned with the 'professional aspects of teaching'. In addition the students also normally study a main subject. It is a common criticism made by teachers that this course as a whole gives too much emphasis to theory and insufficient emphasis to practice.

These teachers also expressed the view that insufficient attention was given to 'fundamental matters such as the teaching of reading'. There was also more detailed criticism on the imbalance of teaching between theory and practice. Many teachers would also argue that the main subject should be chosen not only for its own sake, but also with regard to its relevance for the age range within which the student intends to teach.

(c) Teaching practice

While this is an important part of the student's course 'it is the one means by which teachers continue to have first hand experience of teacher education through the students sent to their schools on practice'. The survey did not set out to discover in what ways the preparation of students for teaching practice might be inadequate, but to get their views on whether they were sufficiently prepared. A significant proportion of the teachers thought the students were badly prepared (26·5 per cent of the primary teachers and 22·6 per cent of the secondary teachers) but also complained of the preoccupations with students' dress, attitudes and behaviour in the staff room as well as their greater concern that students should come to schools better prepared to do the work that the job of teaching involves:

> Students normally do about 60 days of teaching practice during their three year course and views were expressed [by the primary school teachers] that each practice should be spent entirely with one class . . . . There was a strong feeling amongst secondary school teachers that students who intend to teach in the 13-18 age group should spend some of their teaching practice in schools catering for other age groups. There was considerable criticism with regard to the supervision of teaching practice, though much support for the use of a system whereby students are supervised, helped and advised by both the college and the school.

There was also criticism of the inadequate knowledge and experience of the tutors to help the students 'when they did visit the schools . . . . Despite these criticisms it seems likely that many teachers would prefer that teaching practice be given greater prominence in the three-year course'. Various schemes as to who might do the supervision of the student—class teacher, head, teacher with special responsibility, tutor either alone or in various combinations—were all considered. The teachers also seemed to desire a much closer working relationship with the colleges.

(d) The probationary year

> Despite the argument that the teachers' initial training and their work as probationary teachers should be seen and planned as one more or less continuous process, the two are frequently regarded as quite separate and the probationary year has perhaps not received the same critical attention . . . that has been paid to initial training.

Similar questions were asked with regard to guidance and supervision and the majority of the teachers were of the opinion that probationary teachers do not receive enough of either. There were also requests for clarity as regards where the responsibility lies, for instance in relation to the inspectorate.

The report concludes with some implications arising from the survey, in particular the responsibility of the college for initiating and developing closer contacts and understanding between themselves and the schools, and with some suggestions as to how this might be achieved.[25]

Hannam et al.[26] at Bristol University, in writing of young teachers and reluctant learners, describe a scheme whereby students undertaking teacher training are allocated to one or two secondary pupils with learning difficulties and spend one afternoon per week with them on unstructured activities out of school. It is left to the students and their pupils to decide what to do and the task is for the students to get to know and be able to communicate with adolescents who have learning difficulties. Recently, Hannam et al. have also carried out discussions with young teachers in their first post[27] and found that young teachers, while being very vulnerable professionally, are subjected to induction processes which do little to enhance their confidence. Teaching is the only job where young teachers go back to where they have come from, i.e., the school, and this can be a very evocative experience. While they may have survived teaching practice at college, it can also be experienced as very destructive and, as has been shown by the Leeds study, they are often given little help. It is characteristic that young teachers are subjected to a selection interview, often at some central location (e.g., County Hall) and are given no idea where they might be expected to teach. Going into a new staff room can be a fairly chilling experience, as indeed is the entry into most new groups. For the young teacher who is very conscious of his dysfunctions, it can be an intimidating experience, as 'old hands' can show their feelings about the newcomer in many subtle ways. All young teachers are anxious about discipline and control and are often subjected to hair-raising stories of groups which nearly or actually did get out of hand. They are frequently given the worst jobs and rooms. In addition they experience the sharpness of perception common to all newcomers to professional groups, suffering pain and anxiety about situations which older or more experienced teachers have long learned to deal with or defend themselves against. Children are still being beaten in schools, for instance, and this knowledge is often excruciatingly painful for the young teacher who has previously been carefully working out his own views on corporal punishment with his fellow students. Children are superb manipulators and, like most of us, they do not like new people, anyway at first. They find subtle ways of undermining the newcomer, of testing his strengths and limits, of letting him know how much better his predecessor was and of playing him off against the other staff.

Hannam comments that teaching is exhausting as teachers have to swallow so much aggression from the pupils and there comes a time in the lives of most young teachers when they eventually lose their ideals and find themselves acting against their humanitarian principles, whether by losing their temper, hitting out at a child wildly or being overtaken by a despair which it is difficult to keep private. They find they hate the children, the head, the school, or all three. The first year is indeed pretty gruesome, according to the findings. It is a time of initiation rites and of the ultimate induction into the system.

Teaching methods

The model of the child as an empty vessel waiting to be filled with knowledge by a benevolent and paternalistic teacher is seen not only as authoritarian and patronising but also as bad educational practice. This is not to say that didactic teaching has fallen into total disfavour, but educationalists have long struggled to find new and effective teaching methods based on a composite of socialising methods integrated with the imparting of knowledge. This philosophy of itself is subject to considerable debate within the school system, with the primary educationalists more or less coming down on the side of a weighting towards socialisation and the secondary educationalists towards the imparting of 'pure' knowledge. Educationalists, too, have been increasingly concerned about how the authoritarian nature of the structure of the schools influences the teaching methods. This dissatisfaction has led to various 'breakaway' schools, usually outside the state system, where new, more evocative and permissive methods of teaching have evolved.

In writing of teaching as a subversive activity, Postman and Weingartner[28] state 'that the critical conduct of any learning experience is the method or process through which the learning occurs'. They add 'Almost any sensible parent knows this, as does any effective top sergeant . . . . If most teachers have not yet grasped this idea, it is not for lack of evidence.' Postman and Weingartner of course belong to the radical and American 'school' of teaching methods. They go on to write of the enquiry method of teaching in which teaching is considered to be a process, the teacher's goal being 'to engage students in those activities which produce knowledge, defining, questioning, observing, classifying, generalising, verifying, applying'. While many of these radical critiques come from the American educational scene, in this country, too, there is a growing literature of impassioned discontent, such as the Balls'[29] plea to involve the schools in community action. Such teachers and others, too, have long realised that the organisations within which the teaching methods are carried out inevitably and unfailingly enhance or constrain the flexibility of the teaching method. Social workers on the other hand, while they have long been aware of the importance of the process of relationship within which social work intervention occurs, have only recently begun to preoccupy themselves with the important impact which the organisation itself makes upon the intervention.

While it is tempting to try to describe and summarise the ebb and flow of fashion with regard to teaching methods, this is a complex and sophisticated exercise and it must suffice to comment briefly upon some of the obvious differences which prevail in primary and secondary schools. Generally speaking, teachers in primary schools favour teaching methods which are child-centred, starting where the child *is* in terms of learning and enabling and encouraging him outwards and onwards, using such methods as family grouping, projects and the various discovery methods. This enables the child to learn at more or less his own pace, the teacher to give some individual attention and the child to gain the full satisfaction which follows the skill acquisition. However, such methods are only really successful when used in small classes of young children and are enhanced by such accoutrements as open-plan schools designed for the purpose. When the classes get too big, the children too deprived or disturbed, and the buildings outdated and inconvenient, maintaining sufficient control to create such an ambience becomes a real difficulty. It is perhaps interesting to comment here upon a successful introduction of compensatory nurture groups for deprived children where a skilled teacher with a small group of children can give children experiences of some of the early mothering experiences, in particular physical contact and individualised attention, which they have missed.

In secondary schools, however, and particularly in the inner city areas described so vividly by Holman, Hargreaves, Power and Phillipson, the introduction of less authoritarian teaching methods is also highly influenced by the problem of control. However, some interesting methods have begun to develop, although more recently than in the primary schools, which were given additional encouragement following the Plowden Report. The work of Charity James and her associates[30] at the Curriculum Laboratory produced what she describes as 'a mosaic of interdisciplinary enquiry' where children work in clusters with a team of teachers, spending part of their time in the usual class groups with an individual teacher. Special interests and a wish to go into areas at greater depth are possible, as is the opportunity to cater for individual needs. James writes:

These four bases for grouping might be called the macrocosmic aspects of flexible grouping in a diversified curriculum . . . .

Diversity is the essence of I.D.E. for it is in the open, free
wheeling work . . . that one begins to see how narrow has been
our concept of mixed ability.

The development of new teaching methods in secondary education
has also been influenced by the process of comprehensivisation.
While writers such as Elizabeth Richardson[31] have been advocating
the study and use of groups as part of teacher training for some
years, there has been little indication until recently that this has
been taken up in a more general way. Goodacre, for instance,
writing of the need to change attitudes, mentions that 'group
discussions are known to have considerable value in this area', but
comments that 'teachers in their training are given considerable
information about the psychology of young children but not much
about the psychology of small groups and the function of anxiety in
the conduct of groups'. Nevertheless, there are now some indications
that teachers are showing interest, particularly in the various
personal-growth type of groups, though mostly as yet for their own
personal development. While for many years the sophistication of
the psychiatrists' and more recently the social workers' dynamic use
of group processes as an aid in learning has spread to the boundary
areas (for instance in intermediate treatment projects and in
residential schools and schools for the maladjusted), there is still not
much evidence that this has had a spin-off in the ordinary education
sector.

Social work training

Significantly, social work began to develop at about the same time as
schooling during the second half of the nineteenth century and it
also seems to have been related to the work of the social and political
reformers of the time and of the philanthropists who were becoming
increasingly concerned at the results of the industrial revolution.
Indeed the Probation of Offenders Act of 1907, under which the
court missionaries, who later became today's probation officers,
were given statutory recognition, was the direct result of the work of
these reformers. Lady almoners, as they were then called, had
already begun visiting the hospitals, and established their institute
in the same year. The present-day family caseworkers are the direct
heirs to the first Charity Organisation Society social workers and
indeed this organisation, now renamed the Family Welfare Association, is still pioneering new ways of helping in situations of family
breakdown.

The social work training which began to develop in this country
was distinctively related to the function of the agencies in which the

social workers were expected to work and its different aspects were thus separate and apparently unrelated. It seems to have been following the establishment of the Child Care Service in 1948, for which trained social workers were urgently needed, that the generic or general-purpose social worker began to make an appearance. There is little doubt that the early professional training for social work was heavily influenced by the psychodynamic theories of the psychoanalytic schools and particularly by Freudian theory. While these psychodynamically orientated social workers are still often accused of overemphasising the importance of their client's internal psychological world at the expense of the real and appalling social conditions in which they lived, they did develop the values and principles on which most present-day social work practice is based.

By the 1960s it was becoming clear that families experiencing social breakdown were themselves being subjected to partialisation as the result of the exclusive and problem-based functions of the social work agencies whose task it was to help them. Some of the families experiencing tertiary social breakdown, for instance, were subject to social work intervention from up to four or five social work agencies: perhaps the probation service, a child care officer, a welfare officer and a psychiatric or medical social worker. It was by no means uncommon for families to be visited by two or three social workers in addition to the health visitor and the visitor from the National Assistance Board (now the Supplementary Benefits Commission). By that time authorities were themselves employing social workers in the health and welfare departments (psychiatric and medical social workers) and in the children's departments (child care officers). The dissatisfaction with this state of affairs, together with the more general recognition that even a welfare state has its casualties, led to the setting up of the Seebohm Committee[32] to enquire into the local authority and allied personal social services in 1965.

Around the time of the local authority reorganisation into social service departments which followed the Seebohm Report, social work courses acquired a new 'generic' approach, which by now seemed to mean a multiple approach to social work intervention as well as a more eclectic orientation to agency function. At about the same time the CCETSW was founded and funded by the government as a distinct and separate organisation, its main function being to advise, develop and validate social work training.

Since the late 1960s and early 1970s there has been a major expansion in social work education following the 'rediscovery of poverty' and greater awareness and recognition of need. It is perhaps significant that by this time the 'birth rate bulge' children were often parents themselves and experiencing the housing shortage and other undertows of the affluent society. There was also, of course, the longevity of their parents with its accompanying need for care from the community. It is probable that there is a similar body of opinion which is critical of the quality of social work teaching, for while the way social work practice is organised may keep social work students in touch with fieldwork practice, relatively few social tutors have in fact worked in the new social service departments and some indeed have not worked long in practice at all. While there has been as yet no research in social work training comparable to the Leeds study on teacher training, it might be useful to emphasise the comparison between the two groups by commenting on social work training under the same headings, which could be equally appropriately applied to social work.

(a) Entry qualifications for social work education

Qualifications for entry to social work courses is dependent on the prerequisite criteria of the colleges. Some of the non-graduate courses require O or A levels, but others, particularly for older (second career) students, require evidence of an adequate level of education, usually ascertained by a test. Most courses require candidates to have had some experience before they can be considered for application, the most notable exceptions being the four-year courses leading to a degree and a professional qualification and those for older students (many of them married women returning to work). As for the Post Graduate Certificate in Education (PGCE) course, the minimum entry qualification for the graduate courses is, of course, a degree, either 'relevant' (i.e., in the social sciences) or 'non-relevant'. Except for the 'relevant' graduates, who take a one-year course, and those taking the four-year course, most social workers take a two-year course whether they are graduates or not and are awarded the Certificate of Qualification in Social Work (CQSW) by the CCETSW, in addition to their college diploma, certificate or higher degree.

(b) The course of social work education

In the mid 1970s it would be almost true to say that there is no typical social work course, although there are some areas, particularly of practice, knowledge and skills, which most courses encompass. Even so, the emphasis placed upon such knowledge varies and is often dependent upon the history of the course (i.e., its agency and method origin) and on the orientation and experience of the staff. Most social work courses would include social work

218

principles and practice theory. The emphasis on the acknowledged social work methods or work with individuals and families, social group work and community work vary immensely from course to course and may not be accompanied by practice experience in all three methods. Social work in residential care may be considered a method or a setting for social work. While there is frequently a social work amalgam of psychological knowledge (often of psychoanalytic orientation) combined with social psychology and social work practice theory (usually called human growth and development) which aims to enhance the social worker's own insights as well as knowledge and understanding of his (or her) clients, this is also the course which provokes the most criticism, often on the ground that it either 'smuggles' social workers into becoming agents of social control without their thinking around the issues, or indoctrinates them into using the medical sickness/health model with their clients.

Most social work courses also include theoretical teaching in the social sciences—social policy and administration and sociology—often taught with an applied orientation. In addition to psychiatric knowledge, social work students are encouraged to think about people with handicaps (physical and mental) and last of all, but by no means least, there are courses on the vast range of legislation which affects not only the rights of their clients and the day-to-day practice of social work, but also the philosophy underlying such law. As perhaps can be envisaged from such a list, one of the major criticisms of social work courses is not only the amount of knowledge which social workers are expected to acquire, but also the lack of precise knowledge base and the lack of research in social work. Such a gap is beginning to be remedied and many social work courses try to encourage their students to take an analytic and critical stance to social research in relation to social work and also to consider undertaking research themselves. The curricula of social work courses are subject to periodic review by the CCETSW, who are attempting both to maintain qualitative standards and to pioneer new thinking by setting up working parties on various key issues in relation to social work, its reports being available for circulation and comment. Social workers and the law, residential work, community work, values in social work, are some of the issues that have been investigated so far.

The balance of social work teaching methods has been the cause for much debate and argument. Parsloe, Warren and Gauldie,[33] from the University of Aberdeen, given an interesting account of the different perceptions of staff and students as regards the different emphases the many social work courses give to the various social work methods. They write:

> The shift has been not only from specific client groups but also towards a classification of methods based upon the relational system chosen for intervention. Thus since the 1950's when casework reigned supreme in social work courses, we have moved through a brief flirtation with group work into what looks like being a more important and lasting attention to intervention at a community level.

They go on to say that

> to understand some of the intensity which surrounds the argument about casework and community work, we need to look more closely at what these terms convey to some of the participants. They have come to stand for a great deal more than intervention in two different relational systems; they stand for two frequently opposed ideologies. To be successful, caseworkers must be aware of their own internal world as well as that of their client and must understand the way in which past experiences influence present behaviour. Insofar as casework is concerned with the environment it defines this as the people with whom the client relates rather than seeing it in terms of class or the social or political structures within which he or she lives . . . . Community work on the other hand has attached to itself a different set of assumptions, theories and practices. It does not assume that social problems are generated by people's internal world or by their intimate relationships. It considers rather that such problems are created for groups of people by their powerlessness compared to that of more affluent or powerful groups in society. Ultimately *all* problems are caused by poverty and powerlessness. Community work draws upon sociology and political theory. It sees what others call problem behaviour as having structural causes and not as rooted in individual pathology. The aim of community work therefore is to bring people together so that they can participate in changing their society. They obtain greater power first by participation and later through the changes they have pressed for.

(c) Social work practice

All social work students are expected to undertake supervised practice as part of their social work training. While the amount and organisation of the practice varies from course to course, most students would spend half their course undertaking 'fieldwork practice', which may be concurrent with their college work (two or three days a week, perhaps) or blocks of full-time practice of approximately three months' duration, or a mixture of both. Where social work training differs from teacher training is that such practice is carried out under the supervision of a social worker in the agency. Until the past few years this has usually been a senior social work practitioner with some experience and an interest and some skills in teaching. However, following the reorganisation of the social work services, which thrust much greater management responsibilities on such workers in addition to their 'work loads', there has been a development of student units. Such units have been established both in local authorities and in hospital and voluntary social work agencies, where the specific task of the social worker (who is usually experienced in practice and fieldwork training) is to organise the practice and to supervise a group of social work students on placement. Supervision in the social work sense customarily means more than oversight and/or accountability for the work done. Social work students are accustomed to considering with their supervisor their own role and interaction with their clients and how their own attitudes towards social problems—for instance, illegitimacy or mental illness—might possibly affect their work with clients. While there is some criticism of such intrusion or interference into the personal privacy of the social work students, most would regard some such development of self-awareness as to some degree essential both for the protection of their clients and also for the social workers themselves. To be face-to-face daily with the miseries of society can prove emotionally debilitating for social workers, so supervision provides them with opportunity for support as well as constructive criticism. However, since it is difficult to develop criteria for evaluating practice, the quality and orientation of the supervision is variable and inevitably the assessment is to some extent subjective. While the students usually do share in the evaluation of their practice performance, most courses also take clashes of personality or differences of style into account, partly through the mediation of tutors and partly by each student having at least two, if not three, placements. The CCETSW also insists on the appeal procedures being clearly set out as well as the grounds on which appeals may be made.

(d) No probationary year

In social work training there is no probationary year following training. Such probation as there is tends to come before training, both in the selection of trainees, who are paid a salary for one or two years' practice before training and who also undergo a further selection process in order to get on to a course, and whose

221

authorities may then second them on salary. However, there are indications that serious consideration is being given to the recently qualified student undertaking a year of practice prior to the final award of the CQSW.

Many of the points raised by Hannam *et al.* in relation to young teachers would equally apply to young social workers. Social work training aims to fit social workers for good standards of practice, although in such a rapidly changing society such aims are by no means always realised. Since the reorganisation of social service departments, coupled with the changes brought about by the 1969 Children and Young Persons Act and the inadequate resources and cuts, there is little doubt that the standards of practice in the field are very variable. This inevitably leads to a period of disillusionment within the first year of practice following a course. While most social work agencies do build-in general support structures and particular opportunities for the newly trained worker, the pressures on them are considerable. Not only do they have to face high work loads and the inevitable initiation rites to passage like any newcomer to a professional group, but they also have to face the rivalry and envy of their untrained colleagues who may have tried several times to get on training courses but without success. Clients, too, find subtle ways of undermining the newcomer and particularly in busy social service departments may turn up to see the emergency social worker with complaints about the treatment they have received at other hands! While being the steady recipient of aggression may be the stock-in-trade of the teacher, being the steady receptacle for depression could be said to be the stock-in-trade of the social worker, who stands at the interface of society and its casualties.

Conclusion

It is interesting to note that while both professions have their roots in the philanthropic movement which grew up as the result of concern for the families laid waste by the industrial revolution, they have developed very separately. While the reasons for this stem partly from differences in their value base, this separateness seems also to have been exacerbated by the fact that they were not usually trained in the same institutions of higher education. Both teaching and social work are semi-professions which exist somewhat uncomfortably within large bureaucratic structures. This also means that their accountability to their 'clients', rather than always being direct, is often passed upwards and outwards via democratically elected representatives whose ultimate political loyalties may distort or even negate professional opinions and judgments.

While the power of the teacher has generally declined, that of the social worker has steadily increased. Yet, in the current pluralistic society, where authority and power are often called into question, neither the teacher nor the social worker can take for granted the respect which they previously enjoyed, and therefore their credibility has suffered. Perhaps paradoxically, the role of head teacher still retains much of its power although this somewhat anachronistic and total power is being strongly criticised even by teachers themselves. While the value systems of teachers and social workers still differ, there are indications that they are moving closer, particularly in relation to policy issues. Training, too, seems likely to change, though perhaps as much provoked by the economic stringencies as by active intentions to bring the two groups closer together. Social workers have become more concerned with educational policy and, particularly since the rise of the 'free school' movement (which will be further discussed in the concluding chapter), are taking a fresh look at the tasks and organisational structure of schools. They are less inhibited, too, about going into schools, and many neighbourhood teams from social service departments are beginning to form useful liaisons and relationships with the schools of the 'patch'. This has been helped by the developing co-operation of the education social workers, who are slowly emerging from their Cinderella status *vis à vis* both their own system and that of their social work colleagues. Teachers are becoming more interested in the families and social conditions in which their pupils live and in particular those families which do not visit the schools. A recent research project on parents and teachers by Lynch and Pimlott[34] describes the objectives of this Schools Council project as follows:

1 To foster a critical awareness in teachers and parents of the importance of the home environment in successful child education and to increase their sensitivity to the interdependence of the school, the home and the social services.

2 To clarify for parents the values and objectives of formal education and to encourage them to develop an active interest in how, what and why their children were taught, and in the importance of the home environment.

3 To foster a wider community interest in educational values and objectives and to assist the school to play an active and vigorous role in the life and development of the community.

4 To provide teachers and parents with information, instruction and guidance, which would grow into a spirit of self help in order that heightened parent teacher involvement

223

and a more community centred role for the school should be able to continue after the research team had withdrawn.

These brave objectives are indicative of the active interest within the education system in developing closer links with the social work system and with the community which the schools serve. It therefore seems a pity that the research workers involved in this project, when they set up separate groups for teachers and for parents attached to their three project secondary schools, did not also consider the expertise which was probably available from social workers and community workers working in that area. While social workers were indeed invited to the group discussions to talk about their work, their knowledge of group dynamics and community work would have added considerably to the realisation of the objectives. When registering their surprise at the parents' somewhat negative response to the possibility of visits from the head teacher, the child's teacher or school counsellor, the research workers did not appear to consider whether the parents might have reacted more favourably to a call from a more accustomed visitor, the social worker. Nevertheless, the team recommended amongst other things 'that a wider strategy which is being demanded to improve the quality of community life' should include giving teachers 'a wider knowledge and communication with education welfare, legal and social services'. There is a long way to go.

Part four

The challenge of alternatives

Chapter six

Challenges, alternatives and some possible strategies

It may seem a little strange that this book has almost been brought to a conclusion with only the barest reference to de-schooling. This has been deliberate, mainly because the aim of the book has been to describe the boundary areas between the education and social work systems as they exist in the public sector of central and local government systems. But it has also partly been in an attempt to highlight the central issues in relation to the overlap between the functions and tasks of education and social work. Thus the ever-present challenges both to established educational policy and the philosophy underlying it have not been considered. The controversy in social work around the use of the more traditional, psycho-analytically based casework methods employed by many social workers (if not most), as distinct from the more politically based community work methods, has been referred to only in passing. However, it is now necessary to consider the challenges which have been confronting both systems. Such a brief account can barely do justice to philosophical and political issues, which are of considerable importance and which have, in fact, already begun to achieve some quite considerable changes, particularly with regard to social work. It is also significant that these challenges bear a remarkable similarity to each other, stemming from the view that people have a right to have their most basic needs met. With regard to social work, the approach is that the handouts of a capitalist society are not commensurate with equal rights, and going to school is not synonymous with education. Indeed, it could even be said that the education and social work systems are drawing together at last only because in response to these challenges the basic human rights of each individual must be taken into consideration within their policies.

Challenges, alternatives and possibilities

It may perhaps also seem strange that, while many controversial ideas have been considered in this book, the movements from which they have sprung and which present such a challenge to the established systems have barely been mentioned so far. Again, this has been a deliberate choice, not only in order to attempt to provide a description of the education and social work systems as they are functioning, but also to highlight some of the central issues. This final chapter briefly describes some of the challenges to the systems, discusses some of the alternatives which have begun to influence and effect the systems and indicates some of the possibilities for the future.

(a) The challenge from movements of social change

The two most influential movements concerned with schoolchildren and their families are the welfare rights movement and the de-schooling movement. These are descriptive terms for groups of theorists and activists who share philosophical values and whose intentions are to provide a radical challenge to the assumptions and practices of the traditionally established systems. The de-schooling movement presents a disturbing but insightful critique of the educational system and the failure of schools to carry out many of the tasks for which they were established. The welfare rights movement has also challenged the failure of Western societies either to provide equal opportunities or to stem the growing tide of poverty. Underlying both these challenges is a new application of some of the understanding of the theories of social science, which, while they have long formed an integral part of both educational and social work theory, have been less concerned with what might be described as the practice aspects of social work and schooling. Most notably, the influence of sociological thinking, and especially that of a political nature, has led to the confrontations and insights which have proved disturbing and, at times, have achieved changes of attitude and practice which would have been unthinkable a few short years ago. It is not possible or appropriate here to attempt to give an account of the development and scope of these theories and it must suffice to comment that much of the value base which underpins the theory is the same, and also that the uses to which the movements put this understanding are surprisingly similar. For instance, much of the writing of some of the 'prophets' of the de-schooling movement demonstrates the overlap of the tasks of schools and social work. While some of it is ill-informed, confused and polemical, in some cases it has proved as effective in challenging the educationists as that of the community and welfare rights theorists have been in their challenges to social work practice. For instance, Paulo Freire's[1] statement 'education is cultural action for freedom and therefore an act of knowing and not of memorization . . . . The act of knowing involves a dialectical movement which goes from action to reflection and from reflection upon action to new action,' might have been written for social workers. Indeed, Freire's conscientization refers to the process in which men, not as recipients, but as knowing subjects, achieve a deepening awareness both of the sociocultural reality which shapes their lives and their capacity to transform that reality', bears a striking similarity to some social work descriptions of community work. Freire writes of the existence of two interrelated contexts as follows:

one is the context of authentic dialogue between learners and educators as equally knowing subjects. This is what schools should be—the theoretical context of dialogue. The second is the real, concrete context of facts, the social reality in which men exist.

This refers to just the boundary area between the tasks of schools and those of social work. Everitt Reimer,[2] too, in his reference to the gap between the ideologies and the realities of 'equal opportunity, freedom, progress and efficiency', also speaks to teachers and social workers whose tasks are 'to overcome any gross deficiencies in developing which may hinder the child's performance in learning or social functioning. (see Chapter 1). Ivan Illich[3] in his preface to *Celebration of Awareness*, writes:

Institutions create certainties, and taken seriously certainties deaden the heart and shackle the imagination. It is always my hope that my statements angry or passionate, artful or innocent, will also provoke a smile, and thus a new freedom— even though that freedom come at a cost.

While this may provoke some pious hopes, he leaves no doubts at the end of his book on de-schooling society when he writes:

finally, teachers, doctors and social workers realize that their distinct professional ministrations have one aspect—at least— in common. They create further demands for the institutional treatments they provide, faster than they can provide service institutions.[4]

On the other hand, social workers reading the writings of John Holt[5] or George Dennison[6] may find their work with deprived children bears a striking resemblance to that of therapeutic communities for children (such as the Mulberry Bush or Caldecott Community) and therefore will not find such ideas unusual; yet it seems that to many teachers they are almost revolutionary.

When Lister[7] writes of the challenge of the de-schooling movement and its effect on educationalists, he might also have been writing of the welfare rights and community workers and their effect on social work thought and practice during the late 1960s. If the words 'social work' are substituted for 'education' and 'community work' for 'de-schooling', then the similarities are striking:

Many raw nerves [were touched] . . . because of the way education was organised and perceived in many countries and because of the unfolding world crisis in education . . . the history of education, something that might have helped teachers in training to relate the parts to a whole, was a version of Whig history, held together by the idea of progress (organised from above by acts of parliament) and its main end was to celebrate the present. The message, as received from the new holy trinity of educational sub disciplines was: the sociology of education shows us that large sections of the population cannot speak [for themselves] and are virtually ineducable [unhelpable]; educational psychology tells us how to motivate them; and the philosophy of education justifies what we do. In many countries the area of the political economy of education, where de-schooling theory raises some of its most vital questions, is merely a gap in the intellectual training of educationalists and teachers.

The de-schoolers made 'the problems their starting point, not a theory of knowledge', and

the reaction of teachers was either so confused or demoralised, or else they greet[ed] the new theory . . . with what amounted to religious fervour . . . the general crisis in education was first argued by economists who pointed out the growing costs of education in formal institutions.

Such comments bear striking similarities to the reactions of casework-trained social workers when confronted with the new developments in community work. Like some of the teachers and their fervent response to the criticisms of the de-schooling movement, some social workers uncritically grasped at the new thinking, concluding that this might at last prove to be the panacea they had always been seeking. Some community workers, who eschewed the values of social work (and saw themselves as political activists rather than social workers), are now resisting the present, more considered, adoption of this approach by social workers, who describe community work as a method of social work; indeed some even regard this as a takeover bid. Lister goes on to list the challenges of de-schooling society and how these relate to schools. In Table 6 those which seem to link with parallel challenges to social work have been selected and listed opposite their equivalents in relation to social work agencies.

TABLE 6   *De-schooling society—schools and social work*

Schools	*Social work agencies*
1 The shaking of assumptions	The shaking of assumptions
2 Identifying schools as synonymous with education	Identifying social work agencies as synonymous with the promotion of social functioning
3 Their failure to teach what they pretend to teach	Their failure to carry out the social work intervention they pretend to carry out
4 Their labelling of children	Their labelling of clients
5 Their tendency to define situations in their own terms according to their own assumptions	Their tendency to define situations in their own terms according to their own assumptions
6 The assertion that schools are politically neutral	The assertion that social work could or ought to be politically neutral
7 The school as educator for the economy	The social work agency as maintaining the *status quo* of society
8 The school as an institution	The social work agency (most notably social service departments) as a bureaucracy
9 The illusion that most learning is result of teaching	The illusion that most improvements in situations where social workers are involved are the result of their interventions
10 What schools actually do teach (most teachers are actually social workers and political educators without knowing it)	What social workers actually do do (are most social workers actually teachers and political educators without knowing it?)
11 Schooling as part of a service industry	Social work as part of a service industry
12 Schools' failure to do anything effective about elitism or poverty	Social work agencies' failure to do anything effective about equality or poverty
13 Schools' failure to democratise	Social work's failure to democratise
14 Compulsion and therapy (the teachers' preoccupation with maintaining control in the classroom)	Compulsion and therapy (the social workers' statutory responsibilities and society's abdication of its own)

Some of the items in Table 6 illustrate the political aspects of both teaching and social work. Freire has said that 'education cannot be neutral':[8] nor can social work. Yet neither can really do very much about inequality or poverty in our present society. Schools are accused of failing to democratise, and so are social work agencies. Lister writes:[9] 'democratisation would involve positive discrimination on a scale unheard of so far (and it is doubtful . . . if this is a political possibility) or a change in social structures'. Both schools and social work are inevitably drawn into the political arena and yet they have neither the power nor the voice to argue on political terms, nor are teachers and social workers equipped by their training in the use of political skills. Lister mentions Schwartz, an advocate of

> permanent education [who] has argued for education throughout life, not education for life, so that man can keep abreast of the rapidly changing environment, not only in terms of professional re-training, but also in terms of changed values and adapt to new ways of life . . . an important role . . . is resocialisation. Resocialisation is a process in which allegiances, perceptions and habits are altered. It involves a change in personal and social identity.

In the comparison of tasks as between families, schools and social work (discussed in Chapter 1) it was suggested that schools might take a more assertive role as a change agent within society. Sarri has no doubt that 'the school is a people-changing organisation', and points out 'that while these changes are expected to be relatively permanent in the form of new and different modes of behaviour, new identities and new self perceptions', the processes by which these changes are induced have a moral and value-laden quality. So, according to the ideas of the movements of social change, this, too, is an area of shared tasks for teachers and social workers. They share responsibilities, but these include confronting society with the vulnerable position in which society has placed them by abdicating responsibilities to them and then blaming them for failing to carry them out. If, as Illich considers, 'schools have become the repository of society's hopes', then both they and social work agencies have also become the repositories of society's guilt about its failures.

(b) Alternatives

Alternatives not only imply the availability of opportunities outside the institutions of the system (familiar ones are those of alternative education and a radical alternative to prison), but their very existence gives a scope for choice between options. Some of the major criticisms of the state education system are concerned with the fact that not only is education compulsory, but little choice between the types of schools is available to parents who cannot afford to educate their children privately. There are also similar and growing concerns with regard to social work, particularly since the setting up and rapid expansion of the social service departments has been quickly followed by the worsening economic situation, which threatens to jeopardise the actual existence of many specialist independent social work agencies.

Many aspects of the present education and social work systems were first devised as alternatives to the system and developed as challenges to it. For instance, a number of adventure playgrounds began to find that children were hanging around the playground during school hours, and this led to the development of some truancy centres linked with the adventure playground informally but with formalised links with the education system. When such centres proved successful, the education system began to provide various forms of support and eventually either took some of them over or developed its own similar centres, but inside the system. In the area of social work some of the community projects which were developed either by community workers from independent agencies, or even the Home Office-funded Community Development Projects, began to challenge the local authorities in whose area they were working. In some areas the local authorities themselves have begun to employ community workers, not all of them based in the social services departments. However, the adoption of such innovations by the education and social work systems are not without their problems. Education departments have come in for serious criticism on the grounds that they are, in effect, not only condoning truancy, but undermining their own established institution (the schools), when they set up these small centres whose values are at variance with the more traditional ones. In social work, too, social services departments have been criticised by the democratically elected representatives when these challenges about their policies are the result of the community work carried out by their own employees. The efforts to bring about social change are frequently slow and tortuous.

Perhaps the best-known alternatives which remain outside the system are the 'free schools'. Some, though they develop with freshness and vigour, only seem to last a short while before they are overtaken by events (usually lack of resources). Nevertheless, there are some well-established 'free school' alternatives which not only exist outside the system, but even gain support from it in covert ways (such as providing free school meals as part of their general school service). Even those whose existence is short-lived often serve a useful purpose by providing both an alternative and a challenge, with resulting changes in the system. Head[10] writing of re-schooling

233

(as distinct from de-schooling) describes 'free schools as free from the state system, free to be a full time alternative, free to challenge the assumption of schooling and society, free of charge and able to provide free activities within the school and to explore the community'. The White Lion Street Free School is perhaps the best known of the free schools in this country. In writing of their school the contributors describe their roles as follows:

> We do not think that the use of the building or our work can be limited to what is conventionally thought of as education. In other words, we find that one implication of our essentially close relationship with families and others in the immediate area of the school is that our role is far wider than that of 'teacher'. Our way of doing things does not imply a greater number of different professionals 'servicing' families and children. On the contrary, we think that there are already too many. We believe that the fragmentation of these professional roles and their narrow interpretation is both unhelpful and extremely wasteful.

They go on to discuss their aims, some of which are described thus:

> unlike the negative concept of 'freedom from', the positive concept of 'freedom to do' does not at all undermine the role of adults in the school. Their role is vital. They are learners themselves, and then interpreters, and then tentative stage managers or directors of children's learning. A learner will clearly only take initiatives in areas which he finds interest him . . . . Our concept of the teacher's task is one for which we feel there are few, if any, precedents in practice. It is infinitely delicate, and we feel that we still have a great deal to learn about it. In attempting to identify a child's interest we believe that the teacher must never overstep the boundaries of the child's autonomy must never force-feed, but offer only an appropriate menu carefully selected after much reflection on each child's own likes and dislikes, talents and stumbling blocks.

Alison Truefitt[11] writes of educational alternatives within the law, stressing the requirement to register a free school as an institution, and to provide 200 teaching days in a year (or 400 sessions), but pointing out that there is no official guidance either in the 1944 Act or elsewhere as to what 'education' means! This is presumably to be adjudged at the discretion of inspectors from the DES who advise on suitability for registration.

The 1944 Act, she says, gives four headings under which the inspectors must be satisfied:

1 'suitability' of premises,
2 'adequacy' of premises, 'having regard' to the children's ages and sexes,
3 'efficiency and suitability' of the instruction having the same regard,
4 'properness' of the staff.

Free schools which satisfy the criteria may be duly recognised:

> Section 36 of the 1944 Education Act states that 'it shall be the duty of the parents of every child of compulsory school age to cause him to receive efficient full time education suitable to his age, ability and aptitude, either by regular attendance at school or otherwise'.

There are a few alternatives which have been set up by parents themselves. These attempt to give definition to the ambiguous statement 'or otherwise' and to provide alternative education for their children yet remain within the law. Among such parents are the Heads, who, with one or two other families, have provided the education for their own children.

It can be seen that many of these projects indeed reveal a striking similarity and they have in effect developed as a challenge to both systems. Often the differences are merely situational, with a slight emphasis towards challenging the established attitudes and policies of whichever of the systems the project wishes to confront, in order to demonstrate that such alternatives are possible.

Thus there seems to be a growing number of alternatives which function between the education and social work systems, often acting as a bridge or link between them and offering at the same time both a choice to their users and a more specialised service to meet their needs. In the discussion on social functioning in Chapter 1, it was pointed out that there is a period of peak stress for young families at about the time that the elder children start school. Indeed, for some families (notably those whose values are often alien to the state system, which requires compulsory and regular attendance), starting school itself adds to their stress, which is usually compounded by deprivation and poverty. Although the resources are scarce and often inappropriately located, there are various types of opportunities which might be available to such young families of 'rising fives'. If sufficient were provided, families could choose between nursery classes within schools, day centres (provided either for children or mothers and children together and usually financed from social work agencies) or play groups run by mothers themselves (with some financial support from local social service and education authorities and support from the Pre-school

Playgroups Association). Education visitors could be available to support them in the initial stages. Were such choices readily available and families helped to choose according to their own needs, then the alternatives would really be serving a purpose.

The other peak period of family stress, that of adolescent children, elderly grandparents and middle-aged parents, is much less well supported by alternatives to the education and social work systems. Indeed, as has already been noted, the education system in the form of schools withdraws its support at just this time. Although there are counselling services for young people available in most large cities, these often fail to reach those youngsters most in need. Some, like the Young People's Advisory Service, have begun to experiment with community workers who do mainly detached youth and community work from the agency base. Community centres and the youth and community service also attempt to help such young people, either from more formalised clubs or by the detached work described in the section on youth and community work. Once a young person has been convicted of an offence and is put on a probation order, then the probation service, too, plays its part in developing alternative projects. So, too, does the National Association for Care and Resettlement of Offenders, whose New Careers projects not only carry out preventive work for young people at the stage of secondary social breakdown, but also provide opportunities for ex-offenders to devise alternatives using their own values and experience in ways which are constructive for society.

Unfortunately, little seems to be provided for the parents of these young people, although there are old people's visitors and clubs and holidays for the grandparents. Apart from those opportunities, mainly of a social and supportive nature, which develop from settlements and the various councils of social service, neither the education nor the social work systems seem to concern themselves specifically with the needs of middle-aged parents, many of whom seem to lead cheerless and aimless lives whether at home or at work.

The discussion on the boundary areas (Chapter 3) has given some examples of alternatives which exist in the schools system, the social work system or as joint projects between the two, although time and again the lack of communication between the systems has been instanced as a contributory factor in their failure to provide the kind of assistance needed, whether educational or social work intervention, at the right time.

The isolation of one system from the other has been referred to many times throughout this book. The general lack of knowledge of social work on the part of primary school staffs was first publicly commented upon by the Plowden Committee[12] in 1966 and the theme of poor communication was developed by the Seebohm

Committee[13] in 1968. Since then there have been many references to the same state of affairs, most notably in the report of the inquiry on the care given to Maria Colwell.

While it seems sadly inevitable that some children and their families will suffer as the result of social breakdown, it is *not* inevitable that the schools and social work systems which have been developed in order to support them should fail them as they do. There is evidence that too many social work agencies are failing the children in their care. The reasons for these failures are manifold, and only some of them have been outlined in this book. Ignorance and isolation still result in failures of communication between the two systems, but neither appears to have the necessary evidence or the power to confront society with its own failures. In a recent book on the politics of change in relation to the personal social services, Hall writes: 'Whilst the fortunes of the personal social services are not usually seen by policy-makers as of permanent and consuming interest to the general public, the advent of an election may modify this assessment.'[14] She is writing of the pressures to implement the Seebohm proposals, but much of what she describes has relevance for promoting the need for teachers and social workers to work together. While they blame each other for failing to help children in need, instead of working together to bring about needed social change, then more children will proceed to secondary and tertiary breakdown. With appropriate intervention early in the process, the children of underprivileged and deprived families might maintain or even enhance their capacity for social functioning. It is to be hoped that the model of social breakdown developed in Chapter 2 might be clarified and refined, or alternative models conceived which encompass the activities of both systems, so that communication can be promoted and informed by knowledge which is meaningful to all.

The discussion on the people in the system (Chapters 4 and 5) showed that little is done in the training of either teachers or social workers to provide either with information as to the areas of overlap between the two systems, nor are opportunities often provided for each to meet the other so that controversial issues can be discussed. While there does seem to be some evidence that the values of teachers and social workers are coming closer together, little advantage appears to be taken of this.

The senior staff in social service departments have less personal autonomy than heads and in any case are directly accountable through the director of social services to the elected councillors. Many of them have been preoccupied with learning the new management skills required of them since the formation of their departments in 1971. While they may be more familiar with the tasks of the education system than the heads are with the tasks of social work, they have had little time to acquaint themselves with the social science knowledge which is now so relevant in social work and which was almost certainly lacking in their own professional training. Indeed, some of them are not professionally trained social workers but administrators schooled in the bureaucratic methods of local government. School heads, on the other hand, have only recently been introduced to the idea that management skills are an important aspect of their repertoire. Mention has already been made of the heads' absolute power and also of their immense responsibilities, perhaps particularly in the large comprehensive secondary schools. While heads are appointed by democratically elected representatives in the form of school managers or governors—and there is much criticism of these procedures—they have considerable freedom to run their schools in their own way, as the recent events at Tyndale Junior School have shown. What can be done to provide shared or even 'remedial' training opportunities for senior staffs in both the systems? It is at this level that many of the innovative ideas for shared use of resources and projects founder.

As has been shown, both professional associations and unions are often more concerned with enhancing or preserving the interests of their own membership than in promoting dialogues or remedies to common problems which seriously impinge on the way their tasks are carried out. What can be done to ensure by contriving, coaxing or even coercion that such dialogues not only take place, but are openly informative, even provocative, rather than restricted to demarcation discussions?

Finally, what can be offered by way of alternative strategies in order to meet the valid criticisms of both schools and social work? The discussion on social breakdown particularly demonstrated the vitally important roles of both the schools and the social work systems in relation to the process of social breakdown. There are also many problems which specifically result from compulsory school attendance, yet there is little real evidence that de-schooling would resolve many of the problems raised in this book. Nor would further emphasis on community work be sufficient answer. As Lister points out:

> In spite of its profound insights de-schooling theory has its serious weaknesses. The most serious of these are that the arguments lack a firm basis of empirical evidence and practical alternatives; they evade central questions of political power; and they offer critiques, rather than operational strategies or programmes.[15]

The same could be said for the welfare rights movements as regards social work.

238

The school and the community

Throughout this book the problems associated with the schools' responsibilities to the communities they are expected to serve have been pointed out and discussed. Conflicts of values related to the tasks of the family and those of the school have particularly been stressed. An important area which has only been alluded to is the question of parental choice regarding the kind of education they would like for their children. It is not possible to discuss this here, even though it must be pointed out that this, yet again, raises both national and local political issues, which the recent defeat of the Minister of Education (on the appeal of Tameside to the House of Lords, following his directive that they must introduce comprehensive education) has highlighted. What is especially relevant to the subject of this book is the social distance of many schools from the communities within which they are situated. There are many reasons for this, some of them organisational and some of them related to social class, but by and large very little effort is really made specifically to deal with this problem (which can hardly be said to be dealt with by the appointment of parent governors or managers). Many schools make specific efforts to contact the possible parents of their future pupils, both at rising five and at eleven-plus, but this could hardly be considered sufficient. Most members of the community perceive their schools through a prism of fleeting contacts and misinformation based on their own educational experience. It is therefore inevitable that they should form a picture of a stereotyped school, a picture which they have very little opportunity to correct. The school, too, is likely to be functioning from stereotyped views of the community. Considered in terms of systems theory, many schools function as isolated closed systems within the community. A similar situation is implied in the Rose and Marshall[16] research, but not specifically discussed.

Litwak and Meyer[17] have developed both a theory and a practice model of school-community relations, is based on several years' work with the Detroit school system. The purpose of a school community programme as they see it, 'falls within the school's general educational goals', and these they describe in terms similar to those outlined earlier in this book (Chapter 1). They postulate that school community relations can be conceived of 'in terms of the "distance" between the school and its families and neighbourhoods'. There are roughly three positions which are taken by educators in regard to such distance

1 *'The Closed Door'* position—that community involvement is extraneous, if not injurious, to the education of the child.

2 *'The Open Door'* position . . . assumes that many of the

basic educational processes take place outside the building
in family life, peer group and neighbourhood . . . the
motivation for learning in school has its source in the
everyday life of the child.

3   *Balance theory* recognises the validity of both positions, but
argues that optimal social distance is a determinable point
between the extremes of intimacy and isolation.

Litwak and Meyer define the expert and non-expert tasks of teachers
and parents in education and stress the importance of the complementary contributions of both. Again these are not too dissimilar to
the tasks discussed earlier in Chapter 1 as those of families and
schools. They also emphasise that

the organisational settings of bureaucracies and primary groups
present two dangers for appropriate communication between
persons in the community and experts in school. If they are too
close their antithetical structures may lead to reduction of
effective contributions of expertise or of primary group support.
However, if they fail to communicate, the contributions of both
cannot be brought to the common educational purpose.

Such thinking is similar to some of the conclusions drawn from the
EPA projects, although Litwak and Mayer go on to develop a theory
based on some linking mechanisms for regulating school community
relations and to give some guidelines for their use. While their
terminology for such mechanisms inevitably has an American bias,
and thus reads unfamiliarly, there seems no reason why the ideas
expressed within the use of these mechanisms should not be
experimented with by the education system in this country. Litwak
and Meyer describe 'eight mechanisms of co-ordination as approaches a school . . . can use in order to reach and influence the
local community'. These are outlined below, together with comments
and possible opportunities in the UK.

1   *Detached worker:* An organisation uses this mechanism
when it sends a professional person to enter the family or
home territory of those to be influenced so as to develop a
trusting, quasi primary group relationship through which to
bring the groups norms and values into harmony with those
of the organisation.

As Litwak and Meyer point out, teachers and social workers already
use this approach, which is commensurate with the tasks of both
education and social work.

2   *Opinion leader* . . . a professional person from the
organization makes use of natural or indigenous leaders in

the neighbourhood, through whom families and neighbourhood members are influenced in their relationship to the organization.

Such an approach is rarely used directly by schools in this country, although much of the community work carried out by workers from the social work or education system may involve such an approach. (For example, see the section on youth and community work in Chapter 3.)

3 *Settlement House:* this mechanism involves the provision of physical facilities and professional persons located in the home territory of those to be affected so that they are easily accessible. The aim of the settlement house approach is to provide a change-inducing milieu.

This, too, is a familiar approach in this country, where settlements in inner city deprived areas may provide educational facilities as part of their overall provision. In some cases alternative schools are provided in this way, though difficulties arise where the expectation is that eventually the children should return to the schools from which they truanted or have been excluded (in effect if not in fact).

4 *Auxiliary voluntary association:* A voluntary association bringing together members from the organization and from the community can be established for linking the two groups

In the USA the leadership roles are not usually filled by professionals. In this country, parent-teacher associations seem to be feared or else criticised as being dominated by the middle-class parents. However, in view of the success of mothers' clubs at some of the community schools, it may be the schools' lack of expertise in community work skills which has led to this situation.

5 *Common messenger* . . . the use of common members of the organisation and of the community group to be affected to link the two.

The child is the most obvious common messenger, but use might also be made of the indigenous workers who may be employed in the school as auxiliaries, for example the dinner ladies. One of the functions of the school managers or governors is this common messenger function, but, as has already been mentioned, these groups are often dominated by political rather than educational considerations.

6 *Mass media:* the organization tries to influence the members of the community by using public communication, that is by newspapers, television, radio, etc.

Although the great education debate has gone some way to redress this state of affairs, traditionally, educationists in this country could generally be described as timid in their use of the media, particularly on a localised basis. While we are becoming accustomed to seeing national figures discussing their educational views on the television, we are unlikely to read a great deal about our own community schools in the local newspapers, or even in the free shoppers which come through the front doors of many urban dwellers. Here is an opportunity for schools to correct some of the misconceptions regarding their policies and their functions.

7 *Formal authority:* the use of legal authority or the authority of well established custom used by the organization to require members of the community to conform to the expectations or requirements of the school.

The attendance responsibilities of the education social worker/ education welfare officer and the head's power to suspend a pupil are examples of the use of such authority.

8 *Delegated function:* this is not a direct linking mechanism in the same sense as the others; the school in using delegated functions links itself to community groups the school seeks to affect; and links itself to the community through that agency.

Referral to medical agencies or to social service departments are typical examples.

Litwak and Meyer describe some principles for deciding which linking mechanism to use, pointing out that the choice depends on the goals of the school community programme. They describe four principles based on a knowledge of communication theory which they consider are of assistance in assessing the usefulness of the linking mechanisms: initiative to overcome selective listening; intensity to overcome selective retention; focused expertise to provide feedback and flexibility; maximum scope to reach the optimum number. These principles are by no means unfamiliar to either teachers or social workers, although they may describe them in other terms, and teachers particularly may not have considered applying them to their relations with the community outside the school.

The linking mechanisms themselves are also not unfamiliar, although the idea of using them as part of a deliberate strategy and as part of a plan to influence the community seems a novel suggestion. In tabular form, Litwak and Meyer re-examine each mechanism, adding comments as to whether they are useful for opening or closing the social distance relating them to the three positions outlined earlier. Their table is reproduced here as Table 7.

TABLE 7 *Comparative usefulness of linking mechanisms for three positions in school-community relations*

	Open-door position	Closed-door position	Balance-theory Position
Goal:	Close social distance	Create social distance	Create and/or close Social distance
Linking Mechanism			
Detached worker	Very high	Very low	Very high when distance is to be decreased (e.g., when community is hostile), very low when distance is to be increased (e.g. when too involved)
Opinion leader	Potentially moderate e.g., when community is friendly or when coupled with another mechanism (e.g., detached worker, mass media) uses for recruitment	Very low	Potentially moderate when distance is to be decreased through intensity, very low when distance is to be Increased
Settlement (house)	High, potentially very high when community is friendly	Very low	High when distance is to be decreased through focused expertise, very low when distance is to be increased
Voluntary association	Moderate, potentially very high when community is friendly	Moderate	Moderate when distance is to be decreased by scope, moderate when distance is to be increased
Common messenger	Low	High	Moderate when distance is to be decreased by scope, moderate when distance is to be increased
Mass media	Low, potentially high when community is friendly and when coupled with an intense mechanism	High	Very low when distance is to be decreased, high when distance is to be increased
Formal authority	Very low	Very high	Very low when distance is to be decreased, very high when distance is to be increased

SOURCE: E. Litwak and H. J. Meyer, *School, Family and Neighborhood: The Theory and Practice of School-Community Relations,* Columbia University Press, 1974.

Meyer and Litwak stress the importance of values and the implication of ethics in any activity involving the school and the community, and point out that 'the basic goals of the schools may differ from those of the parents'. They also point out that 'schools and communities may have different interests concerning the means', and stress that communication between the experts (teachers) and the non-experts is crucial:

> Because professional persons are experts in the means of achieving certain goals they are expected to know more about teaching, reading, about child development, learning, etc., than parents. But these means cannot be utilized without co-operation from non professionals especially those in families . . . there must be communication in both directions; this is the crux of a community programme . . . [The] adjustments and adaptations [that] will inevitably be necessary [will] usually create some sense of loss or gain in those involved. Conflict will occur over immediate issues and perhaps, more basically, when the values and goals of school and community members seriously differ.

It might be worth developing some similar approach in this country and working with the education and social work systems to devise joint projects that would involve the communities in specific issues, though it would be essential to evaluate these first. Some projects, notably those based on independent agencies, are already being developed. Intermediate treatment provides a useful framework for such opportunities and the many small projects which exist could become part of a co-ordinated strategy if ways could be found.

Heads of schools, teachers, education welfare officers, youth workers, the local area teams of the social service department and local councillors and parents might, for instance, devise a model (involving detached workers, opinion leaders, settlements and common messengers) that would allow them to share with the community their concern over the 15 per cent of schoolchildren who, it is estimated, are out of schools each day.

One such project has been developed from the base of a social work student unit within a social services department. For the past few years a number of student placements, in conjunction with the Education Welfare Department, have been working in a school on a large council estate. They have found that

> Many of the projects in the school continually showed that there was a high degree of school refusal and suspension. The EWO [Education Welfare Officer] involved in these projects undertook some personal research into possible reasons for this school refusal rate; at the same time data were collected from families whose children truanted. The information gained showed that approximately 80% of the yearly intake in the school had low average to ESN [Educationally Subnormal] IQ scores. Education to the majority of families was a low priority

but most felt the Head demanded too high an academic standard of those children who had great difficulty in learning; consequently, the school classed these children as under-achievers based on the school's standards.[18]

The unit was concerned about this state of affairs and attempted to highlight this for the school by offering to work with special groups of school-leavers. This suggestion foundered because of the school's attitude to both the idea and the children in question.

The education welfare officer and the student unit supervisor discussed the situation with other social work agencies and found that this attitude was also affecting their caseloads and, in particular, the number of children received into care:

> Because the child refused school continually, the Education Welfare Department took the family to Court, the Courts placed the children in care or at least made some form of order within which the Social Services Department were statutorily obliged to become involved.

The education welfare officer also discussed the situation with the school psychologist and the senior officers of the Education Welfare Service:

> A joint meeting was arranged at a fairly high level and eventually the school inspectorate were involved in an inquiry . . . it is likely that there will be a change of Head or a re-thinking of the form of education offered to these under-achieving children and how their parents could be involved.

As has been shown by describing this rather controversial project, promoting contacts between the community and the schools can be conflictual and cause discomfort for the people involved; but it is a way of endeavouring to ensure that schools provide a satisfactory educational service for their community.

A future role for the Education Welfare Service

In the discussion of the tasks of education and social work the role of the school as an agent of social change has been considered. At various points throughout the book the opportunities that exist for the development of such a role have also been pointed out. The section on the EPA projects (Chapter 3) also discussed community school models, pointing out some of the difficulties which such a change of role might entail. The description of the Education Welfare Service (Chapter 4) also made reference to developments in the USA in the area of home/school relations, where such tasks are usually carried out by home teachers, who are more like the teacher/social workers described by Craft,[19] or even the education visitors some areas are beginning to introduce. It will be interesting to see whether the education visitor role comes to be seen as similar to that of social workers without statutory duties, and what the public's perception of the role will be. However, in this country there are distinct advantages in the Education Welfare Service playing a large part in such developments, particularly in the relationships of the school with the community, as was demonstrated in the previous sections.

While the education social workers (education welfare officers) are not trained teachers, they have a great deal of knowledge regarding the role and function of the school. As the service becomes more professional in the sense of acquiring the knowledge and skills which are common to social work intervention, then it is also likely to develop an orientation which takes into account its specialist role as the link between the community and the education system. Education social work could become a specialism within social work, taking its place alongside other specialisms based on work with particular client groups—the elderly, mentally ill or the delinquent. It will have to find ways of working out its role in relation to the child care specialism. There are differences, one of which is the Education Welfare Service's responsibility for all schoolchildren (an impossible task) while the child care expertise has been developed in relation to children in need of special care. Teachers, on the other hand, generally know little about social work intervention, nor have they had opportunities to develop the skills as part of their own training, which can be seen from the earlier discussion on their training, which would need to be radically altered in order to equip them to carry out such tasks in relation to the community. However, as has already been noted, following the recent announcement of severe cuts in teacher training many colleges of education are beginning to 'diversify' into some forms of training for community and youth work, and there is no reason why 'graduates' of such courses should not be encouraged to join an extended Education Welfare Service, if they do not wish to teach or become youth workers. The Education Welfare Service has long experience of interpreting the school to the community, although the manner in which it undertakes such tasks may need bringing up-to-date. Social work skills seem more relevant to such a task, than the skills which are more appropriate to the classroom.

At present such community work skills are not readily available in the schools, so this would seem a logical extension of their tasks. While some difficulties will inevitably arise, for instance amongst parents who reject school (see pp. 109-10), at least such parents would have some choice as regards the social work intervention they themselves considered appropriate. Social workers from social services departments and other agencies might be available for consultation or to become involved if it seemed more appropriate or acceptable to the community. Involving the education Welfare Service in such a way might result in involving the school with the families of schoolchildren who are at the stage of primary social breakdown, instead of using the education social worker when the process has almost reached the stage of secondary social breakdown. This, too, might go some way towards reducing the inevitable stigma which seems to result from definitions of social breakdown. However, to use the Education Welfare Service in this way would require a major change of attitude and orientation towards the service on the part of the education system. In relation to its social work colleagues, the Education Welfare Service is emerging from its chrysalis, though it has yet to shed its role as handyman to the teacher (a slightly more appropriate phrase than is suggested by the dainty handmaiden!). Once this has been achieved, there would be added benefits, such as the real development of a consultative social work role, for the benefit of teachers. The need for such consultation is already recognised and specialist teachers (such as teacher/social workers and counsellors) are beginning to be used in such a role as distinct from the more traditional view that the head is responsible for this as well as almost everything else.

Education welfare officers have long made available to the schools their knowledge of the neighbourhoods and of individual families, but this has customarily only been by way of reporting to the head or a senior teacher as part of their pastoral care role. What is needed is the opportunity for social work consultants to be freely available to class teachers by regular contact with them in the staff room. Here is an opportunity for 'educating' teachers into a more community-oriented perspective, by making it possible for them to seek support and consultation as part of their weekly routine, rather than when a crisis is reached in relation to a particular child or family. The opening of the school system in this way, so as to allow knowledge and information regarding the community to flow in can only lead to beneficial results for schoolchildren, providing it is recognised that this is part of the professional role of teachers and education welfare officers and thus the rights of the individuals are safeguarded. Such changes are already developing in some areas.

The dilemma of social control

In a society as ours there seems no way of avoiding the use of some of society's agents in roles where tasks of social control are part of their function. Whether teachers and social workers should play such roles to the extent they are required to do is a matter for debate, but it does not seem inevitable that society should continue to use them to shoulder the burden of trying to bring up to standard or into line those casualties which are the result of its own failures. The model of the process of social breakdown (see Chapter 2) showed that it is not inevitable and that the roles played by society's own agents may play a part in bringing it about. If the model (or something similar) could be developed sufficiently to enable its use by various agents of social control, then it is possible that at least some social breakdowns could be avoided or minimised. Communication and exchange of knowledge and ideas across the system boundaries make co-operation and innovation easier. Definitions and prescriptions of secondary and tertiary social breakdown could perhaps be used more sparingly if the support, mediation, amelioration and correction necessary in the early stages could *really* become part of a co-operative exercise in which the agents of each system could both understand and respect each other's roles.

School social work

The whole question of school social work is perhaps bound up with this dilemma of social control and with the inevitable stigma which seems to accompany definitive actions taken in this area. As has been mentioned earlier, it seems that a decision regarding the organisational location of the Educational Welfare Services has been made by default, in that things are apparently to be left as they are. There are advantages to this situation, some of which were made clear when the service was discussed in Chapter 4, but there may be others. Present resources in social work are in any case inadequate and both the education and the social work systems have recently undergone major organisational changes within which there has been insufficient time to become established.

As an alternative, Rose and Marshall (who also discuss possible organisational location) suggest that School Social Service Centres should be set up jointly, that these should be in premises attached to schools and that they should provide accommodation for counsellors and school social workers, youth workers and community workers:

The functions of such centres might be
    i.   Providing casework type services either for one school or a group of schools according to need.
   ii.   Liaison with police, probation, the social service department, voluntary bodies and other relevant social agencies.

   iii. Fostering positive parent contact with the school.
   iv. Providing and fostering group work services, particularly youth work.
   v. Organising community centre activities.
   vi. Organising social education in schools.
   vii. Providing expert advice where necessary upon vocational and educational guidance.
   viii. Participating in the training of teachers, counsellors, social workers and health service personnel.
   ix. Checking on attendance.

They continue:

> these centres would need to be under the general guidance of the headmaster, but might very well have their own part-time administrative director. They should consist of counsellors, seconded social workers, teachers with relevant training and community workers. Attendance work should be carried out by ancillaries, and education welfare officers should either do this or be retrained as social workers or non-teacher counsellors.

While the idea of having a centre attached to the school where all those professionals engaged in 'school social work' could meet, share ideas, or even work together seems an excellent one, unfortunately there are serious criticisms relating to the suggestion of a School Social Service Centre. First, for it to be under the general guidance of the school head is likely to result in its incorporation into the school system, which would negate much of its usefulness. Nor is it likely that this would be welcomed by social workers or youth and community workers, whose orientations, by their very nature, are likely to differ from those of the head and at times even be diametrically opposed.

Second, the separating of the attendance work as suggested would have major repercussions. One of the major dilemmas of education is how to contain both the caring and the disciplinary aspects which are inherent aspects of its socialising function. The proposal not only splits them, but also indicates that attendance work is of lower standard and therefore less important. The problems relating to attendance enforcement result from society's current view that education should be compulsory from the ages of five to sixteen. That is where the debate should take place and the ramifications of this decision should be considered at all levels, not separated off and carried out by the least trained and the lowest paid.

Third, Rose and Marshall do not seem particularly appreciative of the current role of the Education Welfare Service and their suggestion seems to imply its virtual demise. This is both unrealistic and likely to be unacceptable to the education system as well as to the service itself.

Fourth, as their organisational recommendations imply, there are considerable problems associated with interdisciplinary organisations, although there is increasing interest in such approaches, which are being developed in relation to medicine (health visitors and social workers), in law (community law centres) and in architecture and town planning. All these professions are well established ones and yet they, too, are experiencing the problems of a primary profession, with lesser more dependent professions struggling for equal recognition and power. It may be that some of the models they are developing could be adaptable for school social work.

Opportunities for interdisciplinary education and training

The attitudes of people in higher management positions of both the education and social work systems are a crucial factor in instituting social change. It should be possible for the DES and the DHSS, or the CCETSW and the Schools Council, to jointly sponsor conferences, workshops or even residential courses where heads and senior educational administrators could meet with directors of social services and other senior managers. As this book is going to press the DHSS's Development Group-Social Work Service has published a report of an interdisciplinary project undertaken with South Glamorgan County Council. This pioneering interdisciplinary project, 'Working Together for Children and their Families', not only provided the opportunity for the professionals to get together to work on mutual interests,[20] but also developed a new model for 'in-service training'. Up to 130 people from various professional groups, including elected members, teachers, social workers and others (60 per cent of them 'grass roots' workers) met for an initial residential conference and three follow-up one-day conferences, plus a final residential seminar. In between, various study groups worked together on chosen topics selected from the conference. Such a bold experiment appears not only to have improved local interprofessional understanding and relationships, but also to have seeded ongoing interprofessional activities. This, together with the conferences sponsored by the Gulbenkian Foundation, has blazed a trail for others to follow. Some possible, if controversial, topics to follow the Foundation's 'Education and the Urban Crisis' might be: Compulsory School Attendance; Care v. Control; Violence in the Family; Residential Provision for Adolescents with Behaviour Problems; Is Confidentiality an Outmoded Concept?

As has already been pointed out, both teachers and social workers go through a 'baptism of fire' during the course of their professional training. For social workers this is usually just prior to professional training and for teachers during their first year of teaching. Training courses for teachers and social workers have opportunities for enabling each to gain at least a bird's-eye view of the other. Indeed, this is already happening. Several professional social work courses are enabling students to undertake their practice attached to schools (as was described earlier). At least one PGCE course arranges a short period of attachment to social service departments, where these observational placements are followed up by seminar discussion in which some of the key issues are considered. Such experiments are to be encouraged rather than jeopardised by what are in effect demarcation disputes, though these are usually rationalised as due to 'lack of resources'.

Given the present state of affairs, it is likely that organisational structures and professional tasks and responsibilities will be left much as they are. Social work in relation to schools will thus continue to be a multi-faceted, multiple-method approach. There is no reason, however, why this should remain such a confused, confusing and conflictual boundary area. The increased interest in forms of care for schoolchildren and their families, and also the current concern regarding the failure of many of society's institutions to meet their needs, could be used to promote further co-operative developments across the systems. Those interested in such issues— local Education and Social Services Committees, Child Poverty Action and Family Rights groups, the professional associations and unions (such as BASW and the NUT), organisations like the Advisory Centre for Education, and so on—are already building links to promote the exchange of information. Perhaps joint action will not be far behind. What are also needed are groupings where people can test out with one another the different perceptions as viewed from vantage points at each level in the systems.

Halsey, writing of the views of Illich and Freire in his article 'Is Society Liberated or Repressed by its Educational System?', concludes:

> Both Illich and Freire want to make us all free from these socially structured constraints. From Illich, we have a vivid picture of such an ideal world, but with no convincing plan as to how we might reach it. From Freire, we have an account of educational means towards much the same end, but embedded in a theory of revolutions which I find unacceptable.
>
> Formal systems of education must play a vital part in the road to greater freedom, but this destination can and should be reached by political action other than revolution. It requires

political will to be sure, but it is possible within the framework of traditional Western parliamentary democracies.[21]

From such deliberations, the decisions which need to be made may be refined and clarified, and strategies devised which might lead to their implementation. But they will all need to be political ones—there is no escape!

References

Introduction: some boundary issues

1 A. N. Whitehead, *The Aims of Education*, Ernest Benn, 1962 edn.
2 Werner Boehm, quoted in Harriett Bartlett, *The Common Base of Social Work Practice*, NASW, 1970.
3 R. Parker, 'The Future of the Personal Social Services' in W. Robson and Bernard Crick (eds), *The Future of the Social Services*, Penguin, 1970.
4 Plowden Report, *Children and their Primary Schools*, HMSO, 1966.
5 Newsom Report, *Half our Future*, HMSO, 1963.
6 Seebohm Committee, *Report of the Committee on Local Authority and Allied Personal Social Services*, HMSO, 1968.
7 *Inquiry into the Care Provided in Relation to Maria Colwell*, HMSO, 1974.
8 A. Clegg and B. Megson, *Children in Distress*, Penguin, 1973 edn.
9 H. Goldstein, *Social Work and the Unitary Approach*, University of South Carolina Press, 1973.
10 E. Goodacre, *Home and School*, NFER, 1970.

Chapter one: The area of overlap between school and social work

1 Robin Auld, *William Tyndale Junior and Infants Schools Public Inquiry*, ILEA, 1976.
2 *Inquiry into the Care Provided in Relation to Maria Colwell*, HMSO, 1974.
3 P. Wedge and H. Prosser, *Born to Fail*, Arrow Books, 1971.
4 A. K. Rice and E. J. Miller, *Systems of Organisation*, Tavistock, 1967.
5 H. Goldstein, *Social Work and the Unitary Approach*, University of South Carolina Press, 1973.
6 J. Clausen (ed.), *Socialisation and Society*, Little Brown, 1968.
7 E. McBroom, 'Socialisation and Casework' in R. Roberts and R. Nee, *Theories of Social Casework*, University of Chicago Press, 1970.
8 Werner Boehm, *Objectives of the Social Work Curriculum of the Future*, New York, Council on Social Work Education, 1959; quoted in H. Bartlett, *The Common Base of Social Work Practice*, NASW, 1970.

References

9   K. Rice, *The Enterprise and its Environment*, Tavistock, 1963.
10   J. Clausen, *op. cit.*
11   *A Framework for Expansion*, HMSO, 1972.
12   W. Van der Eyken, *The Pre-School Years*, Penguin, 1974 edn.
13   Ralph Ruddock, *Roles and Relationships*, Routledge & Kegan Paul, 1969.
14   *A Language for Life: The Report of the Committee into Language and Reading*, Report of the Bullock Committee, HMSO, 1975.
15   H. Goldstein, *Social Work and Unitary Approach*, University of South Carolina Press, 1973.
16   Mia Kellmer Pringle, *The Needs of Children*, Hutchinson, 1974.
17   E. Erikson, *Identity, Youth and Crisis*, Faber, 1968.
18   C. Turner, *Family and Kinship in Modern Britain*, Routledge & Kegan Paul, 1969.
19   R. and R. Rapoport, 'Study of Marriage as a Critical Transition Period' in Peter Lomas (ed.), *Predicament of the Family*, Hogarth Press, 1967.
20   H. Perlman, *Persona*, University of Chicago Press, 1970.
21   Gerald Caplan, *An Approach to Community Mental Health*, Tavistock, 1971.
22   P. Marris, *Loss and Change,* Routledge & Kegan Paul, 1974.
23   M. Kellmer Pringle, *op. cit.*
24   H. Bartlett, *op. cit.*

Chapter two: Breakdown in social functioning—social breakdown

1   R. Rowbottom, A. Hey and D. Billis, *Social Services Departments: Developing Patterns of Work and Organization*, Heinemann, 1974.
2   E. Litwak and D. Meyer, *School, Family and Neighborhood: The Theory and Practice of School Community Relations*, Columbia University Press, 1974.
3   Roger Evans, 'Some Implications of an Integrated Model of Social Work for Theory and Practice', *British Journal of Social Work*, Summer 1976, vol. 6, no. 2.
4   Robin Auld, *William Tyndale Junior and Infants School Public Inquiry*, ILEA, 1976.
5   Brian Heraud, *Sociology and Social Work*, Pergamon, 1970.
6   Nina Toren, *Social Work, The Case of a Semi-Profession*, Sage, 1972.
7   *Children and Young Persons Acts 1969, 1975*, HMSO.
8   *Mental Health Act 1969*, HMSO.
9   David Hargreaves, Stephen Hestor and Frank Mellor, *Deviance in Classrooms*, Routledge & Kegan Paul, 1975.
10   Anthony Forder, 'Social Work and System Theory', *British Journal of Social Work*, Spring 1976, vol. 6, no. 1.
11   Robin Skynner, *One Flesh: Separate Persons*, Constable, 1976.
12   H. Goldstein, *Social Work and Unitary Approach*, University of South Carolina Press, 1973.
13   *Inquiry into the Care Provided in Relation to Maria Colwell*, HMSO, 1974.
14   R. Auld, *op. cit.*

15 Mia Kellmer Pringle, *The Needs of Children*, Hutchinson, 1975.
16 Robert Holman, *Socially Deprived Families in Britain*, Bedford Square Press, 1970.
17 Plowden Report, *Children and their Primary Schools*, HMSO, 1966.
18 D. Hargreaves *et al.*, *op. cit.*
19 M. J. Power, R. T. Benn and J. N. Morris, 'Neighbourhood, School and Juveniles Before the Courts', *New Society*, 19 October 1967.
20 Michael Rutter, *Helping Troubled Children*, Penguin, 1975.
21 Michael Phillippson, 'Juvenile Delinquency and the School' in W. F. Carson and P. Wiles (eds), *Crime and Delinquency in Britain*, Martin Robertson, 1970.
22 Frank Field (ed.), *Education and the Urban Crisis*, Routledge & Kegan Paul, 1977.
23 R. Auld, *op. cit.*
24 Rosemary Sarri and Frank Maple (eds), *The School in the Community*, NASW, 1972.
25 David Hargreaves, 'The Delinquent Subculture and the School' in Carson and Wiles, *op. cit.*
26 BBC, 'The Children's Charter', *Man Alive*, March 1975.
27 Leila Berg, *Risinghill: Death of a Comprehensive School*, Penguin, 1968.
28 Erving Goffman, *Asylums*, Penguin, 1968.
29 J. Lynch and J. Pimlott, *Parents and Teachers*, Macmillan Educational, 1976.
30 R. Auld, *op. cit.*
31 Jean Packman, *The Child's Generation*, Basil Blackwell and Martin Robertson, 1976.
32 *Children and Young Persons Act 1969*, HMSO.
33 Phyllida Parsloe, 'Social Work and the Justice Model', *British Journal of Social Work*, Spring 1976, vol. 6, no. 1.
34 Sir Roger Ormrod, 'The Role of the Courts in Relation to Children', *Child Adoption*, 1974, no. 1.
35 M. Kellmer Pringle, *op. cit.*
36 Maria Colwell inquiry, *op. cit.*
37 *Inquiry into the Care Provided in Relation to Stephen Meurs*, Norfolk County Council, 1975.
38 O. Stevenson and C. Desborough, *Case Conferences: A Study of Interprofessional Communication Concerning Children at Risk*, University of Keele, 1977.
39 R. Auld, *op. cit.*
40 *Children and Young Persons Act 1933*, HMSO.
41 *Education Act 1944*, HMSO.
42 Joel Handler, *The Coercive Social Worker*, Markham, 1973.
43 Alec Clegg and Barbara Megson, *Children in Distress*, Penguin, 1973, 2nd edn.
44 Jane Rowe and Lydia Lambert, *Children Who Wait*, Association of British Adoption Agencies, 1973.
45 J. Goldstein, A. Solnit and A. Freud, *Beyond the Best Interests of the Child*, Free Press, 1973.

References

46 Maria Colwell inquiry, *op. cit.*
47 Stephen Meurs inquiry, *op. cit.*
48 *Children and Young Persons Act 1948*, HMSO.
49 Bill Jordan, *Poor Parents*, Routledge & Kegan Paul, 1974.

Chapter three: Some boundary areas and their problems

1 M. Kellmer Pringle, *The Needs of Children*, Hutchinson, 1975.
2 *Inquiry into the Care Provided in Relation to Maria Colwell*, HMSO, 1974.
3 John Paley and David Thorpe, *Children: Handle with Care*, National Youth Bureau, 1974.
4 Norman Tutt, *Care or Custody*, Darton, Longman & Todd, 1974.
5 T. Tuckwell and D. Warrior, 'Home and School', *New Society*, 19 October 1973.
6 Michael Marland, *Pastoral Care*, Heinemann Educational, 1974.
7 Everett Reimer, *School is Dead*, Penguin, 1971.
8 J. B. Douglas, *Home and School*, Panther, 1967.
9 Eric Midwinter, *The Social Environment and the Urban School*, Ward Lock, 1972.
10 Elizabeth Goodacre, *School and Home*, NFER, 1970.
11 Derek Miller, *The Years Between*, Cornmarket Hutchinson, 1969.
12 Mary Saltmarsh, 'Misalliance or Working Partnership', *Social Work Today*, June 1973, vol. 4, no. 6.
13 P. Wedge and H. Prosser, *Born to Fail*, Arrow, 1973.
14 Maurice Craft, 'The School Welfare Team' in M. Craft, J. Rayner and L. Cohen (eds), *Linking Home and School*, Longmans, 1967.
15 L. Green, *Parents and Teachers, Partners or Rivals*, Allen & Unwin, 1968.
16 *The Family in Society, Preparation for Parenthood*, HMSO, 1974.
17 P. Halmos, *The Faith of the Counsellors*, Constable, 1965.
18 M. North, *The Secular Priests*, Allen & Unwin, 1972.
19 Anne Jones, 'School Counselling in Practice', *Concern*, no. 14, Summer 1974.
20 M. Saltmarsh, *op. cit.*
21 Anne Jones, personal communication and the *Guardian*, 20 July 1976.
22 Bill Jordan, *Poor Parents*, Routledge & Kegan Paul, 1974.
23 Gordon Rose and T. Marshall, *Counselling and School Social Work*, Wiley, 1974.
24 *Albemarle Report on the Youth Service for England Wales*, HMSO, 1960.
25 C. Smith, A. Farrant and H. Marchant, *The Wincroft Project*, Tavistock, 1972.
26 Mary Morse, *The Unattached*, Penguin, 1965; G. Goetschius and J. Tash, *Working with Unattached Youth*, Routledge & Kegan Paul, 1967.
27 F. Milson, 'School and the Community', *Education Guardian*, 12 February 1974.
28 Plowden Report, *Children and their Primary Schools*, HMSO, 1966.

29 P. Marris and M. Rein, *Dilemmas of Social Reform*, Penguin, 1974.
30 A. H. Halsey, *Educational Priority vol. 1: Problems and Places*, HMSO, 1972.
31 Karen Lyons, *Social Work and the School*, HMSO, 1973.
32 C. Morrison (ed.), *Educational Priority, vol. 5: A Scottish Study*, HMSO, 1974.
33 DHSS, *The Family in Society—Preparation for Parenthood*, HMSO, 1974.
34 Geoff Poulton in 'Report of the National Conference for Education Home Visitors' (privately circulated), 1977.
35 Teresa Smith and George Smith, 'The Community School—a Base for Community Development' in David Jones and Marjorie Mayo (eds), *Community Work One*, Routledge & Kegan Paul, 1974.
36 Eric Midwinter, *Patterns of Community Education*, Ward Lock, 1973.
37 Report of the Taylor Committee, *A New Partnership for our Schools*, DES and Welsh Office, HMSO, 1977.
38 Smith and Smith, *op. cit.*
39 Michael Rutter, *Helping Troubled Children*, Penguin, 1975.
40 Elizabeth Anderson, 'Special Schools or Special Schooling', *Journal of Child Psychology and Psychiatry*, April 1976, vol. 17, no. 2.
41 *Report of the Underwood Committee on Maladjusted Children*, HMSO, 1955.
42 Sula Wolff, *Children under Stress*, Penguin, 1969.
43 *Inquiry into the Care Provided in Relation to Maria Colwell*, HMSO, 1974.
44 *Times Educational Supplement*, 12 December 1975; 9 April 1976.
45 *Children in Trouble*, HMSO, 1968.
46 Marcel Berlins and Geoffrey Wansell, *Caught in the Act*, Penguin, 1974.
47 *The Child, The Family and the Young Offender*, HMSO, 1965.
48 *Times Educational Supplement*, 24 August 1974.
49 *Observations on the Eleventh Report from the Expenditure Committee, Children and Young Persons Act 1969*, HMSO, 1976.
50 E. Goodacre, *op. cit.*
51 *Intermediate Treatment Projects*, HMSO, 1972, 1973.
52 DHSS, *Intermediate Treatment: A Guide for the Regional Planning of New Forms of Treatment for Children in Trouble*, HMSO, 1972.
53 J. Harding, D. Thorpe *et al.*, 'Intermediate Treatment', *Social Work Today*, 1973, vol. 3, nos 22 and 23.
54 G. Aplin and R. Bamber, 'Groupwork Counselling', *Social Work Today*, 1973, vol. 3.
55 Herschel Prins, 'Intermediate Treatment', *Social Work Today*, 1973, vol. 3.
56 R. Grunsell, quoted in the *Times Educational Supplement*, 15 February 1974.
57 D. Ward, 'Broadening IT Practice: The Child-in-his-living-situation', *Social Work Today*, vol. 8, no. 19, 1977.
58 *Education Act 1944*, HMSO.
59 Maurice Tyerman, *Truancy*, University of London Press, 1968.

References

60 A. Mitchell, Presidential Address to the National Society of Education Welfare Officers, *Times Educational Supplement*, 2 August 1974.

61 Dan Jones, 'The Truant' in *Concern*, National Children's Bureau, 1974.

62 Howard Polsky, *Cottage Six*, Wiley, 1967.

63 Katrin Fitzherbert, *Child Care Services and the Teacher*, Temple Smith, 1977.

64 Mia Kellmer Pringle, 'The Challenge of Prevention' in *Investment in Children*, ed. Mia Kellmer Pringle, Longman, 1965.

65 D. Jones, *op. cit.*

66 O. Stevenson, *Claimant or Client?*, Allen & Unwin, 1973.

67 J. Kahn and Jean Nursten, *Unwillingly to School*, Pergamon, 1968.

68 Colin Pritchard, 'The E.W.O. Truancy and School Phobia', *Social Work Today*, 1974, vol. 5, no. 5.

69 E. Goldschmied at the Inaugural Study Meeting of the Special Interest Group 'Social Work in Education', BASW, 26 March 1976.

70 J. Stritch and P. Crunk, 'School Suspension' in Rosemary Sarri and Frank Maple (eds), *The School in the Community*, NASW, 1972.

71 R. York, J. Heron and S. Wolff, 'Exclusion from School', *Journal of Child Psychology and Psychiatry*, 1972, vol. 13.

72 Gerald Caplan, *An Approach to Community Mental Health*, Tavistock, 1961.

73 Norman Tutt, *Care or Custody*, Dartman, Longman & Todd, 1974.

74 *Care and Treatment in a Planned Environment*, DHSS, 1970.

75 CCETSW Discussion Document, *Training for Residential Work*, 1973.

76 CCETSW, Paper 3, *Residential Work is Part of Social Work*, 1974.

77 Christopher Beedell, *Residential Life with Children*, Routledge & Kegan Paul, 1970.

78 *Observations on the Eleventh Report from the Expenditure Committee*, op. cit.

Chapter four: Education social work: definition of tasks and an educational dilemma

1 *1944 Education Act*, HMSO.

2 Newsom Report, *Half our Future*, HMSO, 1967.

3 Plowden Report, *Children and their Primary Schools*, HMSO, 1966.

4 Katrin Fitzherbert, *Child Care Services and the Teacher*, Temple Smith, 1977.

5 *Report of the Seebohm Committee on the Local Authority and Allied Personal Social Services*, HMSO, 1968.

6 *Report of the Ralphs Committee on the Training of Education Welfare Officers*, Local Government Training Board, 1973.

7 Leonard Davis, 'Education Welfare: The Patchwork Service', *Community Care*, 18 February 1976.

8 *Observations on the Eleventh Report from the Expenditure Committee, Children and Young Persons Act 1969*, HMSO, 1976.

9 *Community Care*, 9 June 1976.

10 Lela Costin, 'An Historical Review of School Social Work', *Social Casework*, October 1969.

11 D. Walker, 'A Study of Elementary School Teachers' Perceptions and Evaluation of the Role of the School Social Worker', doctoral dissertation, University of Pennsylvania, 1963; quoted in Costin, *op. cit.*

12 Robert Taber, 'Children Caught in Cross Currents: The Rights and Responsibilities of Children and Parents', *Bulletin of the National Association of School Social Workers*, 29 June 1954.

13 Alex Clegg and Barbara Megson, *Children in Distress*, 2nd edn, Penguin, 1973.

14 *Education Officer's Reports to Schools Subcommittee*, ILEA, 439/ 439A, 1969.

15 Ralphs Committee, *op. cit.*

16 A. H. Halsey, *Educational Priority vol. 1: Problems and Places*, HMSO, 1972.

17 Karen Lyons, *Social Work and The School: A Study of Some Aspects of the Role of an Education Social Worker*, HMSO, 1973.

18 Katrin Fitzherbert, 'Social Work and School', *New Society*, 8 February 1973.

19 Margaret Robinson, 'Report of the Social Work Consultant on the Professional Staff of the Education Welfare Service of the ILEA', unpublished.

20 *Observations on the Eleventh Report from the Expenditure Committee on the Children and Young Persons Act 1969*, HMSO, 1976.

21 L. Costin, 'The Social Work Contribution to Education in Transition' in R. Sarri and F. Maple (eds), *The School in the Community*, NASW, 1972.

22 Johanna Bielecki, 'Comprehensive Social Work in a Secondary School' in R. Sarri and F. Maple (eds), *The School in the Community*, NASW, 1972.

23 Juliet Cheetham, *Social Work with Immigrants*, Routledge & Kegan Paul, 1972.

24 Gordon Rose and Tony Marshall (with R. F. Adamson and P. Avery), *Counselling and School Social Work*, Wiley, 1974.

25 Derek Miller, *The Years Between*, Cornmarket Hutchinson, 1969.

26 BASW working party on Education Social Work, 1974.

27 BASW, *op. cit.*

28 Mary Saltmarsh, 'Misalliance or Working Partnership', *Social Work Today*, June 1973, vol. 4, no. 6.

29 Reported in *Community Care*, 9 June 1976.

Chapter five: Teachers and social workers

1 Robin Auld, *William Tyndale Junior and Infants Schools Public Inquiry*, ILEA, 1976.

2 *Report of the Taylor Committee: A New Partnership for our Schools*, DES, Welsh Office, 1977.

3 *Inquiry into the Care Provided in Relation to Steven Meurs*, Norfolk County Council, 1976.

References

4   Joan Cooper, 'The Uneasy Response to Social Problems and Private Sorrows', *Social Work Today*, 22 January 1976, vol. 6, no. 21.
5   Nina Toren, 'Semi-Professionalism and Social Work' in A. Etzioni (ed.), *The Semi-Professions and their Organisation*, Free Press, 1972.
6   Dan Lortie, 'The Balance of Control and Autonomy in Elementary School Teaching' in A. Etzioni, *op. cit.*
7   A. Etzioni, *op. cit.*
8   A. Carr Saunders, 'Metropolitan Conditions and Professional Relationships' in Robert Fisher (ed.), *The Metropolis in Modern Life*, Doubleday, 1955; quoted in A. Etzioni, *op. cit.*
9   E. Greenwood, 'Attributes of a Profession', *Social Work*, 2 July 1957; quoted in A. Etzioni, *op. cit.*
10 R. Foren and R. Bailey, *Authority in Social Casework*, Pergamon, 1968.
11 *Handbook of Social Administration*, NUT, 1972.
12 *Code of Ethics*, BASW, 1972.
13 H. Meyer, E. Litwak and D. Warren, 'Occupational and Class Differences in Social Values: a Comparison of Teachers and Social Workers', *Sociology of Education*, 1968, vol. 41, no. 3.
14 M. Craft and A. Craft, 'The Interprofessional Perspectives of Teachers and Social Workers', *Social and Economic Administration*, 1971, vol. 5.
15 Nell Keddie, *Tinker, Tailor . . . The Myth of Cultural Deprivation*, Penguin, 1973.
16 David Street, 'Educators and Social Workers, Sibling Rivalry in the Inner City', *Social Service Review*, June 1967, vol. 4.
17 Eric Midwinter, 'The Educative Community', Conference at Goldsmiths' College, 1975.
18 Katrin Fitzherbert, *Child Care Services and the Teacher*, Temple Smith, 1977.
19 G. Rose and T. Marshall, *Counselling and School Social Work*, Wiley, 1974.
20 Elizabeth Goodacre, *Teachers and their Pupils' Home Background*, NFER, 1968.
21 Sue Lees and Ray Lees, 'Social Work and Teacher Training', *Social Work Today*, 19 October 1972, vol. 3, no. 14.
22 Ann Jones, *Children at Risk in School*, NACRO Crime Prevention Conference, 1975.
23 John Hurt, *Education in Evolution*, Paladin, 1971.
24 G. E. Walley, *The Teacher's Point of View*, Leeds University Institute of Education, NFER, 1974.
25 *James Committee on Teacher Education and Training*, DES, HMSO, 1972.
26 C. Hannam, P. Smyth and N. Stephenson, *Young Teachers and Reluctant Learners*, Penguin, 1971.
27 C. Hannam, P. Smyth and N. Stephenson, *The First Year of Teaching*, Penguin, 1976.
28 N. Postman and C. Weingartner, *Teaching as a Subversive Activity*, Penguin, 1971.

29 C. Ball and M. Ball, *Education for a Change*, Penguin, 1973.
30 Charity James, 'Flexible Grouping for the Secondary School Curriculum' in D. Rubinstein and C. Stoneman (eds), *Education for Democracy*, Penguin, 1970.
31 Elizabeth Richardson, *Group Study for Teachers*, Routledge & Kegan Paul, 1967.
32 Seebohm Report, *Report of the Committee on Local Authority and Allied Personal Social Services*, HMSO, 1968.
33 P. Parsloe, E. Warren and J. Gauldie, 'Social Work as Taught', *New Society*, 4 March 1976, vol. 35, no. 700.
34 J. Lynch and J. Pimlott, *Parents and Teachers*, Macmillan, 1976.

Chapter six: Challenges, alternatives and some possible strategies

1   Paulo Freire, *Cultural Action for Freedom*, Penguin, 1972.
2   Everitt Reimer, *School is Dead*, Penguin, 1971.
3   Ivan Illich, *Celebration of Awareness*, Penguin, 1973.
4   Ivan Illich, *Deschooling Society*, 1971.
5   John Holt, *Freedom and Beyond*, Pelican, 1972.
6   George Dennison, *The Lives of Children*, Penguin, 1972.
7   Ian Lister, *Deschooling: A Reader*, Cambridge University Press, 1974.
8   P. Freire, *op. cit.*
9   I. Lister, *op. cit.*
10 John Head (ed.), 'Community School on the Way: White Lion Street Free School' in J. Head (ed.), *Free Way to Learning*, Penguin, 1973.
11 Alison Truefitt, 'Educational Alternatives Within the Law' in Head, *op. cit.*
12 Plowden Report, *Children and their Primary Schools*, HMSO, 1966.
13 Seebohm Report, *Report of the Committee on Local Authority and Allied Personal Social Services*, HMSO, 1968.
14 Phoebe Hall, *Reforming the Welfare*, Heinemann Educational, 1977.
15 I. Lister, *op. cit.*
16 Gordon Rose and Tony Marshall, *Counselling and School Social Work*, Wiley, 1974.
17 E. Litwak and H. J. Meyer, *School, Family and Neighborhood: The Theory and Practice of School-Community Relations*, Columbia University Press, 1974.
18 D. J. O'Meara, personal communication.
19 Maurice Craft, 'Education and Social Work' in F. H. Hedley (ed.), *Education and Social Work*, Pergamon, 1967.
20 B. Kahan (ed.), *Working Together for Children and their Families*, HMSO, 1977.
21 A. H. Halsey, *Times Higher Education Supplement*, 22 October 1976.

Index

Index